D1353410

Chris Abbott is a writer and researcher specialising in international security and foreign affairs. He is the founder and Executive Director of Open Briefing, the world's first civil society intelligence agency (www.openbriefing.org). He is also an Honorary Visiting Research Fellow in the School of Social and International Studies at the University of Bradford, and Honorary Sustainable Security Consultant to Oxford Research Group (a leading global security think tank, of which he was Deputy Director until 2009). His first book, *Beyond Terror: The Truth About the Real Threats to Our World*, co-authored with Paul Rogers and John Sloboda, was published to worldwide acclaim in 2007 and is now available in six languages. See www.chrisabbott.info for more information.

By the same author:

Beyond Terror (with Paul Rogers and John Sloboda)

21 Speeches That Shaped Our World

*The People and Ideas
That Changed the Way We Think*

Chris Abbott

RIDER

LONDON · SYDNEY · AUCKLAND · JOHANNESBURG

1 3 5 7 9 10 8 6 4 2

First published in 2010 by Rider, an imprint of Ebury Publishing
A Random House Group company

This paperback edition published in 2012

Copyright © Chris Abbott 2010

Chris Abbott has asserted his right to be identified as the author of this Work in
accordance with the Copyright, Designs and Patents Act 1988

All rights reserved. No part of this publication may be reproduced,
stored in a retrieval system or transmitted in any form or by any means,
electronic, mechanical, photocopying, recording or otherwise, without the
prior permission of the copyright owner

The Random House Group Limited Reg. No 954009

Addresses for companies within the Random House Group can be found at:
www.randomhouse.co.uk

The Random House Group Limited supports The Forest Stewardship Council
(FSC®), the leading international forest certification organisation. Our books
carrying the FSC label are printed in FSC® certified paper. FSC is the only forest
certification scheme endorsed by the leading environmental organisations,
including Greenpeace. Our paper procurement policy can be found at:
www.randomhouse.co.uk/environment

Printed and bound by CPI Group (UK) Ltd, Croydon, CR0 4YY

ISBN 9781846042720

Copies are available at special rates for bulk orders. Contact the sales
development team on 020 7840 8487 for more information.

To buy books by your favourite authors and register for offers visit:
www.randomhouse.co.uk

CONTENTS

List of Illustrations

Martin Luther King delivering his 'I have a dream' speech before
the Lincoln Memorial in Washington DC, 28 August 1963
(© Bettman/Corbis) xiv

Video message from Osama bin Laden broadcast on Al-Jazeera,
7 October 2001 (© Patrick Durand/Sygma/Corbis) 74

Margaret Thatcher at the Conservative party conference in Brighton,
12 October 1984 (© Bettman/Corbis) 160

Barack Obama speaking at Cairo University in Egypt, 4 June 2009
(© Larry Downing/Reuters/Corbis) 228

Introduction

Shaping the World

"We see the world the way we do
not because that is the way it is,
but because we have these
ways of seeing."

Ludwig Wittgenstein,
Philosophical Investigations
(1953)

On a hot summer's day in August 1963, Martin Luther King stood on the steps of the Lincoln Memorial in Washington DC and told the world about his dream. His words pointed the way to a different future and painted an image that still captures the imagination now, forty years after his assassination. On that day in 1963, King stood in front of some two hundred thousand people and many more watched him on television or listened on the radio, but millions more will have been moved by his words in the decades since. Truly great speeches can thus survive and inspire long after the crowds have gone home and the words are transcribed to the page. This is part of the power of speeches.

This book is not just about speeches, though. It is about the ideas behind them, the events that surround them and the power of people to inspire others. The twenty-one speeches explored in this book are moments in time – points in history used to illustrate the development of the ways we see the world today. I have split these 'ways of seeing', these world views, into two principal outlooks, which are discussed in the following chapters. Parts I and IV explore the view that all people are created equal and that division and confrontation often lead only to violence. The horror unleashed in Iraq since the 2003 invasion is just the latest in a long line of events that have served to prove this point in people's minds. Parts II and III explore the contrasting view that the world is divided into good and evil, and the powerful therefore have a responsibility to use force to make the world a safer place. The rise of al-Qaida and the so-called clash of civilisations between Islam and the West only serve to reinforce this perception, which led us into a disastrous war on terror. These two outlooks might be characterised, albeit simplistically, as idealist and realist respectively. They are explored here through the contrasting themes of 'all the world is human' with 'you're either with us or against us', and of 'might is right' with 'give peace a chance'. In this way, the speeches are arranged thematically rather than chronologically, which adds to the overall narrative.

These world views did not appear in isolation: they grew out of the events, ideas, politics and people of the last one hundred years or so. This process can be illustrated by examining some of the most influential and inspiring speeches given during that time – and this is the impetus for this book. I reviewed over a hundred speeches in deciding which ones to focus on but decided to limit the final number to twenty-one to represent the current century. It was important that the chosen speeches reflected the narrative framework described above and the final selection encompasses those people and ideas that I feel have shaped our world and the way that we view it today, in the context of this framework. They are the speeches that spoke to me in a powerful way and captured the essence of the ideas that I was exploring. It is for the same reasons that after careful consideration I have not included some equally significant speeches in this book, such as ones by Woodrow Wilson, Sun Yat-sen, Adolf Hitler, Charles de Gaulle, John F. Kennedy, Nelson Mandela, Anwar Sadat, the Dalai Lama and many others. It was also essential that the final selection included some female and non-Western voices (unlike in too many other books). To this end I have included speeches by Emmeline Pankhurst, Margaret Beckett, Margaret Thatcher and Marie Fatayi-Williams, as well as Aleksandr Solzhenitsyn, Osama bin Laden, Salvador Allende and Mohandas Gandhi. This book features politicians, soldiers, activists and ordinary people in extraordinary circumstances. Many of these people brought about tremendous change, or at least came to represent that change. Whether you think they shaped the zeitgeist or grew from it depends on whether you believe in the pre-eminence of the individual or society as a whole. Examples pointing to both are included here.

Speeches can be so much more than just words and, in any case, words are rarely *just* words: they anticipate action. Few have expressed this more clearly than the American politician Deval Patrick during his successful 2006 campaign to become Governor of Massachusetts. He told a crowd of supporters gathered at the Rally for Change on Boston Common on 15 October:

> I will not engage in the politics of fear. Because fear is poisonous. All through history it has been used to hold back progress and limit fairness. Only hope defeats fear. It always has.
>
> At a candidates' forum last week, the moderator asked each of us to say something nice about the other candidates. Kerry Healey rather grudgingly said, 'Well, he can give a good speech.' She would

know this not because she has ever attended a speech of mine, but because she has them filmed. But her dismissive point, and I hear it from her staff, is that all I have to offer is words. Just words.

'We hold these truths to be self-evident, that all men are created equal.' Just words.

'We have nothing to fear but fear itself.' Just words.

'Ask not what your country can do for you. Ask what you can do for your country.' Just words.

'I have a dream.' Just words.

Let me say it before you do: I am no Dr King, no President Kennedy, no FDR, no Thomas Jefferson. But I do know that the right words, spoken from the heart with conviction, with a vision of a better place and a faith in the unseen, are a call to action. So when you hear my words, or speak your own to your neighbours, hear them and speak them as a call to action.

This extract from the last few minutes of his speech clearly articulates the way in which the right words spoken from the heart can inspire people to work for a better future. It is something that Barack Obama understood well during his 2008 bid for the US presidency. His powerful speeches and grassroots campaign saw him beat John McCain to the White House but not before echoing Patrick in a speech in Milwaukee in February 2008: 'Don't tell me words don't matter! "I have a dream." Just words. "We hold these truths to be self-evident, that all men are created equal." Just words! "We have nothing to fear but fear itself." Just words – just speeches!' This prompted accusations of plagiarism but the two men are friends and Patrick did not mind Obama borrowing his words to defend himself from criticism that he was all rhetoric and no substance.

The voices that are strangely silent in this book are the speechwriters'. That may sound counter-intuitive, as politicians in particular often rely on speechwriters and it is their words that are presented here on the page. While it may be the speechwriter who coins the pithy phrase or eloquently describes a course of action, it is the person delivering the speech who truly owns it. It is in the theatre of the event and the skill of the oratory that great speeches are created. It is the speaker who breathes life into the words, while the speechwriter, by nature of their profession, remains behind the scenes. In any case, the process of speechwriting involves a back-and-forth between the speechwriter and politician, with frequent redrafting until the words express exactly what the speaker wishes to say. Obama calls his surprisingly young chief speechwriter Jon Favreau his 'mind-reader' and the man has an obvious ability with words, yet no one would deny that it is Obama's presence and skill as an orator that gives his speeches their power. Of course some of the power of the speech can survive on the page and evidence of that can be found in the transcripts included in this book – a testament to the skill of those who wrote them.

Speeches come in many forms and in selecting those for inclusion in this book I have taken a broad definition of what constitutes a speech. *The Concise Oxford English Dictionary* defines a speech simply as 'a formal address delivered to an audience'. While almost all the speeches included here would be considered speeches in the traditional sense, this book also includes a written last statement, a video message, a radio broadcast and a televised address. There may be surprise at some of the other speeches that have been included: George Bush is not known as the world's greatest orator and bin Laden – while a powerful speaker – is not usually considered to have delivered some of the modern world's most influential speeches, though he has. If, on the other hand, this book is missing some famous speeches, it is because it is not intended to be a collection of the greatest speeches – some excellent anthologies already exist. Even if you have come across some, or all, of these speeches before, they warrant re-reading – and I hope to add to your understanding of how they have shaped the world we live in. In writing this book, I also hope to introduce a new generation of readers to some of the most

❝ I do know that the right words, spoken from the heart with conviction, with a vision of a better place and a faith in the unseen, are a call to action. ❞

important words ever spoken. Many will recognise lines such as 'we will fight on the beaches' or 'I have a dream' but have little understanding of their significance or perhaps not even know who spoke them or, more importantly, why. Hopefully this can be rectified, as each speech is preceded by an introduction exploring the context and wider impact of that moment and the background of the speaker.

The chapters that follow have not been written as detached, objective commentaries. Instead, they are deliberately polemical, designed to provoke critical thinking on key events from the last hundred years. And some incredible events are covered in this book: World Wars I and II; the demise of the British Empire; the partition of India; the assassinations of Gandhi and King; *coups d'état* in Iran, Guatemala, Chile and Argentina; the Cold War and the collapse of the Soviet Union; Israel–Palestine and the wider Arab–Israeli conflict; the Falklands/Malvinas conflict; 9/11, the war on terror and the invasions of Afghanistan and Iraq; Australia's apology to the Stolen Generations; and the election of America's first black President. These events highlight a huge range of important issues, including human rights, racism, slavery, female emancipation, immigration, democracy, colonialism, national identity, capital punishment, non-violence, disarmament, religion, climate change and terrorism. In discussing these I have drawn upon my own background in international security, anthropology and psychology, as well as the lessons of political science, international relations, history and philosophy, in order to shine some light on how we got to where we are today.

Despite the modern desire for sound bites, the best speeches can remind us of Shakespeare: eloquent language and novel phrases are used to impart a message about the human condition that can be understood by almost everyone. They are akin to poetry and, in fact, utilise many of the poet's techniques, from rhythm to repetition. Like the sophist teachers of philosophy and rhetoric in ancient Greece, though, speakers can also use ambiguous language and rhetorical sleight-of-hand to promote weak or false arguments or obscure the truth. A great speaker can use their verbal skills to manipulate our emotions and deceive our thinking. In this way, speeches have the power not only to inspire others to great achievement but also to lead them to great harm (some devastating examples of which are included in this book). In the end, though, this book is about hope: hope for a safer, more equal world, where our differences are not settled by wars and where we are able to work together to overcome the huge social and environmental challenges humanity will face over the course of this century. That may sound a little too idealistic; but is it really? Who, in fact, are the real realists?

AUTHOR'S NOTE

The transcripts of the speeches are taken from official sources wherever possible and have been checked for accuracy where feasible. If sub-headings were included in the original published version of the speech they are also included here in order to break up the text and make reading easier. All transcripts are the full, unedited version of the speech unless stated otherwise in the preceding commentary. However, for consistency I have corrected the occasional typographical error, standardised the transliteration of Arabic words and changed American spellings to British.

Many of these speeches are in the public domain but where permission has been given to reprint a copyrighted transcript the relevant information is provided in the acknowledgements section.

In researching this book I have drawn on hundreds of books, articles, interviews, opinion polls, official reports and other such material, together with meetings and conversations with many different people over the years. Some of these are listed in the references section and readers looking for further information may wish to start there.

Audio and video recordings of many of the speeches featured in this book can be found at **www.21speeches.com**.

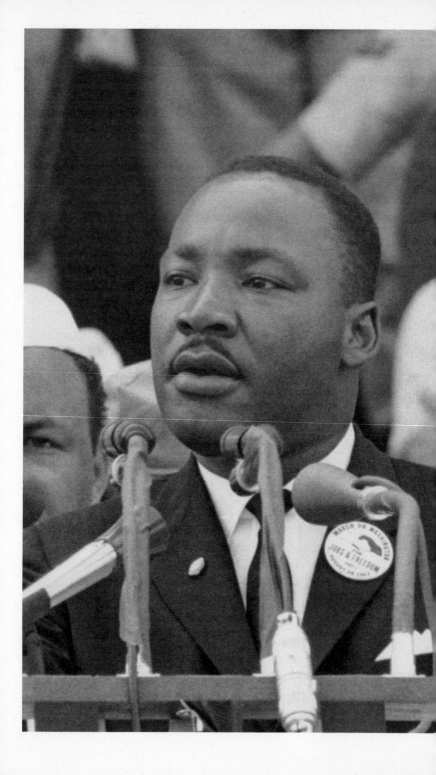

PART I

All the World
is Human

"Every human heart is human."

Henry Wadsworth Longfellow,
The Song of Hiawatha
(1855)

In 1550, King Charles V suspended Spain's wars of conquest in the New World and ordered a group of jurists and theologians to meet in Valladolid to hear arguments over the status of the peoples the Spanish had conquered in the Americas. The colonists were represented by the philosopher Juan Ginés de Sepúlveda, who defended Spain's right to conquest and argued that the indigenous peoples should not be treated as humans but as natural slaves. His opponent, the Dominican friar Bartolemé de las Casas, argued that 'all the world is human' and that the peoples of the Americas should therefore be governed in the same way as the people of Spain. Although both sides claimed victory in the debate, it would prove to be Sepúlveda's point of view that would shape the reality of Spanish behaviour in the Americas. However, Las Casas's arguments had a considerable influence on the King and the Catholic Church, and were an important step forward in the development of human rights and international law.

The Valladolid controversy, as it came to be known, is part of the complex debate over the centuries about our common humanity and the customary legal, political and social rights which that entails. It was not until four hundred years after Las Casas that such rights were finally expressed on a global level. On 10 December 1948, the UN General Assembly adopted the Universal Declaration of Human Rights, guaranteeing certain rights for all people and declaring: 'All human beings are born free and equal in dignity and rights.' This document was key in cementing the position of human rights in international law in the aftermath of World War II. It claimed that 'Everyone is entitled to all the rights and freedoms set forth in this Declaration, without distinction of any kind'. The extent to which all the peoples of our world are considered equal, without distinction, is explored in the chapters that follow.

At least half the world's population are discriminated against to some degree simply because of their gender. All the fine words spoken through history about freedom and equality have only ever been, in truth, about men. This is the argument that the British suffragette Emmeline Pankhurst put forward in a speech she gave in Hartford, Connecticut, on 13 November 1913 and is discussed in the first chapter. Pankhurst saw herself as a solider in the fight to secure women equal voting rights, which at that time they were largely denied. She defended the use of militant tactics such as arson, vandalism, sabotage and acts of civil disobedience and disruption in order to win that struggle. Though female suffrage is now almost universal, women are still discriminated against in many different ways and are frequently denied full autonomy over their own lives and bodies.

The second and third chapters explore aspects of the race debate. Chapter two focuses on the struggle for African-American civil rights as described by Martin Luther King in his speech on the steps of the Lincoln Memorial in Washington DC on 28 August 1963. King's soaring rhetoric captured the shame that racial segregation had brought on the United States but also the potential dream of full civil rights for African Americans. There was, though, a crucial tension within the civil-rights movement. On the one hand there were those like King who promoted non-violence and racial harmony, on the other there were Malcolm X and the Nation of Islam who promoted black nationalism and self-defence against the white enemy. The more radical black-power movement continued to grow in strength following King's assassination in 1968, as the boundaries between racial inequality and other social injustices became increasingly blurred. Today, racial segregation has largely given way to a socio-economic segregation in which race plays a huge part.

Less than three weeks after King's assassination, the British MP Enoch Powell gave an apocalyptic speech to a Conservative Association meeting in Birmingham, on 20 April 1968. This speech, which is explored in the third chapter, highlighted the assumed impact of immigration on national identity. He argued that unbridled immigration was beginning to make the white English majority feel like strangers in their own country and warned that rivers of blood might flow as a result. Although Powell maintained that his arguments were based on national identity not race per se, his warnings were seized upon by extremist and right-wing groups and are still invoked today to underscore the supposed failings of multiculturalism. The debate on immigration is a complex and highly emotive one, marked by much ignorance and prejudice. Perhaps the one universal truth is that we should all have the right to live where we feel safe and happy, wherever that might be and whatever the colour of our skin.

One of the most obvious ways that racial divisions are manifested in the United States and elsewhere is in the legal system. Socio-economic disparity and structural racism ensures that black inmates are disproportionally represented in the prison population as a whole and death row in particular. One such death-row prisoner was Napoleon Beazley, executed on 28 May 2002, and whose last statement is discussed in the fourth chapter. Though Beazley was by his own admission guilty of murder, there are concerns that he may have been subjected to a miscarriage of justice. The right to life is one of the central pillars of human rights, yet Beazley's government disregarded the sanctity of human life and executed him in retaliation for a crime he committed when he was only seventeen years old. The death penalty does not bring about justice and rehabilitation; it is based solely on vengeance. It brutalises society and only creates more victims by perpetuating the very violence it condemns.

The final chapter examines the apology to the Stolen Generations that Kevin Rudd, the Australian Prime Minister, made in parliament in Canberra on 13 February 2008. The Stolen Generations are those tens of thousands of Aboriginal and Torres Strait Islander children who were forcibly removed from their families between the mid-nineteenth century and the 1970s. This was the result of state and federal policies designed to assimilate indigenous children into white Australian society. Their existence demonstrates the fact that judicial and extra-judicial executions are not the only way in which the state can abuse its power over the individual and deny them their human rights. The Stolen Generations policies were part of a wider process of attempted genocide in Australia. Unfortunately, indigenous populations around the world have suffered similar crimes, as governments, missionaries and multi-national corporations work together in the name of so-called civilisation, religion or profit. Rudd and others recognised that the forced removal of Aboriginal and Torres Strait Islander children was wrong and that an apology could be an important step in the healing process.

It is over sixty years since the Universal Declaration of Human Rights was adopted, yet many people are still denied their humanity, let alone even the most basic of human rights. Huge numbers of people across the majority world of Asia, Africa and Latin America are marginalised politically, culturally and economically. Inequality is rife in a world where nearly a billion people must survive on less than a dollar a day and half the world's children live in poverty. People everywhere still face discrimination because of their race, religion, gender or sexual orientation. It would seem that everyone is created equal, but some are created more equal than others.

Freedom or Death

– Emmeline Pankhurst –

Female emancipation is not a minority issue. It is not the concern of a small special-interest group. It is not an issue only for feminists nor is it an issue only for women. It is an issue that concerns everyone; women's rights are human rights.[1] Women account for half the world's population and their emancipation cannot be considered peripheral. There is not a society on Earth where women enjoy entirely equal participation in social, political and economic life. Even in superficially equal societies – with little overt repression – discrimination often remains entrenched in law or custom: denying women the employment opportunities, fair wages, legal justice, sexual freedom, individual autonomy and general respect that they deserve on a par with their male counterparts.

Throughout the early 1900s the struggle for women's rights hinged on suffrage. Some of the first countries to allow women full voting rights were British colonies, such as New Zealand (1893) and Australia (1902, although Aboriginal women were not given the vote until 1967). However, at that time women in Britain, and indeed most other countries, were denied the right to vote in national elections. In 1869, the utilitarian philosopher John Stuart Mill was the first person in the British parliament to call for women to be given full voting rights. Twenty years later, Emmeline Pankhurst and her husband Richard founded the Women's Franchise League. Pankhurst came from a family with a history of radical politics and her husband was a strong advocate of women's rights until his death in 1898. She became frustrated with the more mainstream women's political organisations, such as the National Union of Women's Suffrage Societies, and she sought alternative methods to garner publicity for the suffrage movement. In 1903, she and her daughters founded the more radical Women's Social and Political Union (WSPU).

Pankhurst moved to London in 1907 to join her daughters in the militant struggle for the vote. Over the next seven years she was arrested numerous times, often going on hunger strike in response. She also gave powerful public speeches on both sides of the Atlantic in support of the cause. She gave one of her most famous on 13 November 1913 in a theatre in Hartford, Connecticut (an edited extract of which is reproduced in the pages that follow). By then, she was a well-known figure within the suffrage movement but she started by saying, 'I do not come here as an advocate . . . I am here as a soldier who has temporarily left the field of battle.' It was a powerful image to present to her audience; she was a gifted and entertaining orator – even known to address crowds from a stretcher when she was weak from a hunger strike.

At the time of her Hartford speech, she was on temporary release under the 'Cat and Mouse Act' from a three-year prison sentence for her part in a conspiracy that carried out a bomb attack on the Chancellor of the Exchequer's country house. The 'Cat and Mouse Act' stopped the force-feeding of suffragettes on hunger strike and instead allowed for extremely weak prisoners to be released to recover, whereupon they could be rearrested. Pankhurst told the crowd in Hartford, 'I dare say, in the minds of many of you . . . that I do not look either very like a soldier or very like a convict, and yet I am both'. She thought of the suffragettes as being engaged in a civil war against an unjust government and defended the use of militant tactics such as arson, vandalism, sabotage and acts of civil disobedience and disruption. Five months earlier, Emily Davison, a WSPU member, had thrown herself in front of the King's horse when it was running in the Derby. She was trampled, left unconscious and died four days later. Pankhurst pointed out that were she a man there would be no need to explain such revolutionary tactics in the face of taxation without representation (an injustice that would have been well understood by an American audience). 'We women', she said, 'always have to make as part of our argument, and urge upon men in our audience the fact – a very simple fact – that women are human beings.' She said that women had found that 'all the fine phrases about freedom and liberty were entirely for male consumption'. In fact, she argued, women found that 'every principle of liberty enunciated in any civilised country on earth, with very few exceptions, was intended entirely for men'.

Pankhurst felt certain of her cause and her tactics and was convinced that if she could only explain the situation properly to people then they would surely understand. She told her audience that 'when I have finished you will say . . . that we could not do anything else, that there was no other way, that we had either to submit to intolerable injustice and let the women's movement go back and remain in a worse position than it was before we began, or we had to go on with these methods until victory was secured'. Suffragettes felt that they 'had to rouse the public to such a point that they would say to the government, you must give women the vote'. She told the audience that whether they agreed with her methods or not, 'we have succeeded in making woman suffrage one of the questions which even cabinet ministers now admit cannot indefinitely be neglected. It must be dealt with within a very short period of time. No other methods than ours would have brought about that result.' She told those who thought that they could not succeed that 'we have brought the government of England to this position, that it has to face this alternative: either women are to be killed or women are to have the vote'. 'We will put the enemy in the position where', she said, 'they will have to choose between giving us freedom or giving us death.'

World War I broke out nine months after Pankhurst's speech and campaigning for women's suffrage was suspended in order to support 'King and Country'. It was not until the war ended in 1918 that some women over the age of thirty gained the right to vote in general elections (provided they met certain criteria). This was in recognition of the contribution that women had made to the war effort but the age barrier was set at thirty years, partly to ensure that women did not outnumber men in the post-war electorate. It took another ten years for women to receive the vote on equal terms to men. The Equal Franchise Act came into law on 2 July 1928, but Pankhurst had died three weeks earlier, aged sixty-nine, so was never able to exercise the right she had fought for. The next day, her obituary in *The Times* said: 'Whatever views may be held as to the righteousness of the cause to which she gave her life and the methods by which she tried to bring about its achievement, there can be no doubt about the singleness of her aim and the remarkable strength and nobility of her character.' She was, it said, a 'humble-minded, large-hearted, unselfish woman, of the stuff of which martyrs are made'.[2]

Fast-forward to today and there are those who hold the reactionary view that the pendulum has now swung too far the other way. They argue that men are being emasculated by female authority at home and losing out to positive discrimination at work. It is true that in many countries there is the perception, and occasionally the reality, that men lose out when custody over or access to their children is granted following divorce; suffer from worse health and have lower life expectancy; are less likely to seek support for mental-health problems and more likely to commit suicide; lack suitable male role models at home and in school; and are called upon to fight and die in time of war. But while these issues may be important, they do not in any way detract from the reality that women still suffer far more from legally or culturally embedded discrimination at the social, political and economic levels.

Men and women are equal, but different. However, many of the stereo-typical gender differences have little biological or physiological basis. Many of the differences between men and women are in fact the result of social-isation and cultural conditioning – traditional roles and characteristics rein-forced by society in each generation. It is because gender is such an obvious trait that we still focus on it long after many of the evolutionary and physical differences between men and women have ceased to have much meaningful impact beyond childbearing. That is not, however, to downplay the importance of these social forces. In the worst cases, patri-archal societies maintained through tradition and religious practice con-tinue to inflict suffering on women throughout their lives – from female foeticide, genital mutilation and denial of schooling to forced matrimony, rape in marriage and so-called honour killings. Even in more liberal soci-eties, women are at risk of domestic violence, sexual harassment and rape. In this way, many women are still denied their individual autonomy and ownership over their own lives and bodies.

One of the worst manifestations of this lack of autonomy is the traf-ficking of women for sexual exploitation. One British study found that almost all women trafficked in Europe had been physically or sexually abused during the process.[3] Another study found that 80 per cent of women working in off-street prostitution in London were not from the UK; many of them were being forced to work by traffickers or pimps (a similar figure was found among women working for escort agencies).[4] In the vast majority of cases, prostitution is an especially damaging form of violence against women, particularly as the average age of entry into prostitution for adolescent girls is only thirteen or fourteen.[5]

This discrimination extends from the social realm into the political. Despite the successes of Pankhurst and others, women are still denied equal voting rights in half a dozen countries. The subjugation of women is particularly bad in Saudi Arabia, where, in addition to being denied the right to vote in municipal elections, the policies of male guardianship and sex segregation leave women treated as legal minors.[6] Women are also greatly under-represented as elected officials and in the vast majority of political institutions. Around the world, women usually make up less than one fifth of the MPs in national parliaments (rising to nearly half in some Nordic countries but dropping to a tenth or less in some Arab states).[7] In a world of nearly two hundred countries, there are currently less than twenty female presidents and prime ministers. The first female prime minister was not elected until 1960 (in Sri Lanka) and since then only sixty or so women have been elected heads of state worldwide. Women's involvement in politics is essential because the institutions that govern our lives should be representative of the population as a whole, not just one half of it. Adequate representation of women is necessary to legitimise political systems and make it more likely that issues of particular importance to women will be addressed.

The situation is even worse in the corporate world. At the end of 2009, only three FTSE-100 companies had a woman as chair of the board and only fifteen had female executive directors. In all, only 12 per cent of the directorships on corporate boards were held by women; a quarter of companies had exclusively male boards.[8] The physical and practical restrictions imposed by pregnancy and child-rearing can impact directly on a woman's career if she is unfairly forced out of her job or her employer is unwilling to accept part-time or flexible working patterns. There is also plenty of anecdotal evidence to suggest that many employers are reluctant to employ women of childbearing age because of the perceived difficulties and costs imposed by maternity leave.[9] For those women in employment, there still exists a gender income gap in many countries – with women earning significantly less on average than men, even when employed in similar roles. This difference varies widely between job sector and country but on average women earn less than four-fifths of their male counterparts' salaries.[10] Women are also more likely than men to be employed in the informal economy or to be responsible for food production, household chores, care of children or elderly relatives and other unpaid tasks that help a family to survive but provide little or no income. All this has led to what has been called the feminisation of poverty, whereby women are increasingly those who suffer most from extreme poverty (a 1995 UN study estimated that 70 per cent of the world's 1.3 billion people living in poverty were women).[11]

The work of Pankhurst and the suffragettes is clearly unfinished. Female emancipation does not stop with equal voting rights. While half the world's population still suffer discrimination simply because of their gender, it is the responsibility of all of us to continue to fight for equality. Women's rights are, after all, human rights.

Parsons Theatre, Hartford, Connecticut, United States

13 NOVEMBER 1913

Many people come to Hartford to address meetings as advocates of some reform. Tonight it is not to advocate a reform that I address a meeting in Hartford. I do not come here as an advocate, because whatever position the suffrage movement may occupy in the United States of America, in England it has passed beyond the realm of advocacy and it has entered into the sphere of practical politics. It has become the subject of revolution and civil war, and so tonight I am not here to advocate woman suffrage. American suffragists can do that very well for themselves.

I am here as a soldier who has temporarily left the field of battle in order to explain – it seems strange it should have to be explained – what civil war is like when civil war is waged by women. I am not only here as a soldier temporarily absent from the field of battle; I am here – and that, I think, is the strangest part of my coming – I am here as a person who, according to the law courts of my country, it has been decided, is of no value to the community at all; and I am adjudged because of my life to be a dangerous person, under sentence of penal servitude in a convict prison. So you see there is some special interest in hearing so unusual a person address you. I dare say, in the minds of many of you – you will perhaps forgive me this personal touch – that I do not look either very like a soldier or very like a convict, and yet I am both.

Now, first of all I want to make you understand the inevitableness of revolution and civil war, even on the part of women, when you reach a certain stage in the development of a community's life. It is not at all difficult if revolutionaries come to you from Russia, if they come to you from China, or from any other part of the world, if they are men, to make you understand revolution in five minutes, every man and every woman to understand revolutionary methods when they are adopted by men.

Many of you have expressed sympathy, probably even practical sympathy, with revolutionaries in Russia. I dare say you have followed with considerable interest the story of how the Chinese revolutionary, Sun Yat-sen, conducted the Chinese revolution from England.* It is quite easy for you to understand – it would not be necessary for me to enter into explanations at all – the desirability of revolution if I were a man, in any of these countries, even in a part of the British Empire known to you as Ireland. If an Irish revolutionary had addressed this meeting, and many have addressed meetings all over the United States during the last twenty or thirty years, it would not be necessary for that revolutionary to explain the need of revolution beyond saying that the people of his country were denied – and by people, meaning men – were denied the right of self-government. That would explain the

---

* Sun Yat-sen was a Chinese revolutionary hailed today as the Father of the Nation in the Republic of China (Taiwan). He was forced into exile in Japan, the United States and Britain between 1895 and 1911 following a foiled *coup* attempt. He was kidnapped while in London and held at the Manchu legation (today's embassy of the People's Republic of China) pending his deportation and execution. His former teacher Sir James Cantile started a campaign through *The Times* and after twelve days the Foreign Office secured his release. He returned to China at the end of 1911 following a military uprising that brought an end to the imperial Qing dynasty.

whole situation. If I were a man and I said to you, 'I come from a country which professes to have representative institutions and yet denies me, a taxpayer, an inhabitant of the country, representative rights', you would at once understand that that human being, being a man, was justified in the adoption of revolutionary methods to get representative institutions. But since I am a woman it is necessary in the twentieth century to explain why women have adopted revolutionary methods in order to win the rights of citizenship.

You see, in spite of a good deal that we hear about revolutionary methods not being necessary for American women, because American women are so well off, most of the men of the United States quite calmly acquiesce in the fact that half of the community are deprived absolutely of citizen rights, and we women, in trying to make our case clear, always have to make as part of our argument, and urge upon men in our audience the fact – a very simple fact – that women are human beings. It is quite evident you do not all realise we are human beings or it would not be necessary to argue with you that women may, suffering from intolerable injustice, be driven to adopt revolutionary methods. We have, first of all, to convince you we are human beings, and I hope to be able to do that in the course of the evening before I sit down.

Suppose the men of Hartford had a grievance, and they laid that grievance before their legislature, and the legislature obstinately refused to listen to them, or to remove their grievance, what would be the proper and the constitutional and the practical way of getting their grievance removed? Well, it is perfectly obvious at the next general election, when the legislature is elected, the men of Hartford in sufficient numbers would turn out that legislature and elect a new one: entirely change the personnel of an obstinate legislature which would not remove their grievance. It is perfectly simple and perfectly easy for voting communities to get their grievances removed if they act in combination and make an example of the legislature by changing the composition of the legislature and sending better people to take the place of those who have failed to do justice.

> **❝ I am here as a soldier who has temporarily left the field of battle ❞**

But let the men of Hartford imagine that they were not in the position of being voters at all, that they were governed without their consent being obtained, that the legislature turned an absolutely deaf ear to their demands, what would the men of Hartford do then? They couldn't vote the legislature out. They would have to choose; they would have to make a choice of two evils: they would either have to submit indefinitely to an unjust state of affairs, or they would have to rise up and adopt some of the antiquated means by which men in the past got their grievances remedied. We know what happened when your forefathers decided that they must have representation for taxation, many, many years ago. When they felt they couldn't wait any longer, when they laid all the arguments before an obstinate British government that they could think of, and when their arguments were absolutely disregarded, when every other means had failed, they began by the tea party at Boston, and they went on until they had won the independence of the United States of America. That is what happened in the old days.

Well now, I want to argue with you as to whether our way is the right one; I want to explain all these things that you have not understood; I want to make you understand exactly what our plan of campaign has been because I have always felt that if you could only make people understand most people's hearts are in the right place and most people's understandings are sound and most people are more or less logical – if you could only make them understand.

I am going to talk later on about the grievances, but I want to first of all make you understand that this civil war carried on by women is not the hysterical manifestation which you thought it was, but was carefully and logically thought out, and I think when I have finished you will say, admitted the grievance, admitted the strength of the cause, that we could not do anything else, that there was no other way, that we had either to submit to intolerable injustice and let the woman's movement go back and remain in a worse position than it was before we began, or we had to go on with these methods until victory was secured; and I want also to convince you that these methods are going to win, because when you adopt the methods of revolution there are two justifications which I feel are necessary or to be desired. The first is, that you have good cause for adopting your methods in the beginning, and secondly that you have adopted methods which when pursued with sufficient courage and determination are bound, in the long run, to win.

Now, it would take too long to trace the course of militant methods as adopted by women, because it is about eight years since the word militant was first used to describe what we were doing; it is about eight years since the first militant action was taken by women. It was not militant at all, except that it provoked militancy on the part of those who were opposed to it. When women asked questions in political meetings and failed to get answers, they were not doing anything militant. To ask questions at political meetings is an acknowledged right of all people who attend public meetings; certainly in my country, men have always done it, and I hope they do it in America, because it seems to me that if you allow people to enter your legislatures without asking them any questions as to what they are going to do when they get there you are not exercising your citizen rights and your citizen duties as you ought. At any rate in Great Britain it is a custom, a time-honoured one, to ask questions of candidates for parliament and ask questions of members of the government. No man was ever put out of a public meeting for asking a question until Votes for Women came onto the political horizon. The first people who were put out of a political meeting for asking questions, were women; they were brutally ill-used; they found themselves in jail before twenty-four hours had expired.

But instead of the newspapers, which are largely inspired by the politicians, putting militancy and the reproach of militancy, if reproach there is, on the people who had assaulted the women, they actually said it was the women who were militant and very much to blame. How different the reasoning is that men adopt when they are discussing the cases of men and those of women. Had they been men who asked the questions, and had those men been brutally ill-used, you would have heard a chorus of reprobation on the part of the people toward those who refused to answer those questions. But as they were women who asked the questions, it was not the speakers on the platform who would not answer them, who were to blame, or the ushers at the meeting; it was the poor women who had had their bruises and their knocks and scratches, and who were put into prison for doing precisely nothing but holding a protest meeting in the street after it was all over. We were determined to press this question of the enfranchisement of women to the point where we were no longer to be ignored by the politicians as had been the case for about fifty years, during which time women had patiently used every means open to them to win their political enfranchisement.

We found that all the fine phrases about freedom and liberty were entirely for male consumption, and that they did not in any way apply to women. When it was said taxation without representation is tyranny, when it was 'Taxation of men without representation is tyranny', everybody quite calmly accepted the fact that women had to pay taxes and even were sent to prison if they failed to pay them – quite right. We found that 'Government of the people, by the people and for the people', which is also a time-honoured liberal principle, was again only for male consumption; half of the people were entirely ignored; it was the duty of women to pay their taxes and obey the laws and look as pleasant as they could under the circumstances. In fact, every principle of liberty enunciated in any civilised country on earth, with very few exceptions, was intended entirely for men, and when women tried to force the putting into practice of these principles, for women, then they discovered they had come into a very, very unpleasant situation indeed.

Well, whether you like our methods or not, we have succeeded in making woman suffrage one of the questions which even cabinet ministers now admit cannot indefinitely be neglected. It must be dealt with within a very short period of time. No other methods than ours would have brought about that result. You may have sentimental articles in magazines by the Chancellor of the Exchequer who seems to be able to spare time from his ordinary avocations to write magazine articles telling you that militancy is a drag on the movement for woman suffrage. But our answer to that is, methinks our gentleman doth protest too much, because until militancy became to be known neither Mr Lloyd George nor any statesman, no, nor any member of parliament, ever thought it was necessary to mention the subject of woman suffrage at all.* Now they mention it constantly, to tell us what damage we have done to our cause. They are all urging us to consider the serious position into which we have brought the cause of woman suffrage.

Well now, let me come to the situation as we find it. We felt we had to rouse the public to such a point that they would say to the government, you must give women the vote. We had to get the electors, we had to get the business interests, we had to get the professional interests, we had to get the men of leisure all unitedly saying to the government, relieve the strain of this situation and give women the vote; and that is a problem that I think the most astute politician in this meeting would find very difficult. We have done

* Lloyd George was the Chancellor of the Exchequer (and later Prime Minister). Although an early supporter of women's suffrage, he had been targeted by the Suffragettes – who had destroyed part of his country house in a bomb attack in February 1913.

" every principle of liberty enunciated in any civilised country on earth, with very few exceptions, was intended entirely for men "

it; we are doing it every day; and I think when you take that fact into consideration you will realise why we have been attacking private property, why we have been attacking the property of men so absorbed in their business that they generally forget to vote in ordinary elections, why we have attacked the pleasures of men whose whole life is spent in a round of pleasure, and who think politics so dull and so beneath their distinguished ossification that they hardly know which party is in power. All these people have had to be moved in order to bring enough pressure to bear upon the government to compel them to deal with the question of woman suffrage. And now that in itself is an explanation.

I don't know whether I have used the domestic illustration in Hartford, but it is a very good one: it is quite worth using again. You have two babies very hungry and wanting to be fed. One baby is a patient baby, and waits indefinitely until its mother is ready to feed it. The other baby is an impatient baby and cries lustily, screams and kicks and makes everybody unpleasant until it is fed. Well, we know perfectly well which baby is attended to first. That is the whole history of politics. Putting sentiment aside, people who really want reforms learn that lesson very quickly. It is only the people who are quite content to go on advocating them indefinitely who play the part of the patient baby in politics. You have to make more noise than anybody else, you have to make yourself more obtrusive than anybody else, you have to fill all the papers more than anybody else, in fact you have to be there all the time and see that they do not snow you under, if you are really going to get your reform realised.

Experience will show you that if you really want to get anything done, it is not so much a matter of whether you alienate sympathy; sympathy is a very unsatisfactory thing if it is not practical sympathy. It does not matter to the practical suffragist whether she alienates sympathy that was never of any use to her. What she wants is to get something practical done, and whether it is done out of sympathy or whether it is done out of fear, or whether it is done because you want to be comfortable again and not be worried in this way, doesn't particularly matter so long as you get it. We had enough of sympathy for fifty years; it never brought us anything, and we would rather have an angry man going to the government and saying, my business is interfered with and I won't submit to its being interfered with any longer because you won't give women the vote, than to have a gentleman come onto our platforms year in and year out and talk about his ardent sympathy with woman suffrage.

Now then, let me come to the more serious matters and to some of the more recent happenings. You know when you have war, many things happen that all of us deplore. We fought a great war not very long ago, in South Africa. Women were expected to face with equanimity the loss of those dearest to them in warfare; they were expected to submit to being impoverished; they were expected to pay the war tax exactly like the men for a war about which the women were never consulted at all. When you think of the object of that war it really makes some of us feel very indignant at the hypocrisy of some of our critics. That war was fought ostensibly to get equal rights for all whites in South Africa. The whole country went wild. We had a disease which was called Mafeka, because when the victory of Mafeking was declared everybody in the country, except a few people who tried to keep their heads steady, went absolutely mad with gratification at the sacrifice of thousands of human beings in the carrying on of that war.* That war was fought to get votes for white men in South Africa, a few years sooner than they would have had them under existing conditions, and it was justified on those grounds, to get a voice in the government of South Africa for men who would have had that voice in five or six years if they had waited. That was considered ample justification for one of the most costly and bloody wars of modern times.

Very well, then when you have warfare things happen; people suffer; the noncombatants suffer as well as the combatants. And so it happens in civil war. When your forefathers threw the tea into Boston harbour, a good many

---

* The British settlement of Mafeking in the Cape Colony (now Mafikeng in today's South Africa) was besieged by Boer forces for two hundred and seventeen days from October 1899 to May 1900 during the Second Boer War. The successful defence against far larger enemy forces was led by Colonel Robert Baden-Powell, who became a national hero in Britain and went on to found the Scouting movement.

women had to go without their tea. It has always seemed to me an extraordinary thing that you did not follow it up by throwing the whiskey overboard; you sacrificed the women; and there is a good deal of warfare for which men take a great deal of glorification which has involved more practical sacrifice on women than it has on any man. It always has been so. The grievances of those who have got power, the influence of those who have got power commands a great deal of attention; but the wrongs and the grievances of those people who have no power at all are apt to be absolutely ignored. That is the history of humanity right from the beginning.

If you are dealing with an industrial revolution, if you get the men and women of one class to rising up against the men and women of another class, you can locate the difficulty; if there is a great industrial strike, you know exactly where the violence is, and every man knows exactly how the warfare is going to be waged; but in our war against the government you can't locate it. If any gentleman who is the father of daughters in this meeting went into his home and looked around at his wife and daughters, if he lived in England and was an Englishman, he couldn't tell whether some of his daughters were militants or non-militants. We wear no mark; we belong to every class; we permeate every class of the community from the highest to the lowest; and so you see in the woman's civil war the dear men of my country are discovering it is absolutely impossible to deal with it: you cannot locate it, and you cannot stop it.

'Put them in prison,' they said, 'that will stop it.' But it didn't stop it. They put women in prison for long terms of imprisonment, for making a nuisance of themselves – that was the expression when they took petitions in their hands to the door of the House of Commons; and they thought that sending them to prison, giving them a day's imprisonment, would cause them to all settle down again and there would be no further trouble. But it didn't happen so at all: instead of the women giving it up, more women did it, and more and more and more women did it until there were three hundred women at a time, who had not broken a single law, only 'made a nuisance of themselves' as the politicians say. Well then they thought they must go a little farther, and so then they began imposing punishments of a very serious kind. The judge who sentenced me last May to three years' penal servitude for certain speeches in which I had accepted responsibility for acts of violence done by other women, said that if I could say I was sorry, if I could promise not to do it again, that he would revise the sentence and shorten it, because he admitted that it was a very heavy sentence, especially as the jury recommended me to mercy because of the purity of my motives; and he said he was giving me a determinate sentence, a sentence that would convince me that I would give up my 'evil ways' and would also deter other women from imitating me. But it hadn't that effect at all. So far from it having that effect more and more women have been doing these things and I had incited them to do, and were more determined in doing them: so that the long determinate sentence had no effect in crushing the agitation.

Well then they felt they must do something else, and they began to legislate. I want to tell men in this meeting that the British government, which is not remarkable for having very mild laws to administer, has passed more stringent laws to deal with this agitation than it ever found it necessary during all the history of political agitation in my country. They were able to deal with the revolutionaries of the Chartists' time;* they were able to deal with the trades union agitation; they were able to deal with the revolutionaries later on when the Reform Acts of 1867 and 1884 were passed: but the ordinary law has not sufficed to curb insurgent women. They have had to pass special legislation, and now they are on the point of admitting that that special legislation has absolutely failed. They had to dip back into the Middle Ages to find a means of repressing the women in revolt, and the whole history shows how futile it is for men who have been considered able statesmen to deal with dissatisfied women who are determined to win their citizenship and who will not submit to government until their consent is obtained. That is the whole point of our agitation. The whole argument with the anti-suffragists, or even the critical suffragist man, is this: that you can govern human beings without their consent.

They have said to us government rests upon force, the women haven't force so they must submit. Well, we are showing them that government does not rest upon force at all: it rests upon consent. As long as women consent to be unjustly governed, they can be, but directly women say: 'We withhold our consent, we will not be governed any longer so long as that government is unjust.' Not by the forces of civil war can you govern the very weakest woman. You can kill that woman, but she escapes you then; you cannot govern her. And that is, I think, a most valuable demonstration we have been making to the world.

When they put us in prison at first, simply for taking petitions, we

* The Chartists were an influential movement for political and social reform in Britain during the mid-nineteenth century.

submitted; we allowed them to dress us in prison clothes; we allowed them to put us in solitary confinement; we allowed them to treat us as ordinary criminals, and put us amongst the most degraded of those criminals; and we were very glad of the experience, because out of that experience we learned of the need for prison reform; we learned of the fearful mistakes that men of all nations have made when it is a question of dealing with human beings; we learned of some of the appalling evils of our so-called civilisation that we could not have learned in any other way except by going through the police courts of our country, in the prison vans that take you up to prison and right through that prison experience. It was valuable experience, and we were glad to get it. But there came a time when we said: 'It is unjust to send political agitators to prison in this way for merely asking for justice, and we will not submit any longer.'

And I am always glad to remind American audiences that two of the first women that came to the conclusion that they would not submit to unjust imprisonment any longer were two American girls. One of them came, I believe it was, from Heidelberg, travelling all night, to take part in one of those little processions to parliament with a petition. She was arrested and thrown into prison with about twenty others, and that group of twenty women were the first women who decided they would not submit themselves to the degradation of wearing prison clothes; and they refused, and they were almost the first to adopt the 'hunger strike' as a protest against the criminal treatment. They forced their way out of prison. Well, then it was that women began to withhold their consent.

I have been in audiences where I have seen men smile when they heard the words 'hunger strike', and yet I think there are very few men today who would be prepared to adopt a 'hunger strike' for any cause. It is only people who feel an intolerable sense of oppression who would adopt a means of that kind. I know of no people who did it before us except revolutionaries in Russia – who adopted the hunger strike against intolerable prison conditions. Well, our women decided to terminate those unjust sentences at the earliest possible moment by the terrible means of the hunger strike. It means, you refuse food until you are at death's door, and then the authorities have to choose between letting you die, and letting you go; and then they let the women go.

Now, that went on so long that the government felt they had lost their power, and that they were unable to cope with the situation. Then it was that, to the shame of the British government, they set the example to authorities all over the world of feeding sane, resisting human beings by force. There may be doctors in this meeting: if so, they know it is one thing to treat an insane person, to feed by force an insane person, or a patient who has some form of illness which makes it necessary; but it is quite another thing to feed a sane, resisting human being who resists with every nerve and with every fibre of her body the indignity and the outrage of forcible feeding. Now, that was done in England, and the government thought they had crushed us. But they found that it did not quell the agitation, that more and more women came in and even passed that terrible ordeal, and that they were not able with all their forcible feeding to make women serve out their unjust sentences. They were obliged to let them go.

Then came the legislation to which I have referred, the legislation which is known in England as the 'Cat and Mouse Act'.* It got through the British House of Commons because the Home Secretary assured the House of Commons that he wanted the bill passed in the interests of humanity. He said he was a humane man and he did not like having to resort to forcible feeding; he wanted the House of Commons to give him some way of disposing of them, and this was his way: he said, 'Give me the power to let these women go when they are at death's door, and leave them at liberty under licence until they have recovered their health again and then bring them back; leave it to me to fix the time of their licences; leave it in my hands altogether to deal with this intolerable situation, because the laws must be obeyed and people who are sentenced for breaking the law must be compelled to serve their sentences.' Well, the House of Commons passed the law. They said: 'As soon as the women get a taste of this they will give it up.' In fact, it was passed to repress the agitation, to make the women yield – because that is what it has really come to, ladies and gentlemen. It has come to a battle between the women and the government as to who shall yield first, whether they will yield and give us the vote, or whether we will give up our agitation.

Now, I want to say to you who think women cannot succeed, we have brought the government of England to this position, that it has to face this alternative: either women are to be killed or women are to have the vote. I ask American men in this meeting, what would you say if in your state you were faced with that alternative, that you must either kill them or give them their citizenship – women, many of whom you respect, women whom you

* Officially called the Prisoners (Temporary Discharge for Ill Health) Act 1913.

know have lived useful lives, women whom you know, even if you do not know them personally, are animated with the highest motives, women who are in pursuit of liberty and the power to do useful public service? Well, there is only one answer to that alternative; there is only one way out of it, unless you are prepared to put back civilisation two or three generations: you must give those women the vote. Now that is the outcome of our civil war.

You won your freedom in America when you had the revolution, by bloodshed, by sacrificing human life. You won the civil war by the sacrifice of human life when you decided to emancipate the Negro. You have left it to women in your land, the men of all civilised countries have left it to women, to work out their own salvation. That is the way in which we women of England are doing. Human life for us is sacred, but we say if any life is to be sacrificed it shall be ours; we won't do it ourselves, but we will put the enemy in the position where they will have to choose between giving us freedom or giving us death.

Now whether you approve of us or whether you do not, you must see that we have brought the question of women's suffrage into a position where it is of first-rate importance, where it can be ignored no longer. Even the most hardened politician will hesitate to take upon himself directly the responsibility of sacrificing the lives of women of undoubted honour, of undoubted earnestness of purpose. That is the political situation as I lay it before you today.

Now then, let me say something about what has brought it about because you must realise that only the very strongest of motives would lead women to do what we have done.

Well, I might spend two or three nights dealing with the industrial situation as it affects women, with the legal position of women, with the social position of women. I want very briefly to say a few words about all. First of

66 we will put the enemy in the position where they will have to choose between giving us freedom or giving us death. 99

all there is the condition of the working woman. The industrial workers of Great Britain have an average wage, mind you, not a minimum wage, an average wage, of less than two dollars a week. Think what would happen in any country if the men in industry of that country had to subsist on a wage like that. Thousands upon thousands of these women – because there are over five million wage earners in my country – thousands of these women have dependants. Their average income, taking the highly skilled woman teacher and averaging her wage with the unskilled home worker, the average income is less than two dollars a week. There you have in itself an explanation of an uprising of a very determined kind to secure better conditions; and when you know that the government is the largest employer of all the employers and sets a horribly bad example to the private employer in the wages that it pays to women, there you have another explanation. So much for the industrial situation.

Then there is the legal situation. The marriage laws of our country are bringing hundreds and hundreds of women into the militant ranks because we cannot get reform, the kind of reform that women want, of our marriage laws. First of all, a girl is held marriageable by English law, at the age of twelve years. When I was on trial they produced a little girl as a witness, a little girl who had found something in the neighbourhood of the house of the Chancellor of the Exchequer, which was destroyed by some women, and this little girl was produced as a witness. It was said that it was a terrible thing to bring a little girl of twelve years of age and put her in the witness box in a court of law. I agreed, but I pointed out to the judge and the jury that one of the reasons why women were in revolt was because that little girl, whose head just appeared over the top of the witness box, was considered old enough by the laws of her country to take upon herself the terrible responsibilities of wifehood and motherhood, and women could not get it altered, no politicians would listen to us, when we asked to have the marriage law altered in that particular.

Then, the position of the wife. It is very frequently said that every woman who wants a vote, wants a vote because she has been disappointed, because she has not been chosen to be a wife. Well, I can assure you that if most women made a study of the laws before they decided to get married, a great many women would seriously consider whether it was worthwhile, whether the price was not too heavy, because, according to English law, a woman may toil all her life for her husband and her family, she may work in her husband's business, she may help him to build up the family income, and if he chooses at the end of a long life to take every penny of the money that woman has helped to earn away from her and her children, he can do it, and she has no redress. She may at the end of a long, hard life find herself and her children absolutely penniless because her husband has chosen to will the money away from her. So that you see when you look at it from the legal point of view, it is not such a very, very great gain to become a wife in my country. There are a great many risks that go along with it.

Then take her as a mother. If the child of two parents has any property inherited from relatives, and that child dies before it is of age to make a will, or without making a will, the only person who inherits the property of that child is the child's father; the mother does not exist as her child's heir at all; and during the father's lifetime she not only cannot inherit from her child but she has no voice whatever in deciding the life of her child. Her husband can give the child away to be educated somewhere else or he can bring whomever he pleases into the house to educate the child. He decides absolutely the conditions in which that child is to live; he decides how it is to be educated; he can even decide what religion it is to profess, and the mother's consent is not obtained to any of these decisions. Women are trying to alter it, have tried for generations, but they cannot because the legislatures have no time to listen to the opinions and the desires of people who have no votes.

Well then, when it comes to the question of how people are to get out of marriage, if they are unhappy, under the laws of divorce, the English law of divorce is the most scandalous divorce law in the civilised world. There may be a few states in America, and I believe in Canada, where the same law obtains, but the English divorce law is in itself such a stigma upon women, such a degradation to women, such an invitation to immorality on the part of the married man, that I think that divorce law in itself would justify a rebellion on the part of the women. You get registered in law unequal standards of morals in marriage, and a married man is encouraged by law to think that he can make as many lapses as he thinks fit in marital fidelity; whereas, if one act of infidelity is proved against her the husband can get rid of her by divorce, can take her children away from her and make her an outcast. Women who have been clamouring for an equal divorce law for generations cannot get any attention.

Well, can you wonder that all these things make us more militant? It seems to me that once you look at things from the woman's point of view, once you cease to listen to politicians, once you cease to allow yourself to look at the facts of life through men's spectacles but look at them through your own, every day that passes you are having fresh illustrations of the need there is for women to refuse to wait any longer for their enfranchisement.

I think I have said enough at least to make you understand that this uprising on the part of the British women has as much justification and as much provocation as any uprising on the part of men in their desire for political liberty in the past. We are not working to get the vote. We are not going to prison to get the vote, merely to say we have the vote. We are going through all this to get the vote so that by means of the vote we can bring about better conditions not only for ourselves but for the community as a whole.

Men have done splendid things in this world; they have made great achievements in engineering; they have done splendid organisation work; but they have failed, they have miserably failed, when it has come to dealing with the lives of human beings. They stand self-confessed failures, because the problems that perplex civilisation are absolutely appalling today. Well, that is the function of women in life: it is our business to care for human beings, and we are determined that we must come without delay to the saving of the race. The race must be saved, and it can only be saved through the emancipation of women.

I Have a Dream

– MARTIN LUTHER KING –

In the United States, women finally obtained their full voting rights when the Nineteenth Amendment to the US constitution was ratified in August 1920. In theory African Americans, another discriminated-against sector of the US population, had gained their right to vote fifty years earlier, with the ratification of the Fifteenth Amendment in February 1870 (or at least male African Americans had). However, in reality, it took the best part of another century before they were able to exercise their full voting rights across the whole of the United States.

The history of African Americans is in many ways a history of the United States. Africans first arrived in the Americas with Spanish explorers in the first half of the sixteenth century, and African slaves are recorded in the first English colony of Virginia as early as 1619.[12] Originally Africans, like many white Europeans, were used as indentured labour – under contract for a fixed period of time in return for their travel, food and accommodation – but this gradually changed to a situation of slavery as non-Christian 'imported' servants became slaves for life, and slavery became a permanent state that could be passed on to their children. From the mid-seventeenth century onwards, the heinous situation of hereditary servitude based on race became the norm in the English colonies of North America.[13]

As the demand for labour increased, the Atlantic slave trade developed a vicious circle: goods from Europe were shipped to Africa for sale or trade for enslaved Africans, who were then shipped to the colonies of the Americas, where they were traded for raw materials, which were then returned to Europe to complete the triangular trade.[14] The journey from ordinary life in Africa to enslavement in the Americas was also a three-part process, consisting of the capture and march to the coast, the voyage across the Atlantic from Africa to the Americas and the transfer from the arrival port to the point of resale. The second part, the 'Middle Passage', could take several months and involved terrible conditions for the slaves, who were thought of as little more than cargo.[15] Between 1690 and 1807, English captains took nearly three million slaves from Africa and sold them in foreign ports. During the 1740s and 1750s, five thousand Africans a year were being sold into slavery in America.[16]

Despite the insistence of the Declaration of Independence that 'all men are created equal', the American War of Independence (1775–83) made little difference to the situation of African slaves. It took the American Civil War (1861–65), in which slavery was a key issue, and Abraham Lincoln's 1863 Emancipation Proclamation freeing the slaves of the Confederacy, for the grip of slavery over Africans and their descendants to begin to loosen. Then in 1865 the United States passed the Thirteenth Amendment, abolishing slavery and involuntary servitude. However, this was just the beginning of the African-American struggle for civil rights.

One hundred years after Lincoln's Emancipation Proclamation, a young African-American Baptist minister stood in front of the Lincoln Memorial in Washington DC and told the gathered crowd: 'Five score years ago, a great American, in whose symbolic shadow we stand today, signed the Emancipation Proclamation . . . But one hundred years later, the Negro still is not free. One hundred years later, the life of the Negro is still sadly crippled by the manacles of segregation and the chains of discrimination. One hundred years later, the Negro lives on a lonely island of poverty in the midst of a vast ocean of material prosperity. One hundred years later, the Negro is still languished in the corners of American society and finds himself an exile in his own land.' The minister who spoke that day in August 1963 was Martin Luther King, and he was addressing a crowd of over two hundred thousand people who had converged for the March on Washington for Jobs and Freedom, an attempt to bring civil rights and economic issues to national attention.

The United States at that time was a country profoundly divided by race. This was particularly so in the Deep South, where the Ku Klux Klan was still strong and lynching had continued into the 1950s and 1960s. The Jim Crow laws enacted after the American Civil War, which introduced racial segregation in public places, had not yet been fully dismantled (and would not be until the passing of the Civil Rights Act in the summer of 1964). King had joined the campaign for African-American civil rights in the 1950s and come to national prominence in 1955–56 as the leader of the successful campaign to desegregate public buses in Montgomery, Alabama, after Rosa Parks had refused to give up her seat to a white passenger. In 1957 he was elected as the first President of the Southern Christian Leadership Conference, a loose alliance established to provide leadership for the growing civil-rights movement.

King was a powerful orator and his words helped to galvanise the movement. His speech in Washington on 28 August 1963 was no exception. His soaring rhetoric drew on the Bible, the US Declaration of Independence and Lincoln's Gettysburg Address, and bound them all together in a style that clearly reflected his vocation as a Baptist preacher. His key message was that all people are created equal, and although racial injustice was endemic in the United States at the time he hoped that the future would bring greater harmony. However, King had never spoken to a crowd of this size and the night before the march he had spent hours perfecting what he would say. In front of the huge crowd assembled by the Lincoln Memorial he started out steady and deliberate, if a little nervous. Then, towards the end of his prepared speech, as the energy started to slip away, the gospel singer Mahalia Jackson is reported to have shouted out from behind him on the stage: 'Tell them about the dream, Martin.'[17] King paused and then gave one of the most powerful improvised sermons ever delivered.

He had a dream. He had a dream that one day 'this nation will rise up and live out the true meaning of its creed: we hold these truths to be self-evident, that all men are created equal'. He had a dream that one day 'my four little children will live in a nation where they will not be judged by the colour of their skin but by the content of their character'. He had a dream that one day 'in Alabama little black boys and black girls will be able to join hands with little white boys and white girls as sisters and brothers'. He had a dream that one day 'every valley shall be exalted, and every hill and mountain shall be made low, the rough places will be made plain, and the crooked places will be made straight'. Then, returning to his prepared speech, he ended by saying, 'all of God's children, black men and white men, Jews and Gentiles, Protestants and Catholics, will be able to join hands and sing in the words of the old Negro spiritual: Free at last! Free at last! Thank God Almighty, we are free at last!'

His speech had an electrifying effect on the audience, white and black. All the major television networks had interrupted their normal programming to broadcast King's speech live to millions of Americans. The impact was made even more dramatic by the fact he delivered his words on the steps of the memorial to Lincoln, the President who had defeated the Confederacy over the issue of slavery. His speech was the highlight of the March on Washington for Jobs and Freedom, and placed him firmly at the head of the civil-rights movement.[18] It is remembered as one of the greatest speeches in history, praised for both its content and delivery.

Not everyone involved in the struggle for African-American rights was so supportive of the march on Washington, though. Some felt that it had been controlled by the black bourgeoisie and funded by white liberals, who together had watered down the message in an attempt to avoid upsetting the administration of John F. Kennedy.[19] The militant black nationalist leader Malcolm X used his speech to the Northern Negro Grass Roots Leadership Conference to criticise the civil-rights leaders who, he said, had turned the march into 'a picnic, a circus' and 'a sell-out'.[20] Like many in the black Muslim movement the Nation of Islam, he used 'X' to symbolise the African family name he could never know, since his surname 'Little' had been imposed on his paternal ancestors by a white slave-owner.[21] He promoted the right to self-defence 'by any means necessary' and argued that freedom would come 'by the ballot or the bullet'.[22]

King, on the other hand, had travelled to India in 1959 to visit Mohandas Gandhi's birthplace and learn from his teachings on non-violence. This influence is clearly echoed in his 'I have a dream' speech when he said, 'we must rise to the majestic heights of meeting physical force with soul force' and 'continue to work with the faith that unearned suffering is redemptive'. America's *Time* magazine named him Man of the Year for 1963 and he was awarded the Nobel Peace Prize in 1964.[23] While King and the civil-rights movement fought against racial segregation,

Malcolm X and the Nation of Islam believed in the separation of black people from the white enemy and the creation of a separate African-American territory in the southern United States. The two men represented a crucial tension in the diverse struggle for African-American rights: the United States could be viewed as a potential dream or a realised nightmare.[24]

Malcolm X was assassinated on 21 February 1965 by rivals from the Nation of Islam, which he had turned his back on the previous year.[25] The day before Malcolm X's funeral, King sent a telegram to his widow expressing his sadness and, while admitting that 'we did not always see eye to eye on methods to solve the race problem', he told her that 'he was an eloquent spokesman for his point of view and no one can honestly doubt that Malcolm had a great concern for the problems we face as a race.'[26] Three years later, on 4 April 1968, King was himself assassinated. Standing on the balcony of the Lorraine Motel in Memphis, Tennessee, he was struck by a sniper's bullet and died in hospital soon afterwards. He was thirty-nine years old. Two months later, escaped convict James Earl Ray was arrested at a London airport while trying to leave the United Kingdom for white-ruled Rhodesia using a false passport. He was extradited to Tennessee and charged with King's murder. Despite allegations of a conspiracy, Ray pleaded guilty at his trial and was sentenced to a ninety-nine-year prison term.[27]

The day before his murder, King spoke at a black Pentecostal church in Memphis. In what would be his last speech, he told the crowd: 'Well, I don't know what will happen now. We've got some difficult days ahead. But it really doesn't matter with me now, because I've been to the mountaintop. And I don't mind.' 'Like anybody,' he said, 'I would like to live a long life. Longevity has its place. But I'm not concerned about that now.' He ended by saying, 'I just want to do God's will. And He's allowed me to go up to the mountain. And I've looked over. And I've seen the promised land. I may not get there with you. But I want you to know tonight, that we, as a people, will get to the promised land.'[28] King's assassination led to an eruption of violence and rioting in over a hundred cities across the United States, which in places took the National Guard and federal troops to restore order. The American journalist I. F. Stone wrote that King 'stood in that line of saints which goes back from Gandhi to Jesus' and that 'his violent end, like theirs, reflects the hostility of mankind to those that annoy it by trying hard to pull it one more painful step further up the ladder from ape to angel'.[29] His death left the civil-rights movement without one of its most effective leaders, and as the boundaries between racial inequality and other social injustices became increasingly blurred, the Black Panther party and others in the more radical black-power movement continued to gain greater prominence through the late 1960s and into the 1970s.[30]

Forty years after King's assassination, there are two contrasting images that demonstrate the contemporary position of African Americans in the United States. The first is Barack Obama telling a crowd in Grant Park in Chicago 'change has come to America' after winning the 2008 presidential election and becoming America's first black President.[31] The second is many thousands of poor African Americans trapped in the Louisiana Superdome in New Orleans when the levees broke during Hurricane Katrina in 2005.[32] These examples demonstrate just how far the struggle for racial equality has come and also just how far there still is to go.

Lincoln Memorial, Washington DC, United States

28 AUGUST 1963

I am happy to join with you today in what will go down in history as the greatest demonstration for freedom in the history of our nation.

Five score years ago, a great American, in whose symbolic shadow we stand today, signed the Emancipation Proclamation. This momentous decree came as a great beacon light of hope to millions of Negro slaves who had been seared in the flames of withering injustice. It came as a joyous daybreak to end the long night of their captivity.

But one hundred years later, the Negro still is not free. One hundred years later, the life of the Negro is still sadly crippled by the manacles of segregation and the chains of discrimination. One hundred years later, the

Negro lives on a lonely island of poverty in the midst of a vast ocean of material prosperity. One hundred years later, the Negro is still languished in the corners of American society and finds himself an exile in his own land. And so we've come here today to dramatise a shameful condition.

In a sense we've come to our nation's capital to cash a cheque. When the architects of our republic wrote the magnificent words of the Constitution and the Declaration of Independence, they were signing a promissory note to which every American was to fall heir. This note was a promise that all men, yes, black men as well as white men, would be guaranteed the 'unalienable Rights' of 'Life, Liberty and the pursuit of Happiness'. It is obvious today that America has defaulted on this promissory note, insofar as her citizens of colour are concerned. Instead of honouring this sacred obligation, America has given the Negro people a bad cheque, a cheque which has come back marked 'insufficient funds'.

But we refuse to believe that the bank of justice is bankrupt. We refuse to believe that there are insufficient funds in the great vaults of opportunity of this nation. And so, we've come to cash this cheque, a cheque that will give us upon demand the riches of freedom and the security of justice.

We have also come to this hallowed spot to remind America of the fierce urgency of Now. This is no time to engage in the luxury of cooling off or to take the tranquillising drug of gradualism. Now is the time to make real the promises of democracy. Now is the time to rise from the dark and desolate valley of segregation to the sunlit path of racial justice. Now is the time to lift our nation from the quicksands of racial injustice to the solid rock of brotherhood. Now is the time to make justice a reality for all of God's children.

It would be fatal for the nation to overlook the urgency of the moment. This sweltering summer of the Negro's legitimate discontent will not pass until there is an invigorating autumn of freedom and equality. 1963 is not an end, but a beginning. And those who hope that the Negro needed to blow off steam and will now be content will have a rude awakening if the nation returns to business as usual. And there will be neither rest nor tranquillity in America until the Negro is granted his citizenship rights. The whirlwinds of revolt will continue to shake the foundations of our nation until the bright day of justice emerges.

But there is something that I must say to my people, who stand on the warm threshold which leads into the palace of justice: in the process of gaining our rightful place, we must not be guilty of wrongful deeds. Let us not seek to satisfy our thirst for freedom by drinking from the cup of bitterness and hatred. We must forever conduct our struggle on the high plane of dignity and discipline. We must not allow our creative protest to degenerate into physical violence. Again and again, we must rise to the majestic heights of meeting physical force with soul force.

The marvellous new militancy which has engulfed the Negro community must not lead us to a distrust of all white people, for many of our white brothers, as evidenced by their presence here today, have come to realise that their destiny is tied up with our destiny. And they have come to realise that their freedom is inextricably bound to our freedom.

We cannot walk alone.

And as we walk, we must make the pledge that we shall always march ahead.

We cannot turn back.

There are those who are asking the devotees of civil rights, 'When will you be satisfied?' We can never be satisfied as long as the Negro is the victim of the unspeakable horrors of police brutality. We can never be satisfied as long as our bodies, heavy with the fatigue of travel, cannot gain lodging in the motels of the highways and the hotels of the cities. We cannot be satisfied as long as the Negro's basic mobility is from a smaller ghetto to a larger one. We can never be satisfied as long as our children are stripped of their selfhood and robbed of their dignity by signs stating: 'For Whites Only'. We cannot be satisfied as long as a Negro in Mississippi cannot vote and a Negro in New York believes he has nothing for which to vote. No, no, we are not satisfied, and we will not be satisfied until 'justice rolls down like waters, and righteousness like a mighty stream'.

I am not unmindful that some of you have come here out of great trials

❝ one day this nation will rise up and live out the true meaning of its creed: we hold these truths to be self-evident, that all men are created equal.❞

and tribulations. Some of you have come fresh from narrow jail cells. And some of you have come from areas where your quest for freedom left you battered by the storms of persecution and staggered by the winds of police brutality. You have been the veterans of creative suffering. Continue to work with the faith that unearned suffering is redemptive. Go back to Mississippi, go back to Alabama, go back to South Carolina, go back to Georgia, go back to Louisiana, go back to the slums and ghettos of our northern cities, knowing that somehow this situation can and will be changed.

Let us not wallow in the valley of despair, I say to you today, my friends.

And so even though we face the difficulties of today and tomorrow, I still have a dream. It is a dream deeply rooted in the American dream.

I have a dream that one day this nation will rise up and live out the true meaning of its creed: we hold these truths to be self-evident, that all men are created equal.

I have a dream that one day on the red hills of Georgia, the sons of former slaves and the sons of former slave owners will be able to sit down together at the table of brotherhood.

I have a dream that one day even the state of Mississippi, a state sweltering with the heat of injustice, sweltering with the heat of oppression, will be transformed into an oasis of freedom and justice.

I have a dream that my four little children will one day live in a nation where they will not be judged by the colour of their skin but by the content of their character.

I have a dream today!

I have a dream that one day, down in Alabama, with its vicious racists, with its governor having his lips dripping with the words of 'interposition' and 'nullification' – one day right there in Alabama little black boys and black girls will be able to join hands with little white boys and white girls as sisters and brothers.

I have a dream today!

I have a dream that one day every valley shall be exalted, and every hill and mountain shall be made low, the rough places will be made plain, and the crooked places will be made straight; 'and the glory of the Lord shall be revealed and all flesh shall see it together'.

This is our hope, and this is the faith that I go back to the South with.

With this faith, we will be able to hew out of the mountain of despair a stone of hope. With this faith, we will be able to transform the jangling discords of our nation into a beautiful symphony of brotherhood. With this

> **❝I have a dream** that my four little children will one day live in a nation where they will **not be judged** by the **colour of their skin** but by the **content** of their **character**.**❞**

faith, we will be able to work together, to pray together, to struggle together, to go to jail together, to stand up for freedom together, knowing that we will be free one day.

And this will be the day – this will be the day when all of God's children will be able to sing with new meaning:

> 'My country 'tis of thee, sweet land of liberty, of thee I sing.
> Land where my fathers died, land of the Pilgrim's pride,
> From every mountainside, let freedom ring!'

And if America is to be a great nation, this must become true.
And so let freedom ring from the prodigious hilltops of New Hampshire.
Let freedom ring from the mighty mountains of New York.
Let freedom ring from the heightening Alleghenies of Pennsylvania.
Let freedom ring from the snow-capped Rockies of Colorado.
Let freedom ring from the curvaceous slopes of California.
But not only that:
Let freedom ring from Stone Mountain of Georgia.
Let freedom ring from Lookout Mountain of Tennessee.
Let freedom ring from every hill and molehill of Mississippi.
From every mountainside, let freedom ring.

And when this happens, when we let freedom ring, when we let it ring from every village and every hamlet, from every state and every city, we will be able to speed up that day when all of God's children, black men and white men, Jews and Gentiles, Protestants and Catholics, will be able to join hands and sing in the words of the old Negro spiritual:

'Free at last! Free at last!
Thank God Almighty, we are free at last!'

Rivers of Blood

– Enoch Powell –

Two weeks after Martin Luther King was assassinated, US President Lyndon Johnson signed the Civil Rights Act of 1968, which prohibited discrimination in housing on the grounds of race, colour, religion or national origin. On the other side of the Atlantic, the British parliament was debating a Race Relations Bill that would make it illegal to refuse housing, employment or public services to people because of their ethnic background. However, oil was about to be added to the fire of another aspect of the race debate: national identity and immigration. On the afternoon of 20 April 1968, John Enoch Powell told a Conservative Association meeting in Birmingham, 'Whole areas, towns and parts of towns across England will be occupied by sections of the immigrant and immigrant-descended population.' He argued that the sheer number of immigrants and their children meant 'The discrimination and the deprivation, the sense of alarm and of resentment, lies not with the immigrant population but with those among whom they have come and are still coming.'

Although tempting, it is too simplistic to dismiss Powell as a dyed-in-the-wool racist. On the contrary, he thought that racial categories were meaningless and he did not believe in a hierarchy of racial groups.[33] He maintained that his arguments were based on national identity, not race per se (although it is hard to make such a distinction when his essential argument was that the non-white minority was a threat to the white majority). He also had a powerful intellect: he achieved a double starred first in Latin and Greek at Trinity College, Cambridge, before taking up the post of Professor of Greek at the University of Sydney at only twenty-five years old; while at university he also studied Urdu at the School of Oriental Studies in London and eventually became fluent in eight languages. He returned to England at the outbreak of World War II and enlisted in the army. He became one of the few men to rise through the ranks from private to brigadier during the course of the war. India's post-war independence from the British Empire in 1947 laid waste to his ambition to become viceroy and he instead focused his energies on domestic politics. He joined the Conservative Party, and was elected Member of Parliament for Wolverhampton South West in the 1950 general election – a seat he would hold for twenty-four years before returning to parliament as the Ulster Unionist MP for South Down in 1974.

On 27 July 1959, Powell gave perhaps his most powerful speech in the House of Commons. Several months earlier, eleven suspected insurgents had been beaten to death at the Hola detention camp in Kenya, where they were being held for their part in the Mau Mau uprising against British colonial rule. An emotional Powell railed against his parliamentary colleagues who had called the dead 'sub-human' and told them: 'We cannot, we dare not, in Africa of all places, fall below our own highest standards in the acceptance of responsibility.'[34] Then in 1964 he said, 'I have set and always will set my face like flint against making any difference between one citizen of this country and another on grounds of his origin.'[35] This hardly seems like the same man who would speak of 'wide-grinning piccaninnies' in a speech four years later.

Yet by the late 1960s Powell felt compelled to give voice to a growing fear in the United Kingdom that immigration from the colonies would soon leave the British a 'persecuted minority' and 'strangers in their own country'. He gave speeches in Wolverhampton and Walsall and wrote an article for the *Daily Telegraph*, but it was his speech in Birmingham that has become his most infamous.[36] This time Powell sent the media advance copies of his apocalyptic speech and mixed his own opinions with the blunt views of some of his local constituents: 'If I had the money to go, I wouldn't stay in this country . . . in fifteen or twenty years' time the black man will have the whip hand over the white man.' Paraphrasing Virgil's epic poem the *Aeneid*, Powell warned, 'As I look ahead, I am filled with foreboding; like the Roman, I seem to see the River Tiber foaming with much blood.' He admonished his countrymen, saying, 'We must be mad, literally mad, as a nation to be permitting the annual inflow of some fifty thousand dependants . . . It is like watching a nation busily engaged in heaping up its own funeral pyre.'

Powell's speech had a potent effect. He was immediately branded a racialist in political circles and Edward Heath was forced to sack him from his shadow cabinet post of defence spokesman. However, Powell attracted wide support from the British public: he received over a hundred and twenty thousand letters of support and London dockers and meat porters from Smithfield market went on strike in protest at his sacking. His controversial speech sparked one of the biggest race debates in British history. It was seven months before Powell gave another speech on the issue of immigration and, repeating his view that the only solution was 'by stopping, or virtually stopping, further inflow, and by promoting the maximum outflow', he proposed the creation of a Ministry for Repatriation, arguing that 'The resettlement of a substantial proportion of the Commonwealth immigrants in Britain is not beyond the resources and abilities of this country, if it is undertaken as a national duty.'[37] This would, he argued, be voluntary and in the interests of the immigrants themselves, but was also a matter of great urgency.

Powell's rivers of blood speech cost him his reputation and curtailed his front-bench political career. He has been condemned by history for his views and rightly criticised for stirring up racial tensions. But what motivated Powell to give such an inflammatory speech in the first place; was it simple racism, or was there more to it? He thought that 'people are disposed to mistake predicting troubles for causing troubles' but 'that to see, and not to speak, would be the great betrayal'. In short, he believed that he was doing the right thing – although that is no great defence. He likely had several motivations, including destabilising Heath's leadership of the Conservative Party for his own political gain and attacking the Labour government's plans to pass a Race Relations Act, which he thought would do more harm than good. However, Robert Shepherd, Powell's unofficial biographer, believes that his primary motivation was something much deeper than party politics or racism. Powell's greatest concern, he argues, was communalism: that is, loyalty to the interests of one's own ethnic group rather than to society as a whole. Powell had served in India during World War II and the potentially bloody effect of communalism had been demonstrated to him by the inter-communal violence unleashed during the partition of India in 1947. He feared that immigration would bring communalism to Britain, destroying its supposed homogeneous electorate and threatening its parliamentary system, as individuals in a minority might not accept the majority decision.[38]

Whatever his true motivation, Powell's speech has been seized upon by the political right, many of whom believe his prophecy came to pass with the race riots in Bristol, London, Birmingham, Leeds and Liverpool in the early 1980s and in Bradford and Birmingham in 2001 and 2005 respectively. A section of the white British population now feels overwhelmed by perceived ghettos of Asians, Muslims, Eastern Europeans, refugees, asylum-seekers and migrant workers. However, Britain's minorities do not, on the whole, live in ethnic enclaves. The evidence shows that residential segregation is actually decreasing across Britain and ethnic mixing is on the increase.[39] Furthermore, according to the 2001 census and a 2005 report from the Office for National Statistics, over 90 per cent of the population of the UK described themselves as white; only one in twelve of the population were born overseas; and over the decade from 1994 to 2004, there was a net inflow to the UK of only 1.2 million people (out of a total population of around 60 million).[40] There is a disconnect between perception and reality, but racism and xenophobia have the tabloid press warning of rivers of blood again.

This debate is not just limited to Britain or Europe. Immigration is a highly contentious issue around the world, particularly where there are relatively small, rich populations next to large, poor populations. For example, in the United States some have likened Mexican immigration to an invasion and in Australia the 'yellow peril' of Asian immigration still attracts a great deal of attention. National identity is often formed in opposition to such outside forces; it defines what makes us different to others – and can be manipulated for devastating political effect (as seen time and time again in the Balkans and across Africa, for example). Furthermore, so much of our national identity is based on the flawed collective narrative of our country's past: a national myth with deep symbolic meaning but likely full of exaggerations, omissions and factual errors. In any case, fear that the national identity will be swamped by immigration presupposes that there is a homogeneous, static identity to be swamped in the first place. Culture is not a passive phenomenon; it is creative and created: generated in the context of present activity, rather than simply handed down from past generations.[41]

The United Nations estimates that in the last fifty years the number of people living outside their country of birth has more than doubled to nearly 191 million – larger than at any other time in history.[42] Freedom of movement, both within and between countries, is a basic human right but the debate on immigration is a highly emotive one. Those who oppose immigration in any way are branded racist; those who support immigration are accused of opening the gates to floods of foreigners. However, anyone subscribing to a regressive view of immigration should ask themselves what they would do if the situations were reversed. If they were fleeing rape, torture and murder, seeking refuge from political persecution, or simply looking for a better life for their children, what would they do? Those fortunate enough to have been born in safe and prosperous countries should not deny those looking for the same securities. There are, however, distinctions to be made between unmanaged immigration and cultural diversity; between communalism and multiculturalism; between racism and patriotism; between economic migrants and political and environmental refugees; between newly arrived immigrants and the second- and third-generation children of immigrants. So perhaps in the heated debate over race, national identity and immigration there are no black and white areas, just grey ones. The one universal truth, though, must be that we all have the right to live where we feel safe and happy, wherever that may be and whatever the colour of our skin.

Midland Hotel, Birmingham, England

20 APRIL 1968

The supreme function of statesmanship is to provide against preventable evils. In seeking to do so, it encounters obstacles which are deeply rooted in human nature.

One is that by the very order of things such evils are not demonstrable until they have occurred; at each stage in their onset there is room for doubt and for dispute whether they be real or imaginary. By the same token, they attract little attention in comparison with current troubles, which are both indisputable and pressing: whence the besetting temptation of all politics to concern itself with the immediate present at the expense of the future.

Above all, people are disposed to mistake predicting troubles for causing troubles and even for desiring troubles: 'If only', they love to think, 'if only people wouldn't talk about it, it probably wouldn't happen.'

Perhaps this habit goes back to the primitive belief that the word and the thing, the name and the object, are identical.

At all events, the discussion of future grave but, with effort now, avoidable evils is the most unpopular and at the same time the most necessary occupation for the politician. Those who knowingly shirk it deserve, and not infrequently receive, the curses of those who come after.

A week or two ago I fell into conversation with a constituent, a middle-aged, quite ordinary working man employed in one of our nationalised industries.

After a sentence or two about the weather, he suddenly said: 'If I had the money to go, I wouldn't stay in this country.' I made some deprecatory reply to the effect that even this government wouldn't last for ever; but he took no notice, and continued: 'I have three children, all of them been through grammar school and two of them married now, with family. I shan't be satisfied till I have seen them all settled overseas. In this country in fifteen or twenty years' time the black man will have the whip hand over the white man.'

I can already hear the chorus of execration. How dare I say such a horrible thing? How dare I stir up trouble and inflame feelings by repeating such a conversation?

The answer is that I do not have the right not to do so. Here is a decent, ordinary fellow Englishman, who in broad daylight in my own town says to me, his Member of Parliament, that his country will not be worth living in for his children.

I simply do not have the right to shrug my shoulders and think about something else. What he is saying, thousands and hundreds of thousands are saying and thinking – not throughout Great Britain, perhaps, but in the areas that are already undergoing the total transformation to which there is no parallel in a thousand years of English history.

In fifteen or twenty years, on present trends, there will be in this country three and a half million Commonwealth immigrants and their descendants. That is not my figure. That is the official figure given to parliament by the spokesman of the Registrar General's Office.

"people are disposed to mistake predicting troubles for causing troubles and even for desiring troubles"

There is no comparable official figure for the year 2000, but it must be in the region of five to seven million, approximately one-tenth of the whole population, and approaching that of Greater London. Of course, it will not be evenly distributed from Margate to Aberystwyth and from Penzance to Aberdeen. Whole areas, towns and parts of towns across England will be occupied by sections of the immigrant and immigrant-descended population.

As time goes on, the proportion of this total who are immigrant descendants, those born in England, who arrived here by exactly the same route as the rest of us, will rapidly increase. Already by 1985 the native-born would constitute the majority. It is this fact which creates the extreme urgency of action now, of just that kind of action which is hardest for politicians to take, action where the difficulties lie in the present but the evils to be prevented or minimised lie several parliaments ahead.

The natural and rational first question with a nation confronted by such a prospect is to ask: 'How can its dimensions be reduced?' Granted it be not wholly preventable, can it be limited, bearing in mind that numbers are of the essence: the significance and consequences of an alien element introduced into a country or population are profoundly different according to whether that element is 1 per cent or 10 per cent.

The answers to the simple and rational question are equally simple and rational: by stopping, or virtually stopping, further inflow, and by promoting the maximum outflow. Both answers are part of the official policy of the Conservative Party.

It almost passes belief that at this moment twenty or thirty additional immigrant children are arriving from overseas in Wolverhampton alone every week – and that means fifteen or twenty additional families a decade or two hence. Those whom the gods wish to destroy, they first make mad. We must be mad, literally mad, as a nation to be permitting the annual inflow of some fifty thousand dependants, who are for the most part the material of the future growth of the immigrant-descended population. It is like watching a nation busily engaged in heaping up its own funeral pyre. So insane are we that we actually permit unmarried persons to immigrate for the purpose of founding a family with spouses and fiancés whom they have never seen.

Let no one suppose that the flow of dependants will automatically tail off. On the contrary, even at the present admission rate of only five thousand a year by voucher, there is sufficient for a further twenty-five thousand dependants per annum *ad infinitum*, without taking into account the huge reservoir of existing relations in this country – and I am making no allowance at all for fraudulent entry. In these circumstances nothing will suffice but that the total inflow for settlement should be reduced at once to negligible proportions, and that the necessary legislative and administrative measures be taken without delay.

I stress the words 'for settlement'. This has nothing to do with the entry of Commonwealth citizens, any more than of aliens, into this country, for the purposes of study or of improving their qualifications, like for instance the Commonwealth doctors who, to the advantage of their own countries, have enabled our hospital service to be expanded faster than would otherwise have been possible. They are not, and never have been, immigrants.

I turn to re-emigration. If all immigration ended tomorrow, the rate of growth of the immigrant and immigrant-descended population would be substantially reduced, but the prospective size of this element in the population would still leave the basic character of the national danger unaffected. This can only be tackled while a considerable proportion of the total still comprises persons who entered this country during the last ten years or so.

Hence the urgency of implementing now the second element of the Conservative Party's policy: the encouragement of re-emigration.

Nobody can make an estimate of the numbers which, with generous assistance, would choose either to return to their countries of origin or to go to other countries anxious to receive the manpower and the skills they represent.

Nobody knows, because no such policy has yet been attempted. I can only say that, even at present, immigrants in my own constituency from time to time come to me, asking if I can find them assistance to return home. If such a policy were adopted and pursued with the determination which the gravity of the alternative justifies, the resultant outflow could appreciably alter the prospects.

The third element of the Conservative Party's policy is that all who are in this country as citizens should be equal before the law and that there shall be no discrimination or difference made between them by public authority. As Mr Heath has put it we will have no 'first-class citizens' and 'second-class citizens'. This does not mean that the immigrant and his descendant should be elevated into a privileged or special class or that the citizen should be denied his right to discriminate in the management of his own affairs between one fellow citizen and another or that he should be subjected to imposition as to his reasons and motive for behaving in one lawful manner rather than another.

There could be no grosser misconception of the realities than is entertained by those who vociferously demand legislation as they call it 'against discrimination', whether they be leader writers of the same kidney and sometimes on the same newspapers which year after year in the 1930s tried to blind this country to the rising peril which confronted it, or archbishops who live in palaces, faring delicately with the bedclothes pulled right up over their heads. They have got it exactly and diametrically wrong.

The discrimination and the deprivation, the sense of alarm and of resentment, lies not with the immigrant population but with those among whom they have come and are still coming.

This is why to enact legislation of the kind before parliament at this moment is to risk throwing a match on to gunpowder. The kindest thing that can be said about those who propose and support it is that they know not what they do.

Nothing is more misleading than comparison between the Commonwealth immigrant in Britain and the American Negro. The Negro population of the United States, which was already in existence before the United States became a nation, started literally as slaves and were later given the franchise and other rights of citizenship, to the exercise of which they have only gradually and still incompletely come. The Commonwealth immigrant came to Britain as a full citizen, to a country which knew no discrimination between one citizen and another, and he entered instantly into the possession of the rights of every citizen, from the vote to free treatment under the National Health Service.

Whatever drawbacks attended the immigrants arose not from the law or from public policy or from administration, but from those personal circumstances and accidents which cause, and always will cause, the fortunes and experience of one man to be different from another's.

But while, to the immigrant, entry to this country was admission to privileges and opportunities eagerly sought, the impact upon the existing population was very different. For reasons which they could not comprehend, and in pursuance of a decision by default, on which they were never consulted, they found themselves made strangers in their own country.

They found their wives unable to obtain hospital beds in childbirth, their children unable to obtain school places, their homes and neighbourhoods changed beyond recognition, their plans and prospects for the future defeated; at work they found that employers hesitated to apply to the immigrant worker the standards of discipline and competence required of the native-born worker; they began to hear, as time went by, more and more voices which told them that they were now the unwanted. They now learn that a one-way privilege is to be established by act of parliament; a law which cannot, and is not intended to, operate to protect them or redress their grievances is to be enacted to give the stranger, the disgruntled and the agent-provocateur the power to pillory them for their private actions.

In the hundreds upon hundreds of letters I received when I last spoke on this subject two or three months ago, there was one striking feature which was largely new and which I find ominous. All Members of Parliament are used to the typical anonymous correspondent; but what surprised and alarmed me was the high proportion of ordinary, decent, sensible people, writing a rational and often well-educated letter, who believed that they had to omit their address because it was dangerous to have committed themselves to paper to a Member of Parliament agreeing with the views I had expressed, and that they would risk penalties or reprisals if they were known to have done so. The sense of being a persecuted minority which is growing among ordinary English people in the areas of the country which are affected is something that those without direct experience can hardly imagine.

I am going to allow just one of those hundreds of people to speak for me:

> Eight years ago in a respectable street in Wolverhampton a
> house was sold to a Negro. Now only one white (a woman old-
> age pensioner) lives there. This is her story.* She lost her

---

* Powell kept this woman's identity a secret and many doubted her existence. However, in 2007 a BBC Radio 4 documentary claimed to have identified the woman as Druscilla Cotterill, who lived in Brighton Place in Wolverhampton and died in 1978.

husband and both her sons in the war. So she turned her seven-roomed house, her only asset, into a boarding house. She worked hard and did well, paid off her mortgage and began to put something by for her old age. Then the immigrants moved in. With growing fear, she saw one house after another taken over. The quiet street became a place of noise and confusion. Regretfully, her white tenants moved out.

The day after the last one left, she was awakened at 7 a.m. by two Negroes who wanted to use her 'phone to contact their employer. When she refused, as she would have refused any stranger at such an hour, she was abused and feared she would have been attacked but for the chain on her door. Immigrant families have tried to rent rooms in her house, but she always refused. Her little store of money went, and after paying rates, she has less than £2 per week. She went to apply for a rate reduction and was seen by a young girl, who on hearing she had a seven-roomed house, suggested she should let part of it. When she said the only people she could get were Negroes, the girl said, 'Racial prejudice won't get you anywhere in this country.' So she went home.

The telephone is her lifeline. Her family pay the bill, and help her out as best they can. Immigrants have offered to buy her house – at a price which the prospective landlord would be able to recover from his tenants in weeks, or at most a few months. She is becoming afraid to go out. Windows are broken. She finds excreta pushed through her letter box. When she goes to the shops, she is followed by children, charming, wide-grinning piccaninnies. They cannot speak English, but one word they know. 'Racialist', they chant.

When the new Race Relations Bill is passed, this woman is convinced she will go to prison. And is she so wrong? I begin to wonder.

The other dangerous delusion from which those who are wilfully or otherwise blind to realities suffer is summed up in the word 'integration'. To be integrated into a population means to become for all practical purposes indistinguishable from its other members.

Now, at all times, where there are marked physical differences, especially of colour, integration is difficult though, over a period, not impossible. There are among the Commonwealth immigrants who have come to live here in the last fifteen years or so, many thousands whose wish and purpose is to be integrated and whose every thought and endeavour is bent in that direction.

But to imagine that such a thing enters the heads of a great and growing majority of immigrants and their descendants is a ludicrous misconception, and a dangerous one.

We are on the verge here of a change. Hitherto it has been force of circumstance and of background which has rendered the very idea of integration inaccessible to the greater part of the immigrant population – that they never conceived or intended such a thing, and that their numbers and physical concentration meant the pressures towards integration which normally bear upon any small minority did not operate.

Now we are seeing the growth of positive forces acting against integration, of vested interests in the preservation and sharpening of racial and religious differences, with a view to the exercise of actual domination, first over fellow immigrants and then over the rest of the population. The cloud no bigger than a man's hand, that can so rapidly overcast the sky, has been visible recently in Wolverhampton and has shown signs of spreading quickly. The words I am about to use, verbatim as they appeared in the local press on 17 February, are not mine, but those of a Labour Member of Parliament who is a minister in the present government:

> The Sikh communities' campaign to maintain customs inappropriate in Britain is much to be regretted. Working in Britain, particularly in the public services, they should be prepared to accept the terms and conditions of their employment. To claim special communal rights (or should one say rites?) leads to a dangerous fragmentation within society. This communalism is a canker; whether practised by one colour or another it is to be strongly condemned.

All credit to John Stonehouse for having had the insight to perceive that, and the courage to say it.

For these dangerous and divisive elements the legislation proposed in the Race Relations Bill is the very pabulum they need to flourish. Here is the means of showing that the immigrant communities can organise to

66 As I look ahead,

I am filled with foreboding;

like the Roman, I seem to see

the River Tiber foaming with

much blood. 99

consolidate their members, to agitate and campaign against their fellow citizens, and to overawe and dominate the rest with the legal weapons which the ignorant and the ill-informed have provided. As I look ahead, I am filled with foreboding; like the Roman, I seem to see the River Tiber foaming with much blood.

That tragic and intractable phenomenon which we watch with horror on the other side of the Atlantic but which there is interwoven with the history and existence of the States itself, is coming upon us here by our own volition and our own neglect. Indeed, it has all but come. In numerical terms, it will be of American proportions long before the end of the century.

Only resolute and urgent action will avert it even now. Whether there will be the public will to demand and obtain that action, I do not know. All I know is that to see, and not to speak, would be the great betrayal.

A Second Chance

– Napoleon Beazley –

I t is a basic tenet of morality that it is wrong to take another person's life. The world's religions proscribe murder and human society is built on this fundamental judgement. This is reflected in legal systems across the world and the right to life is a central pillar of human rights. However, we have recognised that there are circumstances in which the taking of life might be justified. This includes, for example, acting proportionately and in self-defence to protect oneself or others from life-threatening harm. The modern state has also granted itself the right to end someone's life. Some instances may be morally justified, such as police officers confronted by an armed suspect or soldiers fighting an invading army. In these examples, agents of the state have been granted dispensation from the laws that govern others under certain, often unavoidable, circumstances. Other examples are not so clear cut and raise complex moral questions. One of the most controversial is the use of the death penalty.

According to Amnesty International, the death penalty is retained by nearly sixty countries. However, the vast majority of the 2,390 people known to have been executed in 2008 were in just five countries: China, Iran, Saudi Arabia, Pakistan and the United States.[43] Punishable crimes include murder, drug-trafficking, kidnapping, treason and, in some Islamic countries, adultery. Throughout history capital punishment has also been applied as a tool of political or religious oppression. The most controversial modern uses of the death penalty have been in cases involving political prisoners, juvenile offenders or those with learning disabilities or mental-health problems. In particular, the execution of those under the age of eighteen at the time of their crime bitterly divides public opinion. Many countries draw a legal line between childhood and adulthood at the age of eighteen. But until 2005, in contravention of

51

international law, the United States was one of the very few countries that allowed for the execution of those who would otherwise be considered minors at the time of their crimes.

One such man was Napoleon Beazley, who was executed in Texas in May 2002. His case attracted international attention and high-profile pleas for clemency because he was just seventeen years old when he committed his crime. On 19 April 1994, he killed sixty-three-year-old John Luttig during a car-jacking in which he shot Luttig twice in the head with a .45-calibre handgun and attempted to kill his wife, Bobbie Luttig.[44] Nearly a year later, Beazley, an African American, was found guilty by an all-white jury based, in part, on dubious testimony from his two accomplices, Cedric and Donald Coleman – who each received a life sentence. Suspicions have been raised, and denied, that prosecutors only sought the death penalty because Luttig's son was an influential federal appeals judge or because the case involved a black offender and a white victim. Racial divisions are painfully reflected in the legal system of the United States, where socio-economic disparity and structural racism ensure that black inmates are disproportionally represented in the prison population as a whole and on death row in particular.[45] Though Beazley was – by his own admission – guilty of a horrendous crime that robbed a family of a husband and father, there are concerns that he may have been subjected to a miscarriage of justice when he received the death penalty, as life imprisonment would have been more appropriate.

There are five methods of execution allowed in the United States: electrocution, lethal gas, hanging, firing squad and lethal injection. Lethal injection is by far the most commonly used and the one that killed Beazley. At 6 p.m. on 28 May 2002 he was brought to the execution chamber of the Texas State Penitentiary and strapped to a hospital trolley. While his parents watched, he was administered a lethal cocktail of drugs consisting of sodium thiopental, a barbiturate that sedated him and induced unconsciousness; pancuronium bromide, a muscle relaxant that paralysed his diaphragm and other respiratory muscles; and potassium chloride, which caused cardiac arrest. He was pronounced dead nine minutes later. By that point he had spent eight years on death row and gone through numerous appeals and last-minute reprieves. He was twenty-five years old at the time of his death. In his last statement he said, 'Tonight we tell the world that there are no second chances in the eyes of justice . . . Tonight, we tell our children that in some instances, in some cases, killing is right.' He was one of the last juvenile offenders to be executed in the United States.

Executions usually follow the same ritualistic pattern. The condemned are offered a last meal, religious counsel and the chance to make any last remarks before being put to death in front of witnesses, which typically include prison officials, family members and journalists. Significantly, members of the victim's family are also often present to witness the execution. The whole ritual is designed to give some semblance of humanity to those involved: the offering of a last meal is a final act of kindness; providing religious counsel helps the condemned go peacefully; the opportunity to say some final words includes the condemned as an almost willing participant in the execution process; and allowing witnesses from the victim's family is supposed to aid the healing process. All the ritual actually does is place a thin veneer over the fact that another life is being taken. Public hangings in front of a baying crowd are at least more honest.

Condemned prisoners in Texas are offered the opportunity to give a last statement, which is either recorded as a written statement prior to their execution or, more commonly, taken down at the execution itself. Most condemned prisoners make last statements and all those made since 1982 have now been published on the website of the Texas Department of Criminal Justice.[46] Beazley's final words were released after his execution in a written statement. It seems fitting to include his last statement, which may have been made in the presence of only one or two people, as it reads so much like a speech – as if while writing it he was addressing a wider audience, albeit one that could not be present in his prison cell. When asked at his execution if he had any final words to add, Beazley reportedly just looked over at Luttig's daughter and said, 'No,' then closed his eyes.[47] So this written statement became his parting address to the world. A dead man talking; a speech from beyond the grave.

Beazley used his statement to rail against the system that ended his life: 'I'm not only saddened, but disappointed that a system that is supposed to protect and uphold what is just and right can be so much like me when I made the same shameful mistake.' While his lawyer and human-rights campaigners had argued for clemency on the grounds that Beazley was a minor at the time of his crime, Beazley himself made no such pleas. He accepted that in murdering Luttig he had committed a heinous and senseless crime that deserved punishment, but said that 'the person that committed that act is no longer here – I am'. There were two sides to the younger Beazley. He came from a loving home and was well liked in his community. He was a gifted athlete and president of his senior year at high school. He had no criminal record, though he admitted to dealing drugs. But one evening he murdered someone in the course of stealing their car. These contradictions inspired a critically acclaimed play, *The Two Lives of Napoleon Beazley*, which explored issues of race and identity to try to understand what drove him to murder.

Beazley's last statement raised issues beyond that of the death penalty: it was concerned with revenge and forgiveness. In a letter dated eight days before his execution, Archbishop Desmond Tutu echoed this sentiment. He told the Texas Board of Pardons and Paroles, 'The State should model the common good it wishes its citizens to follow, not behaviours it condemns.' He went on to say, 'The State has apprehended Napoleon, it has held him accountable for his offence, and it has incarcerated him, preventing him if he were disposed from committing another offence. I feel certain that he is not so disposed. If the State of Texas kills Napoleon Beazley, nothing good will come of it.'[48] As the head of South Africa's post-apartheid Truth and Reconciliation Commission, Tutu understood that revenge is not a suitable motive in handing out justice.

Both Beazley's crime and his state-sponsored execution offend our common humanity. In acquiescing to our primal desire for retribution we deny the chance for true healing – a process that is far more beneficial to the victim and their family, together with society as a whole, than simple revenge. As Beazley himself said, 'No one wins tonight. No one gets closure. No one walks away victorious.' Nonetheless, Beazley's government exercised its self-appointed right to take his life in retaliation for an appalling crime he committed when he was only seventeen years old. Supporters of the death penalty claim it has a deterrent as well as punitive effect. But it is based solely on vengeance and only acts to perpetuate the very violence it condemns. In short, the death penalty does not bring about justice or rehabilitation, it simply creates more victims.

Texas State Penitentiary, Huntsville, Texas, United States

28 MAY 2002

The act I committed to put me here was not just heinous, it was senseless. But the person that committed that act is no longer here – I am.

I'm not going to struggle physically against any restraints. I'm not going to shout, use profanity or make idle threats. Understand though that I'm not only upset, but I'm saddened by what is happening here tonight. I'm not only saddened, but disappointed that a system that is supposed to protect and uphold what is just and right can be so much like me when I made the same shameful mistake.

If someone tried to dispose of everyone here for participating in this killing, I'd scream a resounding, 'No.' I'd tell them to give them all the gift that they would not give me . . . and that's to give them all a second chance.

I'm sorry that I am here. I'm sorry that you're all here. I'm sorry that John Luttig died. And I'm sorry that it was something in me that caused all of this to happen to begin with.

Tonight we tell the world that there are no second chances in the eyes of justice . . . Tonight, we tell our children that in some instances, in some cases, killing is right.

"No one wins tonight.
No one gets closure.
**No one walks away
victorious."**

This conflict hurts us all, there are no sides. The people who support this proceeding think this is justice. The people that think that I should live think that is justice. As difficult as it may seem, this is a clash of ideals, with both parties committed to what they feel is right. But who's wrong if in the end we're all victims?

In my heart, I have to believe that there is a peaceful compromise to our ideals. I don't mind if there are none for me, as long as there are for those who are yet to come. There are a lot of men like me on death row – good men – who fell to the same misguided emotions, but may not have recovered as I have.

Give those men a chance to do what's right. Give them a chance to undo their wrongs. A lot of them want to fix the mess they started, but don't know how. The problem is not in that people aren't willing to help them find out, but in the system telling them it won't matter anyway. No one wins tonight. No one gets closure. No one walks away victorious.

Apology to the
Stolen Generations

– KEVIN RUDD –

A ustralia's indigenous population suffered numerous injustices at the hands of the European invaders of their lands from the late eighteenth century onwards. Crimes against them ranged from discrimination and the appropriation of traditional land and water resources to smallpox pandemics and massacres. But perhaps the most infamous was the state-sponsored forced removal of indigenous children during a period lasting from the mid-nineteenth century until the 1970s. Almost all Aboriginal families have been directly affected by this process. No one knows the exact figures, but between one in ten and one in three Aboriginal and Torres Strait Islander children were forcibly removed from their families by Aboriginal Protection Officers and the police between 1910 and 1970.[49] Most were raised in Church or state institutions, although some were adopted by white parents – with many suffering physical or sexual abuse and long-term mental-health problems. These children became known as the Stolen Generations. Their existence demonstrates the fact that judicial (and extra-judicial) executions are not the only way the state can abuse its power over the individual.

The Stolen Generations were ostensibly removed from their families for their own protection – particularly those children of mixed Aboriginal-European descent. State and federal governments hoped to assimilate indigenous children into European society by removing them from their families and traditional culture. In 1788, the first British settlers encountered the world's oldest living culture – thought to have been in Australia for at least forty thousand to sixty thousand years – but the policies of the colonists' descendants were designed to ensure the disappearance of Australia's indigenous people and culture in only a few generations. Forced child removal played a part in this attempted genocide, as did disease, massacre, forced sterilisation and intermarriage. In short, it was hoped by some that the indigenous population would 'die out' or be 'bred out'.[50]

This period is such a 'stain on the nation's soul' that soon after becoming Prime Minister, Kevin Rudd announced he would be issuing a formal apology. On the morning of 13 February 2008, he tabled a motion in the federal parliament offering an apology to Australia's Stolen Generations. The motion had bipartisan agreement and stated in part:

> We apologise for the laws and policies of successive parliaments and governments that have inflicted profound grief, suffering and loss on these our fellow Australians.
>
> We apologise especially for the removal of Aboriginal and Torres Strait Islander children from their families, their communities and their country.
>
> For the pain, suffering and hurt of these Stolen Generations, their descendants and for their families left behind, we say sorry.
>
> To the mothers and the fathers, the brothers and the sisters, for the breaking up of families and communities, we say sorry.
>
> And for the indignity and degradation thus inflicted on a proud people and a proud culture, we say sorry.[51]

It was such an important event that it was broadcast live on television and radio, and outdoor screens were set up in Canberra, Sydney, Melbourne, Perth and other towns and cities across Australia so that thousands could watch the apology together and take part in the celebrations. After Rudd had read out the motion, he made an extraordinary speech to parliament in which he repeated the apology: 'To the Stolen Generations, I say the following: as Prime Minister of Australia, I am sorry. On behalf of the government of Australia, I am sorry. On behalf of the parliament of Australia, I am sorry. I offer you this apology without qualification.'

During his twenty-minute speech he referred to some of the accounts of those taken from their parents: 'There is something terribly primal about these first-hand accounts. The pain is searing; it screams from the pages. The hurt, the humiliation, the degradation and the sheer brutality of the act of physically separating a mother from her children is a deep assault on our senses and on our most elemental humanity.' He said, 'These stories cry out to be heard; they cry out for an apology.' Instead, he argued, there had been 'stony and stubborn and deafening silence for more than a decade'. He was referring to the fact that in 1997 the Human Rights and Equal Opportunity Commission report *Bringing Them Home* had recommended that acknowledgement and apology form key elements of reparation for the forcible removal of Aboriginal and Torres Strait Islander children.[52] However, the Prime Minister, John Howard, had refused to issue an apology, arguing that the current generation should not be held responsible for the mistakes of the past. Instead, in August 1999 he tabled a motion that simply expressed 'deep and sincere regret that indigenous Australians suffered injustices under the practices of past generations'.[53] This was slightly disingenuous as in some places these practices had continued into the 1970s, so could still be considered the responsibility of the current political generation (Howard himself entered parliament in 1974). As Rudd pointed out, 'The 1970s is not exactly a point in remote antiquity.'

As leader of the opposition, Brendan Nelson – Howard's successor as Liberal Party leader – gave a speech in reply to Rudd's address. However, it was such a half-hearted acceptance of the need for an apology that in protest many turned their backs on the screens broadcasting the event. Nelson angered many with his couched language and historical revisionism: 'Our generation does not own these actions, nor should it feel guilt for what was done in many, but not all cases, with the best of intentions . . . Even when motivated by inherent humanity and decency to reach out to the dispossessed in extreme adversity, our actions can have unintended outcomes.'[54] He was in many ways acting as an apologist for the policies that led to the Stolen Generations, rather than offering an apology to those Stolen Generations – and so was out of step with much of Australia.

Nelson represented a party that, under Howard, had been responsible for some hugely controversial policies in relation to Australia's indigenous peoples. Howard was vehemently opposed to indigenous self-determination and had resisted any moves in this direction.[55] For example, in 2005 he abolished the indigenous representative body the Aboriginal and Torres Strait Islander Commission and in a rushed-through 2006 amendment he seriously weakened the Aboriginal Land Rights Act. Then in June 2007, a government report indicated that widespread child sexual abuse was occurring in Aboriginal communities in the Northern Territory.[56] In response, Howard – who was trailing behind the opposition Labour Party in the opinion polls – intervened in what he described as a national emergency and essentially revoked self-governance for these communities and ordered the police and army to enforce an authoritarian crackdown. While there was an urgent need to ensure the protection of children, by implementing racist policies Howard inflamed sensitivities in the indigenous population and disempowered those communities from addressing the problem themselves (it should be noted that Rudd supported the intervention at the time and many elements of it continued under his premiership). However, the Northern Territory report had concluded that what was required was 'a determined, coordinated effort to break the cycle and provide the necessary strength, power and appropriate support and services to local communities, so they can lead themselves out of the malaise: in a word, *empowerment!*'[57] The report repeatedly stated that there were no quick and easy fixes and that it would take at least fifteen years to make any in-roads into the crisis, using education and other mechanisms to address some of the underlying factors in the breakdown of Aboriginal society, including alcoholism, poverty and unemployment.

In contrast, the apology to the Stolen Generations was one of those rare political moments of genuine hope and renewal. As Rudd acknowledged in his speech, 'The nation is demanding of its political leadership to take us forward.' It was, he said, 'calling on us, the politicians, to move beyond our infantile bickering, our point-scoring and our mindlessly partisan politics and elevate this one core area of national responsibility to a rare position beyond the partisan divide'.

Rudd had become leader of the Labour Party in December 2006 and won the general election a year later by recognising what most

Australians wanted and promising something different from the decade of conservatism Australia had suffered under his predecessor Howard (much as Tony Blair did in Britain in 1997, José Zapatero did in Spain in 2004 and Barack Obama did in the United States in 2009). His first act on taking office in December 2007 was to ratify the Kyoto Protocol on greenhouse-gas emissions. He then made the apology to the Stolen Generations in early 2008 and that summer withdrew Australian combat troops from Iraq. These were all hugely popular policy choices in Australia, but had been firmly resisted by Howard – who was a climate-change sceptic and supporter of big business, opposed to what he called the 'black armband view of history' and a staunch ally of George Bush in the war on terror. The first six months of Rudd's premiership seemed like a breath of fresh air to many Australians but, as so often happens, the harsh reality of politics eventually took its toll – seeing him mired in disagreements over carbon-trading schemes, budget deficits and a controversial mining tax. He eventually resigned in June 2010. However, this should not detract from the fact that he did implement policies in relation to climate change, indigenous peoples and the war in Iraq that the vast majority of Australians had wanted but until then been denied.[58]

The case of the Stolen Generations in Australia is just one example of the horrendous abuses that the indigenous peoples around the world were subjected to as a result of European colonialism from the sixteenth century onwards. After the initial surge of disease and slaughter had decimated an indigenous population, they were often then the victims of deliberate policies designed to eradicate their culture and 'civilise' them, either by assimilating them into the wider population or containing them in state- or Church-run reservations. This approach was often only partially successful – leaving indigenous peoples caught in limbo between the old ways and the new. These 'unpeople' often ended up as part of the rural or urban poor of a country or were relocated to reservations far from their traditional lands.

This process is still happening. In the post-colonial world, European descendants or the dominant ethnic groups continue to treat indigenous peoples as second-class citizens, deemed to be uncivilised and so left disempowered and marginalised.[59] Removed from the lands that have always provided for them and cut off from the social and welfare networks of their traditional communities, people subjected to these policies often turn to alcohol or drugs to escape the despair. Mental-health problems, unemployment, homelessness or domestic violence usually follow. Lacking the 'authenticity' of their traditional culture, they are all too often ignored by indigenous-rights organisations, development charities, government agencies and mainstream society. Governments do not act alone in causing this: missionaries and multinational corporations (particularly oil and mining companies) play their roles, with the three acting as agents for each other's overlapping interests in the name of so-called civilisation, religion or profit.

The result in Australia is that the majority of today's half a million Aboriginal people now live in cities or towns (with only a quarter living in remote areas). Alcoholism, substance abuse and gambling are serious concerns within the indigenous population, which has a higher rate of ill health than any other group in Australia. They suffer much higher rates of infection for many communicable and life-threatening diseases, and experience diseases not usually found in the developed world. They also suffer higher rates of mental-health problems and suicide. The infant-mortality rate is far higher than the national average and their life expectancy is at least ten years less than non-indigenous Australians.[60] They also experience lower rates of schooling, employment and income. Then there are the serious intergenerational social and psychological impacts for the Stolen Generations and their families that risk creating a spiral of harm down through the generations.[61] There is another side to this picture though. Aboriginal people play an important part in Australian society, and elements of their art, music, beliefs, traditions and language are integral to the modern national identity.

This is why the apology to the Stolen Generations was so important – it was a small step on the road to reconciliation. But more must follow. The Stolen Generations and their families deserve compensation and support, and the Aboriginal and Torres Strait Islander peoples as a whole need sustained and well-funded development programmes designed and implemented by the indigenous communities themselves. Progress can also be made in relation to possible reparation from the British and Australian governments, securing permanent land rights for indigenous communities and ending the structural violence that is contributing to the breakdown of Aboriginal society. As Rudd said at the end of his speech, 'let's grasp this opportunity to craft a new future for this great land, Australia'.

Parliament House, Canberra, Australia

13 FEBRUARY 2008

Mr Speaker, there comes a time in the history of nations when their peoples must become fully reconciled to their past if they are to go forward with confidence to embrace their future.

Our nation, Australia, has reached such a time.

That is why the parliament is today here assembled: to deal with this unfinished business of the nation, to remove a great stain from the nation's soul and, in a true spirit of reconciliation, to open a new chapter in the history of this great land, Australia.

Last year I made a commitment to the Australian people that if we formed the next government of the Commonwealth we would in parliament say sorry to the Stolen Generations.

Today I honour that commitment.

I said we would do so early in the life of the new parliament.

Again, today I honour that commitment by doing so at the commencement of this the forty-second parliament of the Commonwealth.

Because the time has come, well and truly come, for all peoples of our great country, for all citizens of our great Commonwealth, for all Australians – those who are indigenous and those who are not – to come together to reconcile and together build a new future for our nation.

Some have asked, 'Why apologise?' Let me begin to answer by telling the parliament just a little of one person's story – an elegant, eloquent and wonderful woman in her eighties, full of life, full of funny stories, despite what has happened in her life's journey, a woman who has travelled a long way to be with us today, a member of the stolen generation who shared some of her story with me when I called around to see her just a few days ago.

Nanna Nungala Fejo, as she prefers to be called, was born in the late 1920s.

She remembers her earliest childhood days living with her family and her community in a bush camp just outside Tennant Creek.

She remembers the love and the warmth and the kinship of those days long ago, including traditional dancing around the camp fire at night.

She loved the dancing. She remembers once getting into strife when, as a four-year-old girl, she insisted on dancing with the male tribal elders rather than just sitting and watching the men, as the girls were supposed to do.

But then, sometime around 1932, when she was about four, she remembers the coming of the welfare men.

Her family had feared that day and had dug holes in the creek bank where the children could run and hide.

What they had not expected was that the white welfare men did not come alone.

They brought a truck, two white men and an Aboriginal stockman on horseback cracking his stockwhip.

The kids were found; they ran for their mothers, screaming, but they could not get away.

They were herded and piled onto the back of the truck.

Tears flowing, her mum tried clinging to the sides of the truck as her children were taken away to the Bungalow in Alice, all in the name of protection.

A few years later, government policy changed.

Now the children would be handed over to the missions to be cared for by the Churches.

But which Church would care for them? The kids were simply told to line up in three lines.

Nanna Fejo and her sisters stood in the middle line, her older brother and cousin on her left.

Those on the left were told that they had become Catholics, those in the middle Methodists and those on the right Church of England.

That is how the complex questions of post-Reformation theology were resolved in the Australian outback in the 1930s.

It was as crude as that.

She and her sister were sent to a Methodist mission on Goulburn Island and then Croker Island.

Her Catholic brother was sent to work at a cattle station and her cousin to a Catholic mission.

Nanna Fejo's family had been broken up for a second time.

She stayed at the mission until after the war, when she was allowed to leave for a prearranged job as a domestic in Darwin.

She was sixteen. Nanna Fejo never saw her mum again.

After she left the mission, her brother let her know that her mum had died years before, a broken woman fretting for the children that had literally been ripped away from her.

I asked Nanna Fejo what she would have me say today about her story.

She thought for a few moments then said that what I should say today was that all mothers are important.

And she added: 'Families – keeping them together is very important. It's a good thing that you are surrounded by love and that love is passed down the generations. That's what gives you happiness.'

As I left, later on, Nanna Fejo took one of my staff aside, wanting to make sure that I was not too hard on the Aboriginal stockman who had hunted those kids down all those years ago.

The stockman had found her again decades later, this time himself to say, 'Sorry.'

And remarkably, extraordinarily, she had forgiven him.

Nanna Fejo's is just one story.

There are thousands, tens of thousands, of them: stories of forced separation of Aboriginal and Torres Strait Islander children from their mums and dads over the better part of a century.

Some of these stories are graphically told in *Bringing Them Home*, the report commissioned in 1995 by Prime Minister Keating and received in 1997 by Prime Minister Howard.

There is something terribly primal about these first-hand accounts.

The pain is searing; it screams from the pages.

The hurt, the humiliation, the degradation and the sheer brutality of the act of physically separating a mother from her children is a deep assault on our senses and on our most elemental humanity.

These stories cry out to be heard; they cry out for an apology.

Instead, from the nation's parliament there has been a stony and stubborn and deafening silence for more than a decade; a view that somehow we, the parliament, should suspend our most basic instincts of what is right and what is wrong; a view that, instead, we should look for any pretext to push this great wrong to one side, to leave it languishing with the historians, the academics and the cultural warriors, as if the Stolen Generations are little more than an interesting sociological phenomenon.

❝ The hurt, the humiliation, the degradation and the sheer brutality of the act of physically separating a mother from her children is a deep assault on our senses ❞

But the Stolen Generations are not intellectual curiosities.

They are human beings; human beings who have been damaged deeply by the decisions of parliaments and governments.

But, as of today, the time for denial, the time for delay, has at last come to an end.

The nation is demanding of its political leadership to take us forward.

Decency, human decency, universal human decency, demands that the nation now step forward to right an historical wrong.

That is what we are doing in this place today.

But should there still be doubts as to why we must now act, let the parliament reflect for a moment on the following facts: that, between 1910 and 1970, between 10 and 30 per cent of indigenous children were forcibly taken from their mothers and fathers; that, as a result, up to fifty thousand children were forcibly taken from their families; that this was the product of the deliberate, calculated policies of the state as reflected in the explicit powers given to them under statute; that this policy was taken to such extremes by some in administrative authority that the forced extractions of children of so-called 'mixed lineage' were seen as part of a broader policy of dealing with 'the problem of the Aboriginal population'.

One of the most notorious examples of this approach was from the Northern Territory Protector of Natives, who stated:

'Generally by the fifth and invariably by the sixth generation, all native characteristics of the Australian aborigine are eradicated. The problem of our half-castes', to quote the Protector, 'will quickly be eliminated by the complete disappearance of the black race, and the swift submergence of their progeny in the white . . .'

The Western Australian Protector of Natives expressed not dissimilar views, expounding them at length in Canberra in 1937 at the first national conference on indigenous affairs that brought together the Commonwealth and state protectors of natives.

These are uncomfortable things to be brought out into the light.

They are not pleasant.

They are profoundly disturbing.

But we must acknowledge these facts if we are to deal once and for all with the argument that the policy of generic forced separation was somehow well motivated, justified by its historical context and, as a result, unworthy of any apology today.

Then we come to the argument of intergenerational responsibility, also used by some to argue against giving an apology today.

But let us remember the fact that the forced removal of Aboriginal children was happening as late as the early 1970s.

The 1970s is not exactly a point in remote antiquity.

There are still serving members of this parliament who were first elected to this place in the early 1970s.

It is well within the adult memory span of many of us.

The uncomfortable truth for us all is that the parliaments of the nation, individually and collectively, enacted statutes and delegated authority under those statutes that made the forced removal of children on racial grounds fully lawful.

There is a further reason for an apology as well: it is that reconciliation is in fact an expression of a core value of our nation – and that value is a fair go for all.

There is a deep and abiding belief in the Australian community that, for the Stolen Generations, there was no fair go at all.

There is a pretty basic Aussie belief that says it is time to put right this most outrageous of wrongs.

It is for these reasons, quite apart from concerns of fundamental human decency, that the governments and parliaments of this nation must make this apology – because, put simply, the laws that our parliaments enacted made the Stolen Generations possible.

We, the parliaments of the nation, are ultimately responsible, not those who gave effect to our laws.

The problem lay with the laws themselves. As has been said of settler societies elsewhere, we are the bearers of many blessings from our ancestors, and therefore we must also be the bearer of their burdens as well.

Therefore, for our nation, the course of action is clear, and therefore, for our people, the course of action is clear: that is, to deal now with what has become one of the darkest chapters in Australia's history.

In doing so, we are doing more than contending with the facts, the evidence and the often rancorous public debate.

In doing so, we are also wrestling with our own soul.

This is not, as some would argue, a black armband view of history; it is just the truth: the cold, confronting, uncomfortable truth – facing it, dealing with it, moving on from it.

Until we fully confront that truth, there will always be a shadow hanging over us and our future as a fully united and fully reconciled people.

It is time to reconcile. It is time to recognise the injustices of the past. It is time to say sorry. It is time to move forward together.

To the Stolen Generations, I say the following: as Prime Minister of Australia, I am sorry.

On behalf of the government of Australia, I am sorry.

On behalf of the parliament of Australia, I am sorry.

I offer you this apology without qualification.

We apologise for the hurt, the pain and suffering that we, the parliament, have caused you by the laws that previous parliaments have enacted.

We apologise for the indignity, the degradation and the humiliation these laws embodied.

We offer this apology to the mothers, the fathers, the brothers, the sisters, the families and the communities whose lives were ripped apart by the actions of successive governments under successive parliaments.

In making this apology, I would also like to speak personally to the

❝ as Prime Minister of Australia, I am sorry. On behalf of the government of Australia, I am sorry. On behalf of the parliament of Australia, I am sorry. ❞

members of the Stolen Generations and their families: to those here today, so many of you; to those listening across the nation – from Yuendumu, in the central west of the Northern Territory, to Yabara, in North Queensland, and to Pitjantjatjara in South Australia.

I know that, in offering this apology on behalf of the government and the parliament, there is nothing I can say today that can take away the pain you have suffered personally.

Whatever words I speak today, I cannot undo that.

Words alone are not that powerful; grief is a very personal thing.

I ask those non-indigenous Australians listening today who may not fully understand why what we are doing is so important to imagine for a moment that this had happened to you.

I say to honourable members here present: imagine if this had happened to us.

Imagine the crippling effect.

Imagine how hard it would be to forgive.

My proposal is this: if the apology we extend today is accepted in the spirit of reconciliation in which it is offered, we can today resolve together that there be a new beginning for Australia.

And it is to such a new beginning that I believe the nation is now calling us.

Australians are a passionate lot. We are also a very practical lot.

For us, symbolism is important but, unless the great symbolism of reconciliation is accompanied by an even greater substance, it is little more than a clanging gong.

It is not sentiment that makes history; it is our actions that make history.

Today's apology, however inadequate, is aimed at righting past wrongs.

It is also aimed at building a bridge between indigenous and non-indigenous Australians – a bridge based on a real respect rather than a thinly veiled contempt.

Our challenge for the future is to now cross that bridge and, in so doing, to embrace a new partnership between indigenous and non-indigenous Australians – embracing, as part of that partnership, expanded Link-up and other critical services to help the Stolen Generations to trace their families if at all possible and to provide dignity to their lives.

But the core of this partnership for the future is the closing of the gap between indigenous and non-indigenous Australians on life expectancy, educational achievement and employment opportunities.

This new partnership on closing the gap will set concrete targets for the future: within a decade to halve the widening gap in literacy, numeracy and employment outcomes and opportunities for indigenous Australians, within a decade to halve the appalling gap in infant-mortality rates between indigenous and non-indigenous children and, within a generation, to close the equally appalling seventeen-year life gap between indigenous and non-indigenous in overall life expectancy.

The truth is, a business as usual approach towards indigenous Australians is not working.

Most old approaches are not working.

We need a new beginning – a new beginning which contains real measures of policy success or policy failure; a new beginning, a new partnership, on closing the gap with sufficient flexibility not to insist on a one-size-fits-all approach for each of the hundreds of remote and regional indigenous communities across the country but instead allowing flexible, tailored, local approaches to achieve commonly-agreed national objectives that lie at the core of our proposed new partnership; a new beginning that draws intelligently on the experiences of new policy settings across the nation.

However, unless we as a parliament set a destination for the nation, we have no clear point to guide our policy, our programmes or our purpose; we have no centralised organising principle.

Let us resolve today to begin with the little children – a fitting place to start on this day of apology for the Stolen Generations.

Let us resolve over the next five years to have every indigenous four-year-old in a remote Aboriginal community enrolled in and attending a proper early childhood education centre or opportunity and engaged in proper pre-literacy and pre-numeracy programmes.

Let us resolve to build new educational opportunities for these little ones, year by year, step by step, following the completion of their crucial pre-school year.

Let us resolve to use this systematic approach to building future educational opportunities for indigenous children and providing proper primary and preventative health care for the same children, to beginning the task of rolling back the obscenity that we find today in infant mortality rates in remote indigenous communities – up to four times higher than in other communities.

None of this will be easy.

Most of it will be hard – very hard. But none of it is impossible, and all of it is achievable with clear goals, clear thinking, and by placing an absolute

❝ It is not sentiment that makes history, it is our actions that make history. ❞

premium on respect, cooperation and mutual responsibility as the guiding principles of this new partnership on closing the gap.

The mood of the nation is for reconciliation now, between indigenous and non-indigenous Australians.

The mood of the nation on indigenous policy and politics is now very simple.

The nation is calling on us, the politicians, to move beyond our infantile bickering, our point-scoring and our mindlessly partisan politics and elevate this one core area of national responsibility to a rare position beyond the partisan divide. Surely this is the unfulfilled spirit of the 1967 referendum.

Surely, at least from this day forward, we should give it a go.

Let me take this one step further, and take what some may see as a piece of political posturing and make a practical proposal to the opposition on this day, the first full sitting day of the new parliament.

I said before the election that the nation needed a kind of war cabinet on parts of indigenous policy, because the challenges are too great and the consequences too great to allow it all to become a political football, as it has been so often in the past.

I therefore propose a joint policy commission, to be led by the Leader of the Opposition and me, with a mandate to develop and implement – to begin with – an effective housing strategy for remote communities over the next five years.

It will be consistent with the government's policy framework, a new partnership for closing the gap.

If this commission operates well, I then propose that it work on the further task of constitutional recognition of the first Australians, consistent with the long-standing platform commitments of my party and the pre-election position of the opposition.

This would probably be desirable in any event because, unless such a proposition were absolutely bipartisan, it would fail at a referendum.

As I have said before, the time has come for new approaches to enduring problems.

> "**reconciliation** across the entire history of the **often bloody** encounter between those who emerged from the Dreamtime a **thousand generations ago** and **those** who, like me, **came** across the seas **only yesterday**"

Working constructively together on such defined projects I believe would meet with the support of the nation.

It is time for fresh ideas to fashion the nation's future.

Mr Speaker, today the parliament has come together to right a great wrong.

We have come together to deal with the past so that we might fully embrace the future.

We have had sufficient audacity of faith to advance a pathway to that future, with arms extended rather than with fists still clenched.

So let us seize the day. Let it not become a moment of mere sentimental reflection.

Let us take it with both hands and allow this day, this day of national reconciliation, to become one of those rare moments in which we might just be able to transform the way in which the nation thinks about itself, whereby the injustice administered to the Stolen Generations in the name of these, our parliaments, causes all of us to reappraise, at the deepest level of our beliefs, the real possibility of reconciliation writ large: reconciliation across all indigenous Australia; reconciliation across the entire history of the often bloody encounter between those who emerged from the Dreamtime a thousand generations ago and those who, like me, came across the seas only yesterday; reconciliation which opens up whole new possibilities for the future.

It is for the nation to bring the first two centuries of our settled history to a close, as we begin a new chapter.

We embrace with pride, admiration and awe these great and ancient cultures we are truly blessed to have among us – cultures that provide a unique, uninterrupted human thread linking our Australian continent to the most ancient prehistory of our planet.

Growing from this new respect, we see our indigenous brothers and sisters with fresh eyes, with new eyes, and we have our minds wide open as to how we might tackle, together, the great practical challenges that indigenous Australia faces in the future.

Let us turn this page together: indigenous and non-indigenous Australians, government and opposition, Commonwealth and state, and write this new chapter in our nation's story together.

First Australians, First Fleeters, and those who first took the oath of allegiance just a few weeks ago – let's grasp this opportunity to craft a new future for this great land, Australia.* Mr Speaker, I commend the motion to the House.

* 'First Fleeters' are the descendants of those people who arrived in Australia on the eleven ships of the British First Fleet and founded the first European colony in Australia at Sydney Cove in 1788.

ن لادن
ظيم القاعدة

Part II

You're Either With Us or Against Us

"He who fights with monsters should look to it that he himself does not become a monster."

Friedrich Nietzsche,
Beyond Good and Evil
(1886)

Many ordinary people are suspicious of and hostile towards those from different religions, cultures, races or political parties. Some of the most powerful forces in human psychology occur within and between groups. Social psychologists have identified several biases that occur once an in-group and an out-group – an 'us' and a 'them' – have been identified. We have, for example, a tendency to see members of other groups as homogeneous and to attribute their failures to internal characteristics. In contrast, we see members of our own group as more varied and attribute our failures to situational factors. Within highly cohesive groups there is a tendency to try to minimise conflict and reach consensus at the expense of independent thinking and the critical assessment of ideas, often resulting in hasty, risky or irrational decision-making. We are also far more likely to give preferential treatment to those whom we perceive to be members of our own group – no matter how arbitrary or random that grouping may be.

In many ways this is reflected on the world stage. With terms like the West, Third World, Iron Curtain, rogue state and Axis of Evil, politicians and others attempt to divide the world up in order to better understand it. In doing so they create a geopolitical them and us, which takes away from our shared humanity. The chapters that follow explore this need to create simplistic divisions and the hostility and conflict that often results from this (in contrast to Part I, which examined our common humanity and shared human rights).

During the second half of the twentieth century the fundamental global division was between the United States, NATO and Western democracy on the one side and the Soviet Union, the Warsaw Pact and communism on the other. This is explored in the first two chapters of Part II. The first chapter examines an address the Russian novelist and dissident Aleksandr Solzhenitsyn gave at Harvard University on 8 June 1978. He used this platform to launch a scathing dissection of Western society, attacking the view that Western democracy is the end point of humanity's ideological evolution and that the Western model of society is superior to all others. This view, Solzhenitsyn argued, fails to recognise the shortcomings in Western society and ignores the presence of multiple deeply rooted cultures in, for example, China, India and Russia and across the Muslim world and Africa.

The second chapter explores a speech given by US President Ronald Reagan to the British parliament on 8 June 1982. The Reagan administration took the confrontation with the Soviet Union to new levels by pursuing aggressive roll-back policies. Reagan himself directly questioned the underlying system of the Soviet Union and believed that Soviet aggression was deeply rooted in the false philosophy of Marxism–Leninism. In doing so he changed the dynamic of the Cold War. After the Soviet Union finally collapsed, there was a brief window during the 1990s when US hegemony looked like it might bring stability to the world system – a perceived unipolar moment. That perception was illusory and short-lived as multiple centres of political and economic power then emerged.

Following the end of the Cold War, some have argued that global conflict now manifests itself between different civilisations rather than ideologies. In the post-9/11 world, considerable attention has focused on the so-called clash of civilisations between Islam and the West. This is explored from opposing perspectives in the third and fourth chapters. First, the fallacy that radical Islamists simply hate Western freedoms is exposed in the chapter discussing US President George Bush's address to a joint session of Congress on 20 September 2001. This was in the aftermath of the 9/11 terrorist attacks that had killed nearly three thousand people and Bush was articulating the war on terror that would be America's response. The Republican hawks and neoconservatives of the Bush administration divided the world into good and evil and made it very clear that you were either allied to the United States or you were with the terrorists. Afghanistan was targeted for immediate retaliation but Iraq was already firmly in their sights.

Bush's speech to Congress is contrasted with a video address recorded by Osama bin Laden and broadcast by Al-Jazeera on 29 October 2004. In the video, bin Laden spoke directly to the American people and explained the motivations behind the 9/11 attacks that al-Qaida had launched three years earlier. He claimed that the inspiration for the attacks came from watching the destruction of high-rise buildings during Israel's US-backed invasion of Lebanon in 1982. Al-Qaida and other violent jihadist movements were, according to bin Laden, simply a reaction to Western aggression. What these movements represent, in part, is a discourse of discontent and anger at the perceived injustices perpetrated against the Muslim world by Western countries and the regional elites allied to them. The war on terror only served to reinforce this sense of marginalisation in some people's minds.

The 9/11 attacks, the war on terror and the invasions and occupations of Afghanistan and Iraq have led to the common misconception that international terrorism is the greatest threat to world stability. However, the evidence points to a far more dangerous development: climate change. This is explored in the final chapter, which discusses a speech on the security implications of climate change that Margaret Beckett gave on 10 May 2007 at the Royal United Services Institute in London. As British Foreign Secretary she argued that climate change has the potential to create division like no other issue, as developing countries will be severely affected by the environmental changes largely caused by rich industrialised countries. This issue is of particular concern in this context given our tendency to divide the world into them and us and the powerful negative forces that then come into play (which is why this speech is included in this part of the book). At the same time, the only truly effective responses will require international action and cooperation. As Beckett argued, climate change may therefore become the issue that drives us apart or, just maybe, brings us together.

Whether we now live in a world with a sole superpower or one with multiple centres of power (both state and non-state), there remains a tendency to confront and attempt to control, or at least contain, those who we perceive to be different from us. In today's interconnected world, overlapping national interests still have the potential to create conflict as powerful states seek to impose their will on the world and others attempt to resist this. Those same powerful states seek to persuade others to choose sides in such conflicts; there can be no middle ground or neutrality for them. Our systems of international governance, such as the United Nations, are still not up to the task of effectively mediating this competitive dynamic. Reforming and strengthening such institutions is, therefore, a matter of great urgency. As climate change and other global forces come into play, we must work to recognise and build upon our common humanity, while respecting the rich diversity that has always been a part of that humanity.

A World Split Apart

– ALEKSANDR SOLZHENITSYN –

The enemy of your enemy is *not* always your friend: the reality is often more complicated than the old proverb would suggest. This was wonderfully demonstrated by the Russian novelist Aleksandr Solzhenitsyn in his commencement day address at Harvard University in June 1978. Over the years, Solzhenitsyn had been imprisoned, attacked and finally exiled by the Soviet Union but instead of railing against his communist oppressors he used his Harvard address to admonish the Western world for its failings.

Solzhenitsyn was born in Kislovodsk in southwest Russia on 11 December 1918. His father was an artillery officer in the imperial Russian army during World War I but was killed in a hunting accident six months before Solzhenitsyn's birth. His mother then worked as a shorthand typist to support herself and her son. In the late 1930s, Solzhenitsyn studied mathematics and physics at Rostov University and completed a correspondence course with the Institute of History, Philosophy and Literature in Moscow. During this time he was a keen Marxist and was awarded a Stalinist scholarship for his work in the Communist Youth League. War broke out between the Soviet Union and Germany in 1941 and shortly after graduating Solzhenitsyn volunteered for the Red Army. He served as a driver of horse-drawn vehicles during the winter of 1941–42 but his mathematical skills were soon recognised and he was transferred to an artillery school, following in his father's footsteps. He was put in command of an artillery-position-finding company and served for over two years on the front line, where he was twice decorated for bravery and achieved the rank of captain.[1]

In February 1945, while serving in East Prussia, Solzhenitsyn was arrested for criticising Joseph Stalin in an intercepted letter to a school friend. Draft stories and some of his other writings found in his map case were used as evidence against him and he was sentenced without trial to eight years in detention camps – the infamous Gulag system. He was imprisoned in various labour camps before being transferred to one of the secret research facilities run by the Ministry of State Security. In 1950, he was sent to a new labour camp for political prisoners. At the end of his sentence in 1953 he was exiled for life to Kok-Terek in southern Kazakhstan.[2] Then in February 1956, the Soviet leader Nikita Khrushchev gave a speech to the party congress in which he criticised Stalin and condemned his cult of personality. Shortly afterwards, Solzhenitsyn's conviction was formally annulled and he was allowed to return from exile. Many of his early poems and stories were composed and memorised while in the Gulag, and his experiences informed his first novels, *One Day in the Life of Ivan Denisovich* and *The First Circle*, and a later three-volume account, *The Gulag Archipelago*.[3]

In the early 1960s, *One Day in the Life of Ivan Denisovich* and several short works were approved by Khrushchev and published in the Soviet Union. This led to overnight fame for Solzhenitsyn, who was compared to the great Russian writers Fyodor Dostoyevsky and Leo Tolstoy.[4] However, at the end of 1964 Khrushchev was removed from power by Leonid Brezhnev, and Solzhenitsyn once again found himself out of favour with the authorities. Printing of his work stopped almost immediately and the KGB seized some of his papers and manuscripts. Solzhenitsyn continued writing in secret and in 1970 was awarded the Nobel Prize in Literature, much to the chagrin of the Soviet authorities. He was such a powerful voice of dissent by this point that in August 1971 the KGB attempted to assassinate him – an attempt that failed but left him seriously ill for months.[5] Then in February 1974 he was arrested on charges of treason, stripped of his Soviet citizenship and deported to West Germany. Living first in Germany and Switzerland, Solzhenitsyn eventually settled in the small town of Cavendish, Vermont, in the United States. He was given an honorary degree by Harvard University and asked to give the 1978 commencement day address at the university.

Commencement day – when degrees are conferred – has been held at Harvard since 1642 and in more modern times features speeches by staff, graduates and invited guest speakers. Recent years have seen addresses from the UN Secretary-General Kofi Annan, Microsoft co-founder Bill Gates and author J. K. Rowling. One of the more memorable was Solzhenitsyn's. He used this platform to launch a scathing dissection of Western society. Though he stressed that the bitterness in his speech 'comes not from an adversary but from a friend' it still caught many of his fans off guard. His denouncement of the Western way of life was an unprecedented event – delivered, as it was, in Russian at an American university during the Cold War.

At that time, the world was divided into a geopolitical tripartite consisting of the US-led West (the capitalist First World), the Soviet-led East (the communist Second World) and the non-aligned countries (the developing Third World, now referred to as the majority world). Solzhenitsyn argued that the West wrongly assumed that other societies would eventually adopt the Western system because it was superior to all others. This assumption existed despite the presence of multiple deeply rooted cultures in China, India and Russia and across the Muslim world and Africa. For Solzhenitsyn, it was a fallacy that had developed out of 'Western incomprehension of the essence of other worlds'.

Furthermore, as Solzhenitsyn pointed out, the West had numerous faults and weaknesses of its own and he explained, 'Even if we are spared destruction by war, our lives will have to change if we want to save life from self-destruction.' Among other things, he criticised the West for being short-sighted and lacking political courage (particularly during the Vietnam War), encouraging unfettered competition in pursuit of material happiness, restricting free thought to that which was fashionable and followed accepted patterns of judgement (a 'petrified armour around people's minds'), allowing the media to 'miseducate' the public with mass prejudices, and relying on a limited method of organisation based primarily on legal systems and the letter of the law. These were, he said, 'a few trends of Western life which surprise and shock a new arrival to this world'. In today's more ecologically aware age, we might also add to his list the fact that Westerners consume more and pollute more than their majority world counterparts.[6]

Solzhenitsyn blamed these failings on a deprivation of spiritual life: 'We have placed too much hope in political and social reforms, only to find out that we were being deprived of our most precious possession:

our spiritual life. In the East, it is destroyed by the dealings and machinations of the ruling party. In the West, commercial interests tend to suffocate it. This is the real crisis.' He called this the 'calamity of a despiritualised and irreligious humanistic consciousness'. For Solzhenitsyn, this calamity was at the very root of Western civilisation – from its birth in the Renaissance and expression in the Enlightenment, when rationalistic humanism and anthropocentricity took hold (that is, the autonomy of humankind from any higher force thus placing humans and their material needs at the centre of the universe). He lamented that 'Everything beyond physical well-being and accumulation of material goods, all other human requirements and characteristics of a subtler and higher nature, were left outside the area of attention of state and social systems, as if human life did not have any superior sense.'

Solzhenitsyn recognised that many people living in the West shared his dissatisfaction but he warned against turning to socialism and made it clear that he was not presenting it as an alternative. Equally, he did not accept that the Western system should be adopted in Russia. He saw people in the East, and in Russia in particular, as having become stronger under decades of repressive rule, which he thought of as a kind of spiritual training. He argued that after suffering decades of violent oppression 'the human soul longs for things higher, warmer and purer than those offered by today's mass living habits, introduced by the revolting invasion of publicity, by TV stupor and by intolerable music'. He did not want to see Russians throw off communism only to replace it with the Western model of civilisation, especially when Russia had a proud heritage of its own to return to.

It is important for Westerners to understand that, despite its positive aspects, the neo-liberal democracy pursued in the West is not the only method of societal organisation nor is it the most suited to every culture. The collapse of the Soviet Union in the early 1990s led many to believe that the Western model was the only way forward. Today, though, there are still many political alternatives – however flawed – across the majority world. These include the communist states of East and Southeast Asia, the Islamic states of Southwest Asia and North Africa, the socialist and social democratic states of Latin America and the egalitarian communitarian nations of indigenous peoples around the world. There are autocracies, oligarchies, democracies and anarchies – with the many different manifestations of each in between.

Solzhenitsyn predicted that 'The Western way of life is less and less likely to become the leading model.' He accused Western thinking of being conservative and argued that 'This debilitating dream of a status quo is the symptom of a society which has come to the end of its development.' Many people are appalled by elements of the culture that has developed in the West – hollow materialism, unbridled consumerism, selfish individualism and superficial celebrity worship – and resist its spread to other parts of the world (of course there are also those who would embrace this Western lifestyle if given the chance). Many disputes in the world today are the result of other countries trying to resist being dominated by what they see as a weak model for society – one that has 'come to the end of its development', to use Solzhenitsyn's words. This stands in stark contrast to the views of people like the conservative philosopher Francis Fukuyama, who famously argued at the end of the Cold War that Western liberal democracy was the end point of humanity's ideological evolution and the final form of human government, in what he, mistakenly, called the end of history.[7]

His reactionary criticism of Western society and mistrust of those around him led Solzhenitsyn to become increasingly isolated during the 1980s.[8] In 1990, Mikhail Gorbachev – the last Soviet leader – restored Solzhenitsyn's citizenship and formally dropped the treason charges against him. Solzhenitsyn finally returned to Russia in May 1994 – two and a half years after the collapse of the Soviet Union and twenty years after he was exiled. He was horrified to discover that after abandoning communism Russia had embraced the Western model of society instead of seeking a return to its pre-communist roots. He continued to attack Western materialism and spiritual decline but much of his energy went into criticising Russian bureaucracy and the rise of the new corporate oligarchy – although fewer people than before were willing to listen to him. His final book, *Two Hundred Years Together*, was published in two volumes in 2001 and controversially dealt with the role Jewish Russians played in the Bolshevik revolution and Soviet purges.[9]

Solzhenitsyn died of heart failure on 3 August 2008, four months short of his ninetieth birthday. On learning of his death, Gorbachev described him as a 'man of unique destiny whose name will remain in Russia's history'.[10] Despite his flaws, Solzhenitsyn is rightly recognised for having done so much to expose the faults in both the Soviet system that sought to suppress his work and the Western one that gave him sanctuary.

Harvard University, Massachusetts, United States

8 JUNE 1978

I am sincerely happy to be here with you on this occasion and to become personally acquainted with this old and most prestigious university. My congratulations and very best wishes to all of today's graduates.

Harvard's motto is *Veritas*. Many of you have already found out and others will find out in the course of their lives that truth eludes us if we do not concentrate with total attention on its pursuit. And even while it eludes us, the illusion still lingers of knowing it and leads to many misunderstandings. Also, truth is seldom pleasant; it is almost invariably bitter. There is some bitterness in my speech today, too. But I want to stress that it comes not from an adversary but from a friend.

Three years ago in the United States I said certain things which at that time appeared unacceptable. Today, however, many people agree with what I then said.

The split in today's world is perceptible even to a hasty glance. Any of our contemporaries readily identifies two world powers, each of them already capable of entirely destroying the other. However, understanding of the split often is limited to this political conception, to the illusion that danger may be abolished through successful diplomatic negotiations or by achieving a balance of armed forces. The truth is that the split is a much profounder and a more alienating one, that the rifts are more than one can see at first glance. This deep manifold split bears the danger of manifold disaster for all of us, in accordance with the ancient truth that a Kingdom – in this case, our Earth – divided against itself cannot stand.

Contemporary Worlds

There is the concept of the Third World: thus, we already have three worlds. Undoubtedly, however, the number is even greater; we are just too far away to see. Any ancient deeply rooted autonomous culture, especially if it is spread on a wide part of the Earth's surface, constitutes an autonomous world, full of riddles and surprises to Western thinking. As a minimum, we must include in this category China, India, the Muslim world and Africa, if indeed we accept the approximation of viewing the latter two as compact units. For one thousand years Russia has belonged to such a category, although Western thinking systematically committed the mistake of denying its autonomous character and therefore never understood it, just as today the West does not understand Russia in communist captivity. It may be that in the past years Japan has increasingly become a distant part of the West, I am no judge here; but as to Israel, for instance, it seems to me that it stands apart from the Western world in that its state system is fundamentally linked to religion.

How short a time ago, relatively, the small new European world was easily seizing colonies everywhere, not only without anticipating any real resistance, but also usually despising any possible values in the conquered peoples' approach to life. On the face of it, it was an overwhelming success, there were no geographic frontiers to it. Western society expanded in a triumph of human independence and power. And all of a sudden in the twentieth century came the discovery of its fragility and friability. We now see that the conquests proved to be short-lived and precarious, and this in turn points to defects in the Western view of the world which led to these conquests. Relations with the former colonial world now have turned into

> ❝ This deep manifold split bears the danger of manifold disaster for all of us, in accordance with the ancient truth that a Kingdom – in this case, our Earth – divided against itself cannot stand. ❞

their opposite and the Western world often goes to extremes of obsequiousness, but it is difficult yet to estimate the total size of the bill which former colonial countries will present to the West, and it is difficult to predict whether the surrender not only of its last colonies, but of everything it owns will be sufficient for the West to foot the bill.

Convergence

But the blindness of superiority continues in spite of all and upholds the belief that vast regions everywhere on our planet should develop and mature to the level of present-day Western systems which in theory are the best and in practice the most attractive. There is this belief that all those other worlds are only being temporarily prevented by wicked governments or by heavy crises or by their own barbarity or incomprehension from taking the way of Western pluralistic democracy and from adopting the Western way of life. Countries are judged on the merit of their progress in this direction. However, it is a conception which developed out of Western incomprehension of the essence of other worlds, out of the mistake of measuring them all with a Western yardstick. The real picture of our planet's development is quite different.

Anguish about our divided world gave birth to the theory of convergence between leading Western countries and the Soviet Union. It is a soothing theory which overlooks the fact that these worlds are not at all developing into similarity; neither one can be transformed into the other without the use of violence. Besides, convergence inevitably means acceptance of the other side's defects, too, and this is hardly desirable.

If I were today addressing an audience in my country, examining the overall pattern of the world's rifts, I would have concentrated on the East's calamities. But since my forced exile in the West has now lasted four years and since my audience is a Western one, I think it may be of greater interest to concentrate on certain aspects of the West in our days, such as I see them.

A Decline in Courage

A decline in courage may be the most striking feature which an outside observer notices in the West in our days. The Western world has lost its civil courage, both as a whole and separately, in each country, each government, each political party and of course in the United Nations. Such a decline in courage is particularly noticeable among the ruling groups and the intellectual elite, causing an impression of loss of courage by the entire society. Of course there are many courageous individuals but they have no determining influence on public life. Political and intellectual bureaucrats show depression, passivity and perplexity in their actions and in their statements and even more so in theoretical reflections to explain how realistic, reasonable as well as intellectually and even morally warranted it is to base state policies on weakness and cowardice. And decline in courage is ironically emphasised by occasional explosions of anger and inflexibility on the part of the same bureaucrats when dealing with weak governments and weak countries, not supported by anyone, or with currents which cannot offer any resistance. But they get tongue-tied and paralysed when they deal with powerful governments and threatening forces, with aggressors and international terrorists.

Should·one point out that from ancient times decline in courage has been considered the beginning of the end?

Well-being

When the modern Western states were created, the following principle was proclaimed: governments are meant to serve man, and man lives to be free to pursue happiness. (See, for example, the American Declaration.) Now at last during past decades technical and social progress has permitted the realisation of such aspirations: the welfare state. Every citizen has been granted the desired freedom and material goods in such quantity and of such quality as to guarantee in theory the achievement of happiness, in the morally inferior sense, which has come into being during those same decades. In the process, however, one psychological detail has been overlooked: the constant desire to have still more things and a still better life and the struggle to obtain them imprints many Western faces with worry and even depression, though it is customary to conceal such feelings. Active and tense competition permeates all human thoughts without opening a way to free spiritual development. The individual's independence from many types of state pressure has been guaranteed; the majority of people have been granted well-being to an extent their fathers and grandfathers could not even dream about; it has become possible to·raise young people according to these ideals, leading them to physical splendour, happiness, possession of material goods, money and leisure, to an almost unlimited freedom of enjoyment. So who should now renounce all this, why and for what should one risk one's precious life in defence of common values, and particularly in such nebulous cases when the security of one's nation must be defended in a distant country?

Even biology knows that habitual extreme safety and well-being are not advantageous for a living organism. Today, well-being in the life of Western society has begun to reveal its pernicious mask.

Legalistic Life
Western society has given itself the organisation best suited to its purposes, based, I would say, on the letter of the law. The limits of human rights and righteousness are determined by a system of laws; such limits are very broad. People in the West have acquired considerable skill in using, interpreting and manipulating law, even though laws tend to be too complicated for an average person to understand without the help of an expert. Any conflict is solved according to the letter of the law and this is considered to be the supreme solution. If one is right from a legal point of view, nothing more is required, nobody may mention that one could still not be entirely right, and urge self-restraint, a willingness to renounce such legal rights, sacrifice and selfless risk: it would sound simply absurd. One almost never sees voluntary self-restraint. Everybody operates at the extreme limit of those legal frames. An oil company is legally blameless when it purchases an invention of a new type of energy in order to prevent its use. A food-product manufacturer is legally blameless when he poisons his produce to make it last longer: after all, people are free not to buy it.

I have spent all my life under a communist regime and I will tell you that a society without any objective legal scale is a terrible one indeed. But a society with no other scale but the legal one is not quite worthy of man either. A society which is based on the letter of the law and never reaches any higher is taking very scarce advantage of the high level of human possibilities. The letter of the law is too cold and formal to have a beneficial influence on society. Whenever the tissue of life is woven of legalistic relations, there is an atmosphere of moral mediocrity, paralysing man's noblest impulses.

And it will be simply impossible to stand through the trials of this threatening century with only the support of a legalistic structure.

The Direction of Freedom
In today's Western society, the inequality has been revealed of freedom for good deeds and freedom for evil deeds. A statesman who wants to achieve something important and highly constructive for his country has to move cautiously and even timidly; there are thousands of hasty and irresponsible

❝ It is time, in the West, **to defend** not so much human rights as human **obligations.❞**

critics around him, parliament and the press keep rebuffing him. As he moves ahead, he has to prove that every single step of his is well founded and absolutely flawless. Actually an outstanding and particularly gifted person who has unusual and unexpected initiatives in mind hardly gets a chance to assert himself; from the very beginning, dozens of traps will be set out for him. Thus mediocrity triumphs with the excuse of restrictions imposed by democracy.

It is feasible and easy everywhere to undermine administrative power and, in fact, it has been drastically weakened in all Western countries. The defence of individual rights has reached such extremes as to make society as a whole defenceless against certain individuals. It is time, in the West, to defend not so much human rights as human obligations.

Destructive and irresponsible freedom has been granted boundless space. Society appears to have little defence against the abyss of human deca-dence, such as, for example, misuse of liberty for moral violence against young people, motion pictures full of pornography, crime and horror. It is consid-ered to be part of freedom and theoretically counter-balanced by the young people's right not to look or not to accept. Life organised legalistically has thus shown its inability to defend itself against the corrosion of evil.

And what shall we say about the dark realm of criminality as such? Legal frames (especially in the United States) are broad enough to encourage not only individual freedom but also certain individual crimes. The culprit can go unpunished or obtain undeserved leniency with the support of thousands of public defenders. When a government starts an earnest fight against terrorism, public opinion immediately accuses it of violating the terrorists' civil rights. There are many such cases.

Such a tilt of freedom in the direction of evil has come about gradually but it was evidently born primarily out of a humanistic and benevolent concept according to which there is no evil inherent to human nature; the world belongs to mankind and all the defects of life are caused by wrong social systems which must be corrected. Strangely enough, though the best social conditions have been achieved in the West, there still is criminality and there even is considerably more of it than in the pauper and lawless Soviet society. (There is a huge number of prisoners in our camps which are termed criminals, but most of them never committed any crime; they merely tried to defend themselves against a lawless state resorting to means outside of a legal framework.)

The Direction of the Press

The press too, of course, enjoys the widest freedom. (I shall be using the word press to include all media.) But what sort of use does it make of this freedom?

Here again, the main concern is not to infringe the letter of the law. There is no moral responsibility for deformation or disproportion. What sort of responsibility does a journalist have to his readers, or to history? If they have misled public opinion or the government by inaccurate information or wrong conclusions, do we know of any cases of public recognition and rectification of such mistakes by the same journalist or the same newspaper? No, it does not happen, because it would damage sales. A nation may be the victim of such a mistake, but the journalist always gets away with it. One may safely assume that he will start writing the opposite with renewed self-assurance.

Because instant and credible information has to be given, it becomes necessary to resort to guesswork, rumours and suppositions to fill in the voids, and none of them will ever be rectified, they will stay on in the readers' memory. How many hasty, immature, superficial and misleading judgements are expressed every day, confusing readers, without any verification. The press can both simulate public opinion and miseducate it. Thus we may see terrorists heroised, or secret matters, pertaining to one's nation's defence, publicly revealed, or we may witness shameless intrusion on the privacy of well-known people under the slogan: 'everyone is entitled to know everything'. But this is a false slogan, characteristic of a false era: people also have the right not to know, and it is a much more valuable one. The right not to have their divine souls stuffed with gossip, nonsense, vain talk. A person who works and leads a meaningful life does not need this excessive burdening flow of information.

Hastiness and superficiality are the psychic disease of the twentieth century and more than anywhere else this disease is reflected in the press. In-depth analysis of a problem is anathema to the press. It stops at sensational formulas.

Such as it is, however, the press has become the greatest power within the Western countries, more powerful than the legislature, the executive and the judiciary. One would then like to ask: by what law has it been elected and to whom is it responsible? In the communist East a journalist is frankly appointed as a state official. But who has granted Western journalists their power, for how long a time and with what prerogatives?

There is yet another surprise for someone coming from the East where the press is rigorously unified: one gradually discovers a common trend of preferences within the Western press as a whole. It is a fashion; there are generally accepted patterns of judgement and there may be common corporate interests, the sum effect being not competition but unification. Enormous freedom exists for the press, but not for the readership because newspapers mostly give enough stress and emphasis to those opinions which do not too openly contradict their own and the general trend.

A Fashion in Thinking

Without any censorship, in the West fashionable trends of thought and ideas are carefully separated from those which are not fashionable; nothing is forbidden, but what is not fashionable will hardly ever find its way into periodicals or books or be heard in colleges. Legally your researchers are free, but they are conditioned by the fashion of the day. There is no open violence such as in the East; however, a selection dictated by fashion and the need to match mass standards frequently prevents independent-minded people from giving their contribution to public life. There is a dangerous tendency to form a herd, shutting off successful development. I have received letters in America from highly intelligent persons, maybe a teacher in a faraway small college who could do much for the renewal and salvation of his country, but his country cannot hear him because the media are not interested in him. This gives birth to strong mass prejudices, blindness, which is most dangerous in our dynamic era. There is, for instance, a self-deluding interpretation of the contemporary world situation. It works as a sort of petrified armour around people's minds. Human voices from seventeen countries of Eastern Europe and Eastern Asia cannot pierce it. It will only be broken by the pitiless crowbar of events.

I have mentioned a few trends of Western life which surprise and shock a new arrival to this world. The purpose and scope of this speech will not allow me to continue such a review, to look into the influence of these Western characteristics on important aspects on the nation's life.

Socialism

It is almost universally recognised that the West shows all the world a way to successful economic development, even though in the past years it has been strongly disturbed by chaotic inflation. However, many people living in the West are dissatisfied with their own society. They despise it or accuse it of not being up to the level of maturity attained by mankind. A number of such critics turn to socialism, which is a false and dangerous current.

I hope that no one present will suspect me of offering my personal criticism of the Western system to present socialism as an alternative. Having experienced applied socialism in a country where the alternative has been realised, I certainly will not speak for it. The well-known Soviet mathematician Shafarevich, a member of the Soviet Academy of Science, has written a brilliant book under the title *Socialism*; it is a profound analysis showing that socialism of any type and shade leads to a total destruction of the human spirit and to a levelling of mankind into death. Shafarevich's book was published in France almost two years ago and so far no one has been found to refute it. It will shortly be published in English in the United States.

Not a Model

But should someone ask me whether I would indicate the West such as it is today as a model to my country, frankly I would have to answer negatively. No, I could not recommend your society in its present state as an ideal for the transformation of ours. Through intense suffering our country has now achieved a spiritual development of such intensity that the Western system in its present state of spiritual exhaustion does not look attractive. Even those characteristics of your life which I have just mentioned are extremely saddening.

A fact which cannot be disputed is the weakening of human beings in the West while in the East they are becoming firmer and stronger. Six decades for our people and three decades for the people of Eastern Europe; during that time we have been through a spiritual training far in advance of Western experience. Life's complexity and mortal weight have produced stronger, deeper and more interesting characters than those produced by standard-ised Western well-being. Therefore if our society were to be transformed into yours, it would mean an improvement in certain aspects, but also a change for the worse on some particularly significant scores. It is true, no doubt, that a society cannot remain in an abyss of lawlessness, as is the case in our country. But it is also demeaning for it to elect such mechanical legalistic smoothness as you have. After the suffering of decades of violence and oppression, the human soul longs for things higher, warmer and purer than those offered by today's mass living habits, introduced by the revolting invasion of publicity, by TV stupor and by intolerable music.

All this is visible to observers from all the worlds of our planet. The Western way of life is less and less likely to become the leading model.

There are meaningful warnings that history gives a threatened or perishing society. Such are, for instance, the decadence of art, or a lack of great statesmen. There are open and evident warnings, too. The centre of your democracy and of your culture is left without electric power for a few hours only, and all of a sudden crowds of American citizens start looting and creating havoc. The smooth surface film must be very thin, then, the social system quite unstable and unhealthy.

But the fight for our planet, physical and spiritual, a fight of cosmic proportions, is not a vague matter of the future; it has already started. The forces of Evil have begun their decisive offensive, you can feel their pressure, and yet your screens and publications are full of prescribed smiles and raised glasses. What is the joy about?

Short-sightedness

Very well-known representatives of your society, such as George Kennan, say: we cannot apply moral criteria to politics.* Thus we mix good and evil, right and wrong and make space for the absolute triumph of absolute Evil in the world. On the contrary, only moral criteria can help the West against communism's well-planned world strategy. There are no other criteria. Practical or occasional considerations of any kind will inevitably be swept away by strategy. After a certain level of the problem has been reached, legalistic thinking induces paralysis; it prevents one from seeing the size and meaning of events.

In spite of the abundance of information, or maybe because of it, the West has difficulties in understanding reality such as it is. There have been

---

* George Kennan was a US diplomat and historian who advocated the policy of containment in response to Soviet expansionism and whose thinking was particularly influential during the early stages of the Cold War.

" This **debilitating** dream of a **status quo** is the **symptom** of a society which has **come** to the **end** of its **development**. "

naive predictions by some American experts who believed that Angola would become the Soviet Union's Vietnam or that Cuban expeditions in Africa would best be stopped by special US courtesy to Cuba. Kennan's advice to his own country – to begin unilateral disarmament – belongs to the same category. If you only knew how the youngest of the Moscow Old Square officials laugh at your political wizards! As to Fidel Castro, he frankly scorns the United States, sending his troops to distant adventures from his country right next to yours.

However, the most cruel mistake occurred with the failure to understand the Vietnam War. Some people sincerely wanted all wars to stop just as soon as possible; others believed that there should be room for national, or communist, self-determination in Vietnam, or in Cambodia, as we see today with particular clarity. But members of the US anti-war movement wound up being involved in the betrayal of Far Eastern nations, in a genocide and in the suffering today imposed on thirty million people there. Do those convinced pacifists hear the moans coming from there? Do they understand their responsibility today? Or do they prefer not to hear? The American intelligentsia lost its nerve and as a consequence thereof danger has come much closer to the United States. But there is no awareness of this. Your short-sighted politicians who signed the hasty Vietnam capitulation seemingly gave America a carefree breathing pause; however, a hundredfold Vietnam now looms over you. That small Vietnam had been a warning and an occasion to mobilise the nation's courage. But if a full-fledged America suffered a real defeat from a small communist half-country, how can the West hope to stand firm in the future?

I have had occasion already to say that in the twentieth century democracy has not won any major war without help and protection from a powerful continental ally whose philosophy and ideology it did not question.

In World War II against Hitler, instead of winning that war with its own forces, which would certainly have been sufficient, Western democracy grew and cultivated another enemy who would prove worse and more powerful yet, as Hitler never had so many resources and so many people, nor did he offer any attractive ideas, or have such a large number of supporters in the West – a potential fifth column – as the Soviet Union. At present, some Western voices already have spoken of obtaining protection from a third power against aggression in the next world conflict, if there is one; in this case the shield would be China. But I would not wish such an outcome to any country in the world. First of all, it is again a doomed alliance with Evil; also, it would grant the United States a respite, but when at a later date China with its billion people would turn around armed with American weapons, America itself would fall prey to a genocide similar to the one perpetrated in Cambodia in our days.

Loss of Willpower

And yet – no weapons, no matter how powerful, can help the West until it overcomes its loss of willpower. In a state of psychological weakness, weapons become a burden for the capitulating side. To defend oneself, one must also be ready to die; there is little such readiness in a society raised in the cult of material well-being. Nothing is left, then, but concessions, attempts to gain time and betrayal. Thus at the shameful Belgrade conference free Western diplomats in their weakness surrendered the line where enslaved members of Helsinki watch groups are sacrificing their lives. *

Western thinking has become conservative: the world situation should stay as it is at any cost, there should be no changes. This debilitating dream of a status quo is the symptom of a society which has come to the end of its development. But one must be blind in order not to see that oceans no longer belong to the West, while land under its domination keeps shrinking.

* The Helsinki Accords (or Final Act) were signed at the Conference on Security and Cooperation in Europe (CSCE) on 1 August 1975. They were an attempt to improve relations between the Eastern Bloc and the West as part of *détente* and related primarily to respect for sovereignty, human rights and international law. Various non-governmental groups were established to monitor the Soviet Union's compliance with the Accords (what Solzhenitsyn called the 'Helsinki watch groups'). The first follow-up meeting to the CSCE was held in Belgrade from 4 October 1977 to 8 March 1978. The meeting was marked by tensions between the United States and the Soviet Union, particularly during discussions over human rights, and consensus was not reached on a number of proposals.

The two so-called world wars (they were by far not on a world scale, not yet) have meant internal self-destruction of the small, progressive West which has thus prepared its own end. The next war (which does not have to be an atomic one and I do not believe it will) may well bury Western civilisation forever.

Facing such a danger, with such historical values in your past, at such a high level of realisation of freedom and apparently of devotion to freedom, how is it possible to lose to such an extent the will to defend oneself?

Humanism and Its Consequences

How has this unfavourable relation of forces come about? How did the West decline from its triumphal march to its present sickness? Have there been fatal turns and losses of direction in its development? It does not seem so. The West kept advancing socially in accordance with its proclaimed intentions, with the help of brilliant technological progress. And all of a sudden it found itself in its present state of weakness.

This means that the mistake must be at the root, at the very basis of human thinking in the past centuries. I refer to the prevailing Western view of the world which was first born during the Renaissance and found its political expression from the period of the Enlightenment. It became the basis for government and social science and could be defined as rationalistic humanism or humanistic autonomy: the proclaimed and enforced autonomy of man from any higher force above him. It could also be called anthropocentricity, with man seen as the centre of everything that exists.

The turn introduced by the Renaissance evidently was inevitable historically. The Middle Ages had come to a natural end by exhaustion, becoming an intolerable despotic repression of man's physical nature in favour of the spiritual one. Then, however, we turned our backs upon the Spirit and embraced all that is material with excessive and unwarranted zeal. This new way of thinking, which had imposed on us its guidance, did not admit the existence of intrinsic evil in man nor did it see any higher task than the attainment of happiness on earth. It based modern Western civilisation on the dangerous trend to worship man and his material needs. Everything beyond physical well-being and accumulation of material goods, all other human requirements and characteristics of a subtler and higher nature, were left outside the area of attention of state and social systems, as if human life did not have any superior sense. That provided access for evil, of which in our days there is a free and constant flow. Merely freedom does not in the least solve all the problems of human life and it even adds a number of new ones.

However, in early democracies, as in American democracy at the time of its birth, all individual human rights were granted because man is God's creature. That is, freedom was given to the individual conditionally, in the assumption of his constant religious responsibility. Such was the heritage of the preceding thousand years. Two hundred or even fifty years ago, it would have seemed quite impossible, in America, that an individual could be granted boundless freedom simply for the satisfaction of his instincts or whims. Subsequently, however, all such limitations were discarded everywhere in the West; a total liberation occurred from the moral heritage of Christian centuries with their great reserves of mercy and sacrifice. State systems were becoming increasingly and totally materialistic. The West ended up by truly enforcing human rights, sometimes even excessively, but man's sense of responsibility to God and society grew dimmer and dimmer. In the past decades, the legalistically selfish aspect of Western approach and thinking has reached its final dimension and the world wound up in a harsh spiritual crisis and a political impasse. All the glorified technological achievements of progress, including the conquest of outer space, do not redeem the twentieth century's moral poverty which no one could imagine even as late as in the nineteenth century.

An Unexpected Kinship

As humanism in its development became more and more materialistic, it made itself increasingly accessible to speculation and manipulation at first by socialism and then by communism. So that Karl Marx was able to say in 1844 that 'communism is naturalised humanism'.

This statement turned out not to be entirely senseless. One does see the same stones in the foundations of a despiritualised humanism and of any type of socialism: endless materialism; freedom from religion and religious responsibility, which under communist regimes reach the stage of anti-religious dictatorship; concentration on social structures with a seemingly scientific approach. (This is typical of the Enlightenment in the eighteenth century and of Marxism.) Not by coincidence all of communism's meaningless pledges and oaths are about Man, with a capital M, and his earthly happiness. At first glance it seems an ugly parallel: common traits in the thinking and way of life of today's West and today's East? But such is the logic of materialistic development.

The interrelationship is such, too, that the current of materialism which is most to the left always ends up by being stronger, more attractive and victorious, because it is more consistent. Humanism without its Christian heritage cannot resist such competition. We watch this process in the past centuries and especially in the past decades, on a world scale as the situation becomes increasingly dramatic. Liberalism was inevitably displaced by radicalism, radicalism had to surrender to socialism and socialism could never resist communism. The communist regime in the East could stand and grow due to the enthusiastic support from an enormous number of Western intellectuals who felt a kinship and refused to see communism's crimes. When they no longer could do so, they tried to justify them. In our Eastern countries, communism has suffered a complete ideological defeat; it is zero and less than zero. But Western intellectuals still look at it with interest and with empathy, and this is precisely what makes it so immensely difficult for the West to withstand the East.

Before the Turn

I am not examining here the case of a world-war disaster and the changes which it would produce in society. As long as we wake up every morning under a peaceful sun, we have to lead an everyday life. There is a disaster, however, which has already been under way for quite some time. I am referring to the calamity of a despiritualised and irreligious humanistic consciousness.

To such consciousness, man is the touchstone in judging and evaluating everything on earth. Imperfect man, who is never free of pride, self-interest, envy, vanity and dozens of other defects. We are now experiencing the consequences of mistakes which had not been noticed at the beginning of the journey. On the way from the Renaissance to our days we have enriched our experience, but we have lost the concept of a Supreme Complete Entity which used to restrain our passions and our irresponsibility. We have placed too much hope in political and social reforms, only to find out that we were being deprived of our most precious possession: our spiritual life. In the East, it is destroyed by the dealings and machinations of the ruling party. In the West, commercial interests tend to suffocate it. This is the real crisis. The split in the world is less terrible than the similarity of the disease plaguing its main sections.

If humanism were right in declaring that man is born to be happy, he would not be born to die. Since his body is doomed to die, his task on earth evidently must be of a more spiritual nature. It cannot be unrestrained

" Only **voluntary,** inspired self-restraint can **raise** man **above** the world **stream** of **materialism.** "

enjoyment of everyday life. It cannot be the search for the best ways to obtain material goods and then cheerfully get the most out of them. It has to be the fulfilment of a permanent, earnest duty so that one's life journey may become an experience of moral growth, so that one may leave life a better human being than one started it. It is imperative to review the table of widespread human values. Its present incorrectness is astounding. It is not possible that assessment of the President's performance be reduced to the question of how much money one makes or of unlimited availability of gasoline. Only voluntary, inspired self-restraint can raise man above the world stream of materialism.

It would be retrogression to attach oneself today to the ossified formulas of the Enlightenment. Social dogmatism leaves us completely helpless in front of the trials of our times.

Even if we are spared destruction by war, our lives will have to change if we want to save life from self-destruction. We cannot avoid revising the fundamental definitions of human life and human society. Is it true that man is above everything? Is there no Superior Spirit above him? Is it right that man's life and society's activities have to be determined by material expansion in the first place? Is it permissible to promote such expansion to the detriment of our spiritual integrity?

If the world has not come to its end, it has approached a major turn in history, equal in importance to the turn from the Middle Ages to the Renaissance. It will exact from us a spiritual upsurge, we shall have to rise to a new height of vision, to a new level of life where our physical nature will not be cursed as in the Middle Ages, but, even more importantly, our spiritual being will not be trampled upon as in the Modern era.

This ascension will be similar to climbing onto the next anthropologic stage. No one on earth has any other way left but – upward.

Ash Heap
of History

– Ronald Reagan –

Four years to the day after Aleksandr Solzhenitsyn's Harvard address, a very different man stood in a very different place and spoke out against a system he hated. While Solzhenitsyn had spoken of the demise of the West, US President Ronald Reagan used his speech to the British parliament on 8 June 1982 to talk of the downfall of the Soviet Union – a country that, he argued, ran 'against the tide of history'.

The Union of Soviet Socialist Republics (USSR) had emerged from the ashes of Imperial Russia following the revolutions of 1917 and the civil war of 1918–23 that had brought Vladimir Lenin and the Bolsheviks to power. Established in December 1922 as a union of four Soviet socialist republics, by 1945 the Soviet Union had become a highly centralised entity consisting of sixteen republics under the control of Moscow. At the end of World War II, the Soviet Union occupied much of central and Eastern Europe, including the Baltic states and some German, Polish, Czechoslovakian and Romanian territory. These areas were either annexed by existing Soviet republics, became new Soviet republics or became satellite states with communist governments, forming an Eastern Bloc of countries under Soviet control and influence.

In February 1945, as the war in Europe was reaching its end, Winston Churchill, Franklin D. Roosevelt and Joseph Stalin – the leaders of Britain, the United States and the Soviet Union – met in the Black Sea resort of Yalta to discuss the reorganisation of post-war Europe. Then in July and August 1945, Clement Attlee and Harry S. Truman – the new leaders of Britain and the United States – met Stalin in Potsdam in occupied Germany to discuss the administration of the defeated Germany and the on-going war with Japan. The agreements reached during these conferences resulted in a divided Europe, with the one-time allies facing each other through what Churchill described as an Iron Curtain across the continent from the Baltic to the Adriatic – the British, Americans and French on one side and the Soviets on the other.[11] This gave geographical manifestation to the political and ideological divide that would result in the Cold War.

The 1940s and 1950s saw the United States implement the Truman doctrine of containment and the Marshall Plan of aid to Western Europe, and the creation of the North Atlantic Treaty Organisation (NATO) as a political and military alliance. These decades also saw the Soviet Union seal off East Germany and blockade West Berlin, develop its own nuclear weapons and form the Warsaw Pact as a counterbalance to NATO. While the Soviet Union focused on consolidating and expanding communist control within its sphere of influence, the United States sought to use its economic and military power to mould the post-war world and promote capitalism and Western democracy. Then in June 1950, war broke out between North and South Korea. The Korean Peninsula had been ruled by Japan until the end of the Pacific War in 1945, at which point it had been divided along the 38th parallel between the Soviet occupying forces in the north and the American occupying forces in the south. On 25 June 1950, North Korean forces attacked the south in an attempt to reunify the country. The intervention of the United States and the United Nations on the side of South Korea and China and the Soviet Union on the side of North Korea quickly turned the conflict into a proxy war between the Cold War superpowers.

This pattern of proxy wars would be repeated over the next three decades in Vietnam, Angola, Afghanistan and Lebanon, as well as through direct or indirect political interference across the majority world. At least ten million people were killed and thirty million injured in these conflicts.[12] As such, the popular belief that the Cold War was an era in which nuclear weapons kept the peace between the superpowers is a fallacy. Furthermore, at the height of the Cold War around seventy thousand nuclear weapons were deployed and numerous early warning errors and false alarms, together with more than forty accidents involving nuclear weapons or military nuclear reactors, made this a highly unstable period.[13] As more information has come to light about the Cuban Missile Crisis of 1962 (which followed the discovery of Soviet medium-range nuclear missiles on Cuba) and NATO's Able Archer exercise in 1983 (which the Soviet Union mistook as preparations for a nuclear first strike) it is clear just how close to nuclear confrontation the superpowers came.[14]

During this period, serious efforts were made to reduce the tensions between the United States and NATO on one side and the Soviet Union and the Warsaw Pact on the other. *Détente* gave rise to a series of summits between the US and Soviet leaders and a number of important arms-control agreements, including SALT I and the Anti-Ballistic Missile Treaty. By the end of the 1970s, though, relations between the Americans and Soviets had begun to break down and the Soviet intervention in Afghanistan in December 1979 and the rise of Reagan to the US presidency in January 1981 effectively led to the end of détente. Reagan, together with the British Prime Minister, Margaret Thatcher, adopted a more hard-line stance against the Soviet Union – increasing defence spending and denouncing communism. Reagan also signalled a shift from a policy of containment to one of roll-back as the United States sought to topple Soviet-backed left-wing governments in the Third World by providing overt and covert support to right-wing guerrillas and resistance movements.[15]

On 8 June 1982, Reagan gave an address to both houses of the British parliament. It has become famous for a line in which he described 'the march of freedom and democracy which will leave Marxism–Leninism on the ash heap of history'. The expression 'ash heap of history' was likely used to paraphrase Leon Trotsky, who had used a similar choice of words in reference to moderate socialist opponents of the October 1917 Bolshevik revolution: 'You are pitiful isolated individuals; you are miserable bankrupts; your role is played out. Go where you belong from now on – into the dustbin of history!'[16] Reagan's 'ash heap of history' speech was a seminal moment because never before had an American President so openly questioned the underlying philosophy of the Soviet system. According to Richard Pipes, a member of Reagan's National Security Council at the time, until then the dominant view in the West was that it was only the Soviet Union's actions that were of concern, not the system per se; but Reagan believed that Soviet aggression was deeply rooted in the false philosophy of Marxism–Leninism – a system he viewed as unnatural and wicked. By attacking the Soviet system directly he was at odds with his predecessors as well as officials and academics on both sides of the Atlantic; but he persisted and, together with Thatcher, changed the dynamic of the Cold War from trying to negotiate with and contain the Soviet Union to trying to defeat it .[17]

Reagan's speech to the British parliament is sometimes mistakenly referred to as the Evil Empire speech. While Reagan did refer to 'totalitarian evil' in that speech, he did not actually use the phrase 'an evil empire' until eight months later, in a speech to the National Association of Evangelicals in Orlando.[18] By then, Reagan and others had recast the Cold War into a war of good against evil. In his Orlando speech he urged people to resist 'the temptation of blithely declaring yourselves above it all and label both sides equally at fault, to ignore the facts of history and the aggressive impulses of an evil empire, to simply call the arms race a giant misunderstanding and thereby remove yourself from the struggle between right and wrong and good and evil'. There was, however, no 'good' and 'evil' as such in the Cold War. Put simply, both sides were nuclear-armed imperiums that committed gross wrongs at home and abroad as they sought to impose their differing world views and political and economic systems on others. Nonetheless, it was a popular stance with the American electorate and Reagan was re-elected in 1984 in a landslide victory. Part of his success was due to the homely, almost con- versational, style that the former Hollywood actor used in his speeches – delivering the lines of his principal speechwriters Anthony Dolan and Peggy Noonan with just the right amount of emotion and showbiz charm.

Reagan argued in his 'ash heap of history' speech, 'If history teaches anything it teaches self-delusion in the face of unpleasant facts is folly.' Yet blind to the horrors that the West had unleashed during various proxy wars or US-backed *coups d'état*, he told parliament, 'Historians looking back at our time will note the consistent restraint and peaceful intentions of the West.' 'They will note', he said, 'it was not the democracies that invaded Afghanistan . . . or used chemical and toxin warfare in Afghanistan and Southeast Asia'. He was referring to accusations that the Soviets had supplied a weaponised trichothecene mycotoxin to Vietnam, which may have been used against the Hmong in Laos in 1975 and the

Khmer Rouge in Cambodia in 1978, and that the Soviets had deployed the weapon themselves against the mujahedin in Afghanistan in the early 1980s (attacks that became known as 'yellow rain'). However, these claims remain unconfirmed to this day.[19]

In turn, though, it is well known that the US military used highly toxic defoliants, including Agent Orange, on vegetation and food crops in South Vietnam in the 1960s, causing dioxin-related deformities in children over several generations. There is a lesser-known accusation that sarin nerve gas was used during a US special forces attack on a village in Laos in 1970 (although this is denied by the Pentagon).[20] There are also suspicions that the United States used biological weapons during the Korean War and on several occasions against Cuba.[21] Furthermore, the United States is the only country to have ever used nuclear weapons: when it bombed the Japanese cities of Hiroshima and Nagasaki in August 1945. To suggest that democracies are in some way more restrained and peaceful than countries with other systems of government is to fundamentally misrepresent history. Self-delusion in the face of unpleasant facts is, indeed, folly.

The pseudo-bipolar world of the Cold War came to an end with the collapse of the Soviet Union. The centrally planned economy of the Soviet Union had been in decline and proved to be inefficient and unable to adapt to change. The Soviet political system was unable to accommodate the growth of nationalism within the Soviet republics or satellite states of the Eastern Bloc, which one after another turned their backs on Moscow. The Soviet military was unable to maintain pace with technological developments and was placing a considerable strain on the Soviet economy. The foreign policy of the Soviet Union met several setbacks following the disastrous military intervention in Afghanistan, the failure of Marxism–Leninism in several Third World countries and the aggressive roll-back policies of Reagan.[22] Mikhail Gorbachev pursued policies of *glasnost* (greater civil liberties and better governance) and *perestroika* (political and economic reform) throughout the late 1980s but the Soviet Union weakened even further and eventually disintegrated. The Soviet flag was lowered over the Kremlin for the last time on 25 December 1991 and by the end of the month the Soviet Union had ceased to exist.

The Cold War period had involved a forty-five-year diversion of scientific and intellectual effort and financial and other resources from civil use into an ideological, political and military confrontation.[23] This was at a time of great human need following World War II, the decolonisation of the majority world, the energy and food crises of the 1970s and deep poverty and socio-economic divisions in many parts of the world. With the end of the Cold War, there was a brief window during the 1990s when US hegemony looked like it might bring stability to the world system – a perceived unipolar moment. That perception was illusory and short-lived as multiple centres of political and economic power emerged and the so-called clash of civilisations developed between the Western and Muslim worlds.[24] At his nomination hearing for the post of CIA director in February 1993, James Woolsey gave this description of the post-Cold War situation: 'We have slain a large dragon. But we live now in a jungle filled with a bewildering variety of poisonous snakes. And in many ways, the dragon was easier to keep track of.'[25] Many of the same conservatives who had fought the old 'dragon' of the Soviet Union with Reagan would re-emerge at the beginning of the twenty-first century to fight a war on terror against the new 'poisonous snakes' of al-Qaida and radical Islam. If, for many, the Cold War had been World War III, this would be their World War IV.

Royal Gallery, Palace of Westminster, London, England

8 JUNE 1982

The journey of which this visit forms a part is a long one. Already it has taken me to two great cities of the West, Rome and Paris, and to the economic summit at Versailles. And there, once again, our sister democracies have proved that even in a time of severe economic strain, free peoples can work together freely and voluntarily to address problems as serious as inflation, unemployment, trade and economic development in a spirit of cooperation and solidarity.

Other milestones lie ahead. Later this week, in Germany, we and our

NATO allies will discuss measures for our joint defence and America's latest initiatives for a more peaceful, secure world through arms reductions. Each stop of this trip is important, but among them all, this moment occupies a special place in my heart and in the hearts of my countrymen – a moment of kinship and homecoming in these hallowed halls.

Speaking for all Americans, I want to say how very much at home we feel in your house. Every American would, because this is, as we have been so eloquently told, one of democracy's shrines. Here the rights of free people and the processes of representation have been debated and refined. It has been said that an institution is the lengthening shadow of a man. This institution is the lengthening shadow of all the men and women who have sat here and all those who have voted to send representatives here.

This is my second visit to Great Britain as President of the United States. My first opportunity to stand on British soil occurred almost a year and a half ago when your Prime Minister graciously hosted a diplomatic dinner at the British Embassy in Washington. Mrs Thatcher said then that she hoped I was not distressed to find staring down at me from the grand staircase a portrait of His Royal Majesty King George III. She suggested it was best to let bygones be bygones, and in view of our two countries' remarkable friendship in succeeding years, she added that most Englishmen today would agree with Thomas Jefferson that 'a little rebellion now and then is a very good thing'.

Well, from here I will go on to Bonn and then Berlin, where there stands a grim symbol of power untamed. The Berlin Wall, that dreadful grey gash across the city, is in its third decade. It is the fitting signature of the regime that built it.

And a few hundred kilometres behind the Berlin Wall, there is another symbol. In the centre of Warsaw, there is a sign that notes the distances to two capitals. In one direction it points toward Moscow; in the other, it points toward Brussels, headquarters of Western Europe's tangible unity. The marker says that the distances from Warsaw to Moscow and Warsaw to Brussels are equal. The sign makes this point: Poland is not East or West. Poland is at the centre of European civilisation. It has contributed mightily to that civilisation. It is doing so today by being magnificently unreconciled to oppression.

Poland's struggle to be Poland, and to secure the basic rights we often take for granted, demonstrates why we dare not take those rights for granted. Gladstone, defending the Reform Bill of 1866, declared: 'You cannot fight against the future. Time is on our side.'* It was easier to believe in the march of democracy in Gladstone's day – in that high noon of Victorian optimism.

We're approaching the end of a bloody century plagued by a terrible political invention – totalitarianism. Optimism comes less easily today, not because democracy is less vigorous, but because democracy's enemies have refined their instruments of repression. Yet optimism is in order, because day by day democracy is proving itself to be a not-at-all-fragile flower. From Stettin on the Baltic to Varna on the Black Sea, the regimes planted by totalitarianism have had more than thirty years to establish their legitimacy. But none – not one regime – has yet been able to risk free elections. Regimes planted by bayonets do not take root.

The strength of the Solidarity Movement in Poland demonstrates the truth told in an underground joke in the Soviet Union.‡ It is that the Soviet Union would remain a one-party nation even if an opposition party were permitted, because everyone would join the opposition party.

America's time as a player on the stage of world history has been brief. I think understanding this fact has always made you patient with your younger cousins – well, not always patient. I do recall that on one occasion, Sir Winston Churchill said in exasperation about one of our most distinguished diplomats: 'He is the only case I know of a bull who carries his china shop with him.'

But witty as Sir Winston was, he also had that special attribute of great statesmen – the gift of vision, the willingness to see the future based on the experience of the past. It is this sense of history, this understanding of the past that I want to talk with you about today, for it is in remembering what we share of the past that our two nations can make common cause for the future.

We have not inherited an easy world. If developments like the Industrial Revolution, which began here in England, and the gifts of science and technology have made life much easier for us, they have also made it more dangerous. There are threats now to our freedom, indeed to our very existence, that other generations could never even have imagined.

There is first the threat of global war. No President, no Congress, no Prime Minister, no parliament can spend a day entirely free of this threat.

* William Gladstone was a nineteenth-century Liberal Party politician and four times Prime Minister of Britain.

‡ The Solidarity movement was an anti-Soviet trade union federation founded in Poland in 1980.

❝ Optimism comes **less easily today,** not because democracy is less vigorous, but **because democracy's enemies** have **refined** their instruments of **repression. ❞**

And I don't have to tell you that in today's world the existence of nuclear weapons could mean, if not the extinction of mankind, then surely the end of civilisation as we know it. That's why negotiations on intermediate-range nuclear forces now underway in Europe and the START talks – Strategic Arms Reduction Talks – which will begin later this month are not just critical to American or Western policy; they are critical to mankind. Our commitment to early success in these negotiations is firm and unshakable, and our purpose is clear: reducing the risk of war by reducing the means of waging war on both sides.

At the same time there is a threat posed to human freedom by the enormous power of the modern state. History teaches the dangers of government that overreaches – political control taking precedence over free economic growth, secret police, mindless bureaucracy, all combining to stifle individual excellence and personal freedom.

Now, I'm aware that among us here and throughout Europe there is legitimate disagreement over the extent to which the public sector should play a role in a nation's economy and life. But on one point all of us are united – our abhorrence of dictatorship in all its forms, but most particularly total-itarianism and the terrible inhumanities it has caused in our time – the Great Purge, Auschwitz and Dachau, the Gulag, and Cambodia.

Historians looking back at our time will note the consistent restraint and peaceful intentions of the West. They will note that it was the democracies who refused to use the threat of their nuclear monopoly in the forties and early fifties for territorial or imperial gain. Had that nuclear monopoly been in the hands of the communist world, the map of Europe – indeed, the world – would look very different today. And certainly they will note it was not the democracies that invaded Afghanistan or suppressed Polish Solidarity or used chemical and toxin warfare in Afghanistan and Southeast Asia.

If history teaches anything it teaches self-delusion in the face of unpleasant facts is folly. We see around us today the marks of our terrible dilemma – predictions of doomsday, anti-nuclear demonstrations, an arms race in which the West must, for its own protection, be an unwilling participant. At the same time we see totalitarian forces in the world who seek subversion and conflict around the globe to further their barbarous assault on the human spirit. What, then, is our course? Must civilisation perish in a hail of fiery atoms? Must freedom wither in a quiet, deadening accommodation with totalitarian evil?

Sir Winston Churchill refused to accept the inevitability of war or even that it was imminent. He said: 'I do not believe that Soviet Russia desires war. What they desire is the fruits of war and the indefinite expansion of their power and doctrines. But what we have to consider here today while time remains is the permanent prevention of war and the establishment of conditions of freedom and democracy as rapidly as possible in all countries.'

Well, this is precisely our mission today: to preserve freedom as well as peace. It may not be easy to see; but I believe we live now at a turning point.

In an ironic sense Karl Marx was right. We are witnessing today a great revolutionary crisis, a crisis where the demands of the economic order are conflicting directly with those of the political order. But the crisis is happening not in the free, non-Marxist West, but in the home of Marxist – Leninism, the Soviet Union. It is the Soviet Union that runs against the tide of history by denying human freedom and human dignity to its citizens. It also is in deep economic difficulty. The rate of growth in the national product has been steadily declining since the '50s and is less than half of what it was then.

The dimensions of this failure are astounding: a country which employs one-fifth of its population in agriculture is unable to feed its own people. Were it not for the private sector, the tiny private sector tolerated in Soviet agriculture, the country might be on the brink of famine. These private plots occupy a bare 3 per cent of the arable land but account for nearly one-quarter of Soviet farm output and nearly one-third of meat products and vegetables. Over-centralised, with little or no incentives, year after year the Soviet system pours its best resource into the making of instruments of destruction. The constant shrinkage of economic growth combined with the growth of military production is putting a heavy strain on the Soviet people. What we see here is a political structure that no longer corresponds to its economic base, a society where productive forces are hampered by political ones.

The decay of the Soviet experiment should come as no surprise to us. Wherever the comparisons have been made between free and closed societies – West Germany and East Germany, Austria and Czechoslovakia, Malaysia and Vietnam – it is the democratic countries that are prosperous and responsive to the needs of their people. And one of the simple but overwhelming facts of our time is this: of all the millions of refugees we've seen in the modern world, their flight is always away from, not toward the communist world. Today on the NATO line, our military forces face east to prevent a possible invasion. On the other side of the line, the Soviet forces also face east to prevent their people from leaving.

The hard evidence of totalitarian rule has caused in mankind an uprising of the intellect and will. Whether it is the growth of the new schools of economics in America or England or the appearance of the so-called new philosophers in France, there is one unifying thread running through the intellectual work of these groups – rejection of the arbitrary power of the state, the refusal to subordinate the rights of the individual to the superstate, the realisation that collectivism stifles all the best human impulses.

Since the exodus from Egypt, historians have written of those who sacrificed and struggled for freedom – the stand at Thermopylae, the revolt of Spartacus, the storming of the Bastille, the Warsaw uprising in World War II. More recently, we've seen evidence of this same human impulse in one of the developing nations in Central America. For months and months the world news media covered the fighting in El Salvador. Day after day we were treated to stories and films slanted toward the brave freedom fighters battling oppressive government forces on behalf of the silent, suffering people of that tortured country.

And then one day those silent, suffering people were offered a chance to vote, to choose the kind of government they wanted. Suddenly the freedom fighters in the hills were exposed for what they really are – Cuban-backed guerrillas who want power for themselves and their backers, not democracy for the people.* They threatened death to any who voted, and destroyed hundreds of buses and trucks to keep the people from getting to the polling places. But on election day, the people of El Salvador, an unprece-

---

* The civil war in El Salvador lasted from 1980 until 1992 and was fought between the US-backed military government and a coalition of left-wing groups. The conflict resulted in the deaths of at least seventy-five thousand civilians.

dented 1.4 million of them, braved ambush and gunfire and trudged for miles to vote for freedom.

They stood for hours in the hot sun waiting for their turn to vote. Members of our Congress who went there as observers told me of a woman who was wounded by rifle fire on the way to the polls, who refused to leave the line to have her wound treated until after she had voted – a grand-mother, who had been told by the guerrillas she would be killed when she returned from the polls, and she told the guerrillas: 'You can kill me; you can kill my family, kill my neighbours, but you can't kill us all.' The real freedom fighters of El Salvador turned out to be the people of that country – the young, the old, the in-between.

Strange, but in my own country there's been little if any news coverage of that war since the election. Now, perhaps they'll say it's – well, because there are newer struggles now: on distant islands in the South Atlantic young men are fighting for Britain. And, yes, voices have been raised protesting their sacrifice for lumps of rock and earth so far away. But those young men aren't fighting for mere real estate. They fight for a cause – for the belief that armed aggression must not be allowed to succeed, and the people must participate in the decisions of government – the decisions of government under the rule of law. If there had been firmer support for that principle some forty-five years ago, perhaps our generation wouldn't have suffered the bloodletting of World War II.

In the Middle East now the guns sound once more, this time in Lebanon, a country that for too long has had to endure the tragedy of civil war, terrorism and foreign intervention and occupation. The fighting in Lebanon on the part of all parties must stop and Israel should bring its forces home. But this is not enough. We must all work to stamp out the scourge of terrorism that in the Middle East makes war an ever-present threat.

But beyond the trouble spots lies a deeper, more positive pattern. Around the world today, the democratic revolution is gathering new strength. In India, a critical test has been passed with the peaceful change of governing political parties. In Africa, Nigeria is moving into remarkable and unmistakable ways to build and strengthen its democratic institutions. In the Caribbean and Central America, sixteen of twenty-four countries have freely elected governments. And in the United Nations, eight of the ten developing nations which have joined that body in the past five years are democracies.

In the communist world as well, man's instinctive desire for freedom and self-determination surfaces again and again. To be sure, there are grim reminders of how brutally the police state attempts to snuff out this quest for self-rule – 1953 in East Germany, 1956 in Hungary, 1968 in Czechoslovakia, 1981 in Poland. But the struggle continues in Poland. And we know that there are even those who strive and suffer for freedom within the confines of the Soviet Union itself. How we conduct ourselves here in the Western democracies will determine whether this trend continues.

No, democracy is not a fragile flower. Still, it needs cultivating. If the rest of this century is to witness the gradual growth of freedom and democratic ideals, we must take actions to assist the campaign for democracy.

Some argue that we should encourage democratic change in right-wing dictatorships, but not in communist regimes. Well, to accept this preposterous notion – as some well-meaning people have – is to invite the argument that once countries achieve a nuclear capability, they should be allowed an undisturbed reign of terror over their own citizens. We reject this course.

As for the Soviet view, Chairman Brezhnev repeatedly has stressed that the competition of ideas and systems must continue and that this is entirely consistent with relaxation of tensions and peace. Well, we ask only that these systems begin by living up to their own constitutions, abiding by their own laws and complying with the international obligations they have undertaken. We ask only for a process, a direction, a basic code of decency, not for an instant transformation.

We cannot ignore the fact that even without our encouragement there has been and will continue to be repeated explosions against repression and dictatorships. The Soviet Union itself is not immune to this reality. Any system is inherently unstable that has no peaceful means to legitimise its leaders. In such cases, the very repressiveness of the state ultimately drives people to resist it, if necessary, by force.

While we must be cautious about forcing the pace of change, we must not hesitate to declare our ultimate objectives and to take concrete actions to move toward them. We must be staunch in our conviction that freedom is not the sole prerogative of a lucky few, but the inalienable and universal right of all human beings. So states the United Nations Universal Declaration of Human Rights, which, among other things, guarantees free elections.

The objective I propose is quite simple to state: to foster the infrastructure of democracy, the system of a free press, unions, political parties, universities, which allows a people to choose their own way to develop their own culture, to reconcile their own differences through peaceful means.

This is not cultural imperialism. It is providing the means for genuine self-determination and protection for diversity. Democracy already flourishes in countries with very different cultures and historical experiences. It would be cultural condescension, or worse, to say that any people prefer dictatorship to democracy. Who would voluntarily choose not to have the right to vote, decide to purchase government propaganda handouts instead of independent newspapers, prefer government to worker-controlled unions, opt for land to be owned by the state instead of those who till it, want government repression of religious liberty, a single political party instead of a free choice, a rigid cultural orthodoxy instead of democratic tolerance and diversity?

Since 1917 the Soviet Union has given covert political training and assistance to Marxist-Leninists in many countries. Of course, it also has promoted the use of violence and subversion by these same forces. Over the past several decades, West European and other Social Democrats, Christian Democrats, and leaders have offered open assistance to fraternal, political, and social institutions to bring about peaceful and democratic progress. Appropriately, for a vigorous new democracy, the Federal Republic of Germany's political foundations have become a major force in this effort.

We in America now intend to take additional steps, as many of our allies have already done, toward realising this same goal. The chairmen and other leaders of the national Republican and Democratic Party organisations are initiating a study with the bipartisan American Political Foundation to determine how the United States can best contribute as a nation to the global campaign for democracy now gathering force. They will have the cooperation of congressional leaders of both parties, along with representatives of business, labour and other major institutions in our society. I look forward to receiving their recommendations and to working with these institutions and the Congress in the common task of strengthening democracy throughout the world.

It is time that we committed ourselves as a nation – in both the public and private sectors – to assisting democratic development. We plan to consult with leaders of other nations as well. There is a proposal before the Council of Europe to invite parliamentarians from democratic countries to a meeting next year in Strasbourg. That prestigious gathering could consider ways to help democratic political movements.

This November in Washington there will take place an international meeting on free elections. And next spring there will be a conference of world authorities on constitutionalism and self-government hosted by the chief justice of the United States. Authorities from a number of developing and developed countries – judges, philosophers and politicians with practical experience – have agreed to explore how to turn principle into practice and further the rule of law.

At the same time, we invite the Soviet Union to consider with us how the competition of ideas and values – which it is committed to support – can be conducted on a peaceful and reciprocal basis. For example, I am prepared to offer President Brezhnev an opportunity to speak to the American people on our television if he will allow me the same opportunity with the Soviet people. We also suggest that panels of our newsmen periodically appear on each other's television to discuss major events.

Now, I don't wish to sound overly optimistic, yet the Soviet Union is not immune from the reality of what is going on in the world. It has happened in the past – a small ruling elite either mistakenly attempts to ease domestic unrest through greater repression and foreign adventure, or it chooses a wiser course. It begins to allow its people a voice in their own destiny. Even if this latter process is not realised soon, I believe the renewed strength of the democratic movement, complemented by a global campaign for freedom, will strengthen the prospects for arms control and a world at peace.

I have discussed on other occasions, including my address on May 9th, the elements of Western policies toward the Soviet Union to safeguard our interests and protect the peace. What I am describing now is a plan and a hope for the long term – the march of freedom and democracy which will leave Marxism–Leninism on the ash heap of history, as it has left other tyrannies which stifle the freedom and muzzle the self-expression of the people. And that's why we must continue our efforts to strengthen NATO even as we move forward with our Zero Option initiative in the negotiations on intermediate-range forces and our proposal for a one-third reduction in strategic ballistic-missile warheads.

Our military strength is a prerequisite to peace, but let it be clear we maintain this strength in the hope it will never be used, for the ultimate determinant in the struggle that's now going on in the world will not be bombs and rockets, but a test of wills and ideas, a trial of spiritual resolve, the values we hold, the beliefs we cherish, the ideals to which we are dedicated.

The British people know that, given strong leadership, time, and a little bit of hope, the forces of good ultimately rally and triumph over evil. Here among you is the cradle of self-government, the Mother of Parliaments.

" What I am describing now is a plan and a **hope** for the long-term – the **march** of **freedom** and **democracy** which will leave Marxism–Leninism on the **ash heap** of history **"**

Here is the enduring greatness of the British contribution to mankind, the great civilised ideas: individual liberty, representative government and the rule of law under God.

I've often wondered about the shyness of some of us in the West about standing for these ideals that have done so much to ease the plight of man and the hardships of our imperfect world. This reluctance to use those vast resources at our command reminds me of the elderly lady whose home was bombed in the Blitz. As the rescuers moved about, they found a bottle of brandy she'd stored behind the staircase, which was all that was left standing. And since she was barely conscious, one of the workers pulled the cork to give her a taste of it. She came around immediately and said, 'Here now – there now, put it back. That's for emergencies.' Well, the emergency is upon us. Let us be shy no longer. Let us go to our strength. Let us offer hope. Let us tell the world that a new age is not only possible but probable.

During the dark days of the Second World War, when this island was incandescent with courage, Winston Churchill exclaimed about Britain's adversaries: 'What kind of a people do they think we are?' Well, Britain's adversaries found out what extraordinary people the British are. But all the democracies paid a terrible price for allowing the dictators to underestimate us. We dare not make that mistake again. So, let us ask ourselves: 'What kind of people do *we* think we are?' And let us answer: 'Free people, worthy of freedom and determined not only to remain so but to help others gain their freedom as well.'

Sir Winston led his people to great victory in war and then lost an election just as the fruits of victory were about to be enjoyed. But he left office honourably, and, as it turned out, temporarily, knowing that the liberty of his people was more important than the fate of any single leader. History recalls his greatness in ways no dictator will ever know. And he left us a message of hope for the future, as timely now as when he first uttered it, as opposition leader in the Commons nearly twenty-seven years ago, when he said, 'When we look back on all the perils through which we have passed and at the mighty foes that we have laid low and all the dark and deadly designs that we have frustrated, why should we fear for our future? We have', he said, 'come safely through the worst.'

Well, the task I've set forth will long outlive our own generation. But together, we too have come through the worst. Let us now begin a major effort to secure the best – a crusade for freedom that will engage the faith and fortitude of the next generation. For the sake of peace and justice, let us move toward a world in which all people are at last free to determine their own destiny.

Our War
on Terror

– George Bush –

'They misunderestimate me.'[26] It is hard to believe that the man who spoke these words would coin a phrase that would define American foreign policy for nearly a decade. But that is exactly what George Bush did when he articulated a 'war on terror' in his address to a joint session of Congress on 20 September 2001. While Ronald Reagan had a way with words, Bush was not blessed with a silver tongue; yet this simple phrase – war on terror – became to the first years of the twenty-first century what Iron Curtain and Evil Empire had been to the Cold War era. The Soviet Union had been defeated, but America now faced a new enemy in international Islamic terrorism. The world could once again be divided into good and evil, and according to President Bush there was no room for neutrality: 'Either you are with us, or you are with the terrorists.'

This enemy had revealed itself in the form of Saudi-born millionaire Osama bin Laden and his al-Qaida network. Although most Americans had never heard of al-Qaida, in the previous few years groups associated with it had bombed US embassies in Kenya and Tanzania and attacked a US Navy warship docked in Yemen (and had attempted attacks in Jordan, Yemen and the United States that failed or were foiled). In August 1998, President Clinton had controversially ordered cruise-missile strikes against a pharmaceutical factory in Sudan and several of bin Laden's compounds in Afghanistan in retaliation for the embassy bombings. By the summer of 2001, US intelligence agencies were reportedly receiving a stream of warnings that al-Qaida associates were planning a massive attack on America and the CIA's daily briefing to

Bush on 6 August 2001 warned the President of the threat posed by bin Laden.[27] However, no one foresaw what was just over the horizon.

On the morning of 11 September 2001 the al-Qaida network launched a series of coordinated strikes against America in which nineteen terrorists hijacked four passenger airliners and used them as ballistic missiles to attack economic, military and political targets in the Eastern United States. American Airlines Flight 11 and United Airlines Flight 175 were each flown into one of the Twin Towers of the World Trade Center in New York, bringing down both buildings and killing 2,749 people. American Airlines Flight 77 was flown into the Pentagon in Arlington, Virginia, killing 184 people and severely damaging the western face of the building. Some of the passengers attempted to retake control of the fourth plane – United Airlines Flight 93, probably en route to the White House or the US Capitol – but it crashed into a field near Shanksville, Pennsylvania, killing all forty passengers and crew on board. The nineteen hijackers also died in the attacks that became known collectively as 9/11.[28]

The events of that day completely changed the course of Bush's presidency. Less than a year earlier he had narrowly beaten the incumbent Vice-President Al Gore in a controversial election in which he won the electoral vote despite losing the popular vote. His nomination and subsequent victory somewhat surprised outsiders but Bush came from one of the few American political dynasties: his grandfather Prescott Bush had been a US senator; his father, George Bush Sr., had been head of the CIA under Gerald Ford, Vice-President under Ronald Reagan and President from 1989 until 1993; and his brother Jeb Bush was Governor of Florida at the time. Bush himself had been Governor of Texas for six years before he entered the White House in January 2001. His southern upbringing and folksy manner of speaking helped him to connect with ordinary people and hid the reality of a privileged background in which he had studied at Yale and Harvard before going on to earn a personal fortune in oil exploration and other business ventures. The months that followed 9/11 were in many ways the making of Bush and, for better or worse, transformed the former hard-drinking frat boy into a controversial war President.

America had never experienced anything like 9/11 before; in fact, no country had experienced a terrorist attack on such a horrific scale. In his 20 September address to Congress, Bush was trying to answer the questions of a confused nation: 'Who attacked our country?' and 'Why do they hate us?', and preparing America for what was to come: 'How will we fight and win this war?' and 'What is expected of us?' People wanted answers and this address was Bush's chance to provide them. However, in answering the question 'Why do they hate us?', Bush repeated a fallacy: 'They hate our freedoms – our freedom of religion, our freedom of speech, our freedom to vote and assemble and disagree with each other.' There is no doubt that those who share al-Qaida's world view find America's promiscuous and consumerist society abhorrent, but they do not hate America's freedoms, they hate America's policies – they hate what America does.[29] What Bush was suggesting with his global war on terror was not just more of the same. Over the next few years it would take American policies to a whole new level of confrontation: the extraordinary rendition of foreign citizens; detention without trial at Guantánamo Bay and secret CIA prisons around the world; torture, abuse and sexual humiliation at the Abu Ghraib prison in Iraq; extra-judicial killings using unmanned combat drones in Afghanistan and Pakistan; and the occupation of Muslim lands by Western forces in Iraq and Afghanistan. The war on terror would evolve into the 'long war against Islamofascism' and bring about the deaths and injuries of many tens of thousands and the detention of well over a hundred thousand people, primarily in Afghanistan and Iraq. As Bush warned, 'Americans should not expect one battle, but a lengthy campaign, unlike any other we have ever seen.'

A number of other incidents occurred before the end of 2001 that served to feed American paranoia that they were a country under attack. Starting only a week after 9/11, letters containing anthrax spores were posted to media offices in New York and Florida and to two US senators in Washington DC, killing five people and injuring seventeen others over several weeks. The letters were dated 11 September 2001 and ended with the lines: 'Death to America. Death to Israel. Allah is great.'[30] At the time, the White House desperately tried to link the attacks to al-Qaida or Iraq, but the FBI eventually concluded that they were the sole work of disgruntled US Army microbiologist Dr Bruce Ivins, who committed suicide in 2008 shortly before the Department of Justice was about to file criminal charges against him.

Then on the morning of 12 November, American Airlines Flight 587 crashed into Belle Harbor, New York, killing all two hundred and sixty people on board and five people on the ground. The Queens neighbourhood was home to a large number of New York City police officers and firefighters and the area was already mourning the loss of dozens of residents who had died in the attack on the World Trade Center. Media speculation immediately pointed to a terrorist plot but the National Transportation Safety Board later concluded that pilot error on the part of the first officer was to blame. Then on 22 December, Richard Reid tried to bring down American Airlines Flight 63 en route from Paris to Miami by igniting explosives hidden in his shoe. This time it was a terrorist incident and at his trial in 2003 the so-called shoe-bomber declared his loyalty to bin Laden and al-Qaida.

At the same time, unfounded but persistent conspiracy theories began circulating. Some claimed that 9/11 was a covert operation led by elements within the Bush administration: controlled demolitions brought down the Twin Towers, the Pentagon was hit by a guided missile and Flight 93 was shot down by US fighter jets. Others claimed that the US government had facilitated al-Qaida's operation: insider trading in the stocks of United Airlines and American Airlines in the days before 11 September indicated advance knowledge of the attacks and US air defences were stood down in order to allow them to happen. None of these theories were true but all distracted from the real conspiracy that lay in some of the things that happened after the attacks: the rushing through Congress of the controversial USA PATRIOT Act that expanded law-enforcement powers and threatened civil liberties; the timely political manipulation of the terror alert level to high or severe; the falsification or exaggeration of intelligence to justify the invasion of Iraq; and the nearly $800 billion that was spent on the war on terror, largely secured through emergency supplemental appropriations for the Defense Department.[31]

Such events helped create the climate of fear that the war on terror fed off and fed into, and enabled Bush's foreign policy to adopt the neoconservative principles that had lain dormant early in his administration. The neoconservatives saw the world as divided into good and evil, and advocated the unilateral use of military force to shape the world to America's advantage and export democracy to other countries. An overlapping alliance of neoconservatives and hawkish Republicans in the White House and Defense Department, including Donald Rumsfeld, Paul Wolfowitz, Douglas Feith, Dick Cheney, Lewis Libby, John Ashcroft, Condoleezza Rice and Karl Rove, together with prominent outsiders from the Project for the New American Century, the Committee on the Present Danger and the Christian right, began to exert a greater influence and dominate the policymaking process.

One of the most controversial strategies to emerge was the Bush doctrine of pre-emption, whereby the United States would use force to remove hostile regimes that represented a perceived threat to US security (even though they posed no immediate threat). The primary targets of this strategy were singled out by Bush in his 2002 State of the Union address in which he identified an 'Axis of Evil' comprising North Korea, Iran and Iraq.[32] The notion that there are rogue states that operate outside the accepted norms of the international community is a pervasive one but ignores the fact that many states that consider themselves part of the international community routinely flout international law and norms of behaviour in their own national interests. Nevertheless, tackling this axis was an essential part of the war on terror and right from the beginning the neoconservatives argued that the United States should not stop with al-Qaida and their Taliban hosts but move to overthrow Saddam Hussein as well.

First, though, the Bush administration needed to retaliate for 9/11. They focused their immediate attention on Afghanistan, toppling the Taliban regime of Mohammed Omar in a relatively brief aerial bombing campaign in conjunction with a ground offensive by Afghan Northern Alliance troops with support from CIA paramilitary operatives and American and British special forces. Despite the initial success of the US-led campaign, neither bin Laden nor Mullah Omar was captured and by the summer of 2003 the remnants of al-Qaida and a renewed Taliban had emerged from their new mini-state in the Waziristan tribal areas of northwest Pakistan and begun an insurgency that within two years would draw Afghan, Pakistani and American,

British and other NATO forces into some of the fiercest fighting since World War II. By this time, the United States and a small coalition of countries had launched a disastrous invasion and occupation of Iraq, finally achieving what the neoconservatives had been demanding but provoking a bitter insurgency that would cost many thousands of lives. As combat troops began to be withdrawn from Iraq in 2009, the conflict in Afghanistan was still being waged and had become what many considered to be an unwinnable war in the face of widespread insurrection by local warlords and Taliban militias. By then, Bush had been replaced in the White House by Barack Obama and the world was hopeful of a change of direction from the United States.

The phrase 'war on terror' has now been dropped from political discourse, first by the British government and then by the Obama administration, who prefer to use the more nondescript 'overseas contingency operations' to distance themselves from Bush-era policies. Instead of a war on terror, America's response to 9/11 could have been limited to targeted military strikes and a sustained law-enforcement and intelligence-led campaign against terrorist networks and their financing, coupled with international diplomatic efforts to isolate and contain rogue states and address long-standing Muslim grievances. Unfortunately, Bush chose instead to embark on a costly geopolitical agenda to reshape the world. We certainly did 'misunderestimate' him, but his was an agenda that history will likely judge to have failed.

US Capitol, Washington DC, United States

20 SEPTEMBER 2001

Mr Speaker, Mr President Pro Tempore, members of Congress, and fellow Americans:

In the normal course of events, Presidents come to this chamber to report on the state of the Union. Tonight, no such report is needed. It has already been delivered by the American people.

We have seen it in the courage of passengers, who rushed terrorists to save others on the ground – passengers like an exceptional man named Todd Beamer. And would you please help me to welcome his wife, Lisa Beamer, here tonight. We have seen the state of our Union in the endurance of rescuers, working past exhaustion. We've seen the unfurling of flags, the lighting of candles, the giving of blood, the saying of prayers – in English, Hebrew, and Arabic. We have seen the decency of a loving and giving people who have made the grief of strangers their own. My fellow citizens, for the last nine days, the entire world has seen for itself the state of our Union – and it is strong.

Tonight we are a country awakened to danger and called to defend freedom. Our grief has turned to anger, and anger to resolution. Whether we bring our enemies to justice, or bring justice to our enemies, justice will be done. I thank the Congress for its leadership at such an important time. All of America was touched on the evening of the tragedy to see Republicans and Democrats joined together on the steps of this Capitol, singing 'God Bless America'. And you did more than sing; you acted, by delivering $40 billion to rebuild our communities and meet the needs of our military. Speaker Hastert, Minority Leader Gephardt, Majority Leader Daschle, and Senator Lott, I thank you for your friendship, for your leadership, and for your service to our country. And on behalf of the American people, I thank the world for its outpouring of support. America will never forget the sounds of our National Anthem playing at Buckingham Palace, on the streets of Paris, and at Berlin's Brandenburg Gate.

We will not forget South Korean children gathering to pray outside our embassy in Seoul, or the prayers of sympathy offered at a mosque in Cairo. We will not forget moments of silence and days of mourning in Australia and Africa and Latin America. Nor will we forget the citizens of eighty other nations who died with our own: dozens of Pakistanis; more than a hundred and thirty Israelis; more than two hundred and fifty citizens of India; men and women from El Salvador, Iran, Mexico, and Japan; and hundreds of British citizens. America has no truer friend than Great Britain. Once again, we are joined together in a great cause – so honoured the British Prime Minister has crossed an ocean to show his unity with America. Thank you for coming, friend.

On September the 11th, enemies of freedom committed an act of war against our country. Americans have known wars – but for the past hundred and thirty-six years, they have been wars on foreign soil, except for one

Sunday in 1941.* Americans have known the casualties of war – but not at the centre of a great city on a peaceful morning. Americans have known surprise attacks – but never before on thousands of civilians. All of this was brought upon us in a single day – and night fell on a different world, a world where freedom itself is under attack. Americans have many questions tonight. Americans are asking: who attacked our country? The evidence we have gathered all points to a collection of loosely affiliated terrorist organisations known as al-Qaida. They are some of the murderers indicted for bombing American embassies in Tanzania and Kenya, and responsible for bombing the USS *Cole*. Al-Qaida is to terror what the Mafia is to crime. But its goal is not making money; its goal is remaking the world – and imposing its radical beliefs on people everywhere.

The terrorists practise a fringe form of Islamic extremism that has been rejected by Muslim scholars and the vast majority of Muslim clerics, a fringe movement that perverts the peaceful teachings of Islam. The terrorists' directive commands them to kill Christians and Jews, to kill all Americans, and make no distinctions among military and civilians, including women and children. This group and its leader – a person named Osama bin Laden – are linked to many other organisations in different countries, including the Egyptian Islamic Jihad and the Islamic Movement of Uzbekistan. There are thousands of these terrorists in more than sixty countries. They are recruited from their own nations and neighbourhoods and brought to camps in places like Afghanistan, where they are trained in the tactics of terror. They are sent back to their homes or sent to hide in countries around the world to plot evil and destruction.

The leadership of al-Qaida has great influence in Afghanistan and supports the Taliban regime in controlling most of that country. In Afghanistan, we see al-Qaida's vision for the world. Afghanistan's people have been brutalised; many are starving and many have fled. Women are not allowed to attend school. You can be jailed for owning a television. Religion can be practised only as their leaders dictate. A man can be jailed in Afghanistan if his beard is not long enough.

The United States respects the people of Afghanistan. After all, we are currently its largest source of humanitarian aid; but we condemn the Taliban regime. It is not only repressing its own people, it is threatening

---

* The Japanese attack on the US naval base at Pearl Harbor, Hawaii, on 7 December 1941.

people everywhere by sponsoring and sheltering and supplying terrorists. By aiding and abetting murder, the Taliban regime is committing murder.

And tonight, the United States of America makes the following demands on the Taliban: deliver to United States authorities all the leaders of al-Qaida who hide in your land. Release all foreign nationals, including American citizens, you have unjustly imprisoned. Protect foreign journalists, diplomats, and aid workers in your country. Close immediately and permanently every terrorist training camp in Afghanistan, and hand over every terrorist, and every person in their support structure, to appropriate authorities. Give the United States full access to terrorist training camps, so we can make sure they are no longer operating. These demands are not open to negotiation or discussion. The Taliban must act, and act immediately. They will hand over the terrorists, or they will share in their fate.

I also want to speak tonight directly to Muslims throughout the world. We respect your faith. It's practised freely by many millions of Americans, and by millions more in countries that America counts as friends. Its teachings are good and peaceful, and those who commit evil in the name of Allah blaspheme the name of Allah. The terrorists are traitors to their own faith, trying, in effect, to hijack Islam itself. The enemy of America is not our many Muslim friends; it is not our many Arab friends. Our enemy is a radical network of terrorists, and every government that supports them. Our war on terror begins with al-Qaida, but it does not end there. It will not end until every terrorist group of global reach has been found, stopped, and defeated.

Americans are asking, why do they hate us? They hate what they see right here in this chamber – a democratically elected government. Their leaders are self-appointed. They hate our freedoms – our freedom of religion, our freedom of speech, our freedom to vote and assemble and disagree with each other. They want to overthrow existing governments in many Muslim countries, such as Egypt, Saudi Arabia and Jordan. They want to drive Israel out of the Middle East. They want to drive Christians and Jews out of vast regions of Asia and Africa. These terrorists kill not merely to end lives, but to disrupt and end a way of life. With every atrocity, they hope that America grows fearful, retreating from the world and forsaking our friends. They stand against us, because we stand in their way.

We are not deceived by their pretences to piety. We have seen their kind before. They are the heirs of all the murderous ideologies of the twentieth century. By sacrificing human life to serve their radical visions

– by abandoning every value except the will to power – they follow in the path of fascism, Nazism and totalitarianism. And they will follow that path all the way, to where it ends: in history's unmarked grave of discarded lies. Americans are asking: how will we fight and win this war? We will direct every resource at our command – every means of diplomacy, every tool of intelligence, every instrument of law enforcement, every financial influence and every necessary weapon of war – to the disruption and to the defeat of the global terror network.

Now this war will not be like the war against Iraq a decade ago, with a decisive liberation of territory and a swift conclusion. It will not look like the air war above Kosovo two years ago, where no ground troops were used and not a single American was lost in combat. Our response involves far more than instant retaliation and isolated strikes. Americans should not expect one battle, but a lengthy campaign, unlike any other we have ever seen. It may include dramatic strikes, visible on TV, and covert operations, secret even in success. We will starve terrorists of funding, turn them one against another, drive them from place to place, until there is no refuge or no rest. And we will pursue nations that provide aid or safe haven to terrorism. Every nation, in every region, now has a decision to make. Either you are with us, or you are with the terrorists. From this day forward, any nation that continues to harbour or support terrorism will be regarded by the United States as a hostile regime.

Our nation has been put on notice: we're not immune from attack. We will take defensive measures against terrorism to protect Americans. Today, dozens of federal departments and agencies, as well as state and local governments, have responsibilities affecting homeland security. These efforts must be coordinated at the highest level. So tonight I

> **❝** Our **war on terror** begins with al-Qaida, but it does not end there. **It will not end** until **every terrorist** group of global reach has been **found,** **stopped,** and **defeated.❞**

announce the creation of a cabinet-level position reporting directly to me – the Office of Homeland Security. And tonight I also announce a distinguished American to lead this effort, to strengthen American security: a military veteran, an effective governor, a true patriot, a trusted friend – Pennsylvania's Tom Ridge. He will lead, oversee and coordinate a comprehensive national strategy to safeguard our country against terrorism, and respond to any attacks that may come.

These measures are essential. But the only way to defeat terrorism as a threat to our way of life is to stop it, eliminate it and destroy it where it grows. Many will be involved in this effort, from FBI agents to intelligence operatives to the reservists we have called to active duty. All deserve our thanks, and all have our prayers. And tonight, a few miles from the damaged Pentagon, I have a message for our military: be ready. I've called the armed forces to alert, and there is a reason. The hour is coming when America will act, and you will make us proud. This is not, however, just America's fight. And what is at stake is not just America's freedom. This is the world's fight. This is civilisation's fight. This is the fight of all who believe in progress and pluralism, tolerance and freedom.

We ask every nation to join us. We will ask, and we will need, the help of police forces, intelligence services and banking systems around the world. The United States is grateful that many nations and many international organisations have already responded – with sympathy and with support. Nations from Latin America, to Asia, to Africa, to Europe, to the Islamic world. Perhaps the NATO Charter reflects best the attitude of the world: an attack on one is an attack on all. The civilised world is rallying to America's side. They understand that if this terror goes unpunished, their own cities, their own citizens may be next. Terror, unanswered, cannot only bring down buildings, it can threaten the stability of legitimate governments. And you know what? We're not going to allow it.

Americans are asking: what is expected of us? I ask you to live your lives, and hug your children. I know many citizens have fears tonight, and I ask you to be calm and resolute, even in the face of a continuing threat. I ask you to uphold the values of America, and remember why so many have come here. We are in a fight for our principles, and our first responsibility is to live by them. No one should be singled out for unfair treatment or unkind words because of their ethnic background or religious faith. I ask you to continue to support the victims of this tragedy with your contributions. Those who want to give can go to a central source of information, libertyunites.org, to find the names of groups providing direct help in New York, Pennsylvania and Virginia.

The thousands of FBI agents who are now at work in this investigation may need your cooperation, and I ask you to give it. I ask for your patience, with the delays and inconveniences that may accompany tighter security; and for your patience in what will be a long struggle. I ask your continued participation and confidence in the American economy. Terrorists attacked a symbol of American prosperity. They did not touch its source. America is successful because of the hard work, and creativity and enterprise of our people. These were the true strengths of our economy before September 11th, and they are our strengths today. And, finally, please continue praying for the victims of terror and their families, for those in uniform and for our great country. Prayer has comforted us in sorrow, and will help strengthen us for the journey ahead.

Tonight I thank my fellow Americans for what you have already done and for what you will do. And ladies and gentlemen of the Congress, I thank you, their representatives, for what you have already done and for what we will do together. Tonight, we face new and sudden national challenges. We will come together to improve air safety, to dramatically expand the number of air marshals on domestic flights and take new measures to prevent hijacking. We will come together to promote stability and keep our airlines flying, with direct assistance during this emergency. We will come together to give law enforcement the additional tools it needs to track down terror here at home. We will come together to strengthen our intelligence capabilities to know the plans of terrorists before they act, and to find them before they strike.

We will come together to take active steps that strengthen America's economy, and put our people back to work. Tonight we welcome two leaders who embody the extraordinary spirit of all New Yorkers: Governor George Pataki, and Mayor Rudolph Giuliani. As a symbol of America's resolve, my administration will work with Congress, and these two leaders, to show the world that we will rebuild New York City.

After all that has just passed – all the lives taken, and all the possibilities and hopes that died with them – it is natural to wonder if America's future is one of fear. Some speak of an age of terror. I know there are struggles ahead, and dangers to face. But this country will define our times, not be defined by them. As long as the United States of America is determined and strong, this will not be an age of terror; this will be an age of liberty, here and across the world.

Great harm has been done to us. We have suffered great loss. And in our grief and anger we have found our mission and our moment. Freedom and fear are at war. The advance of human freedom – the great achievement of our time, and the great hope of every time – now depends on us. Our nation, this generation will lift a dark threat of violence from our people and our future. We will rally the world to this cause by our efforts, by our courage. We will not tire, we will not falter, and we will not fail.

It is my hope that in the months and years ahead, life will return almost to normal. We'll go back to our lives and routines, and that is good. Even grief recedes with time and grace. But our resolve must not pass. Each of us will remember what happened that day, and to whom it happened. We'll remember the moment the news came – where we were and what we were doing. Some will remember an image of a fire, or a story of rescue. Some will carry memories of a face and a voice gone forever.

And I will carry this: it is the police shield of a man named George Howard, who died at the World Trade Center trying to save others. It was given to me by his mother, Arlene, as a proud memorial to her son. This is my reminder of lives that ended, and a task that does not end. I will not forget this wound to our country or those who inflicted it. I will not yield; I will not rest; I will not relent in waging this struggle for freedom and security for the American people. The course of this conflict is not known, yet its outcome is certain. Freedom and fear, justice and cruelty, have always been at war, and we know that God is not neutral between them.

> **The course of this conflict is not known, yet its outcome is certain. Freedom and fear, justice and cruelty, have always been at war, and we know that God is not neutral between them.**

Fellow citizens, we'll meet violence with patient justice – assured of the rightness of our cause, and confident of the victories to come. In all that lies before us, may God grant us wisdom, and may He watch over the United States of America.

Thank you.

**❝ As long as the
United States of America
is determined and strong,
this will not be an age of terror;
this will be an age of liberty,
here and across the world. ❞**

Your Security is in Your Own Hands

– Osama bin Laden –

I n the last few days of the 2004 US presidential election race, the incumbent George Bush received a boost from an unlikely source. On 29 October, the Qatar-based television station Al-Jazeera broadcast excerpts of a new video-tape message from a man known to his supporters as the Sheikh: Osama bin Laden, one of the key architects of the 9/11 attacks that had rocked America three years earlier. Although bin Laden used the opportunity to condemn Bush's policies, the criticism – unsurprisingly given where it was coming from – did not drive voters into the arms of his Democrat opponent John Kerry, but instead reminded Americans of the danger posed by international terrorism and therefore increased support for Bush, who was seen at the time as the candidate most likely to confront the terrorist threat.

It may seem counter-intuitive to suggest that bin Laden hoped for a Bush victory; Bush had, after all, declared a war against terrorism and al-Qaida in particular. But in many ways, the two men needed each other. During his first term, Bush had used the threat of international terrorism and rogue states to implement neoconservative plans to reshape the Middle East and push through controversial domestic security laws. On the other side of the coin, bin Laden relied on the occupation of Iraq and Afghanistan and America's continued backing of Israel to increase support for al-Qaida and other militant groups and draw the far enemy (the United States) into protracted local conflicts. There was a somewhat symbiotic relationship that may have been broken, or at least weakened, if Kerry had entered the White House. The appearance of bin Laden's tape helped Bush to gain a lead in the opinion polls and he won re-election. Al-Qaida then benefited from four more years of recruitment propaganda courtesy of the impact of American policies and military actions across the Muslim world.

Bin Laden made dozens of audio- and video-tapes over the years that were broadcast on Al-Jazeera or posted on various radical websites (mediated through a network of jihadist production and dissemination groups).[33] They began in earnest a few weeks after 9/11 and continued into Barack Obama's presidency, with an unexplained hiatus during 2005 that led many to speculate he had died. The tapes cover a wide range of issues and were sometimes timed to coincide with important international events, such as presidential elections.[34] He used these messages to offer truces with Europe (in April 2004) and America (in January 2006) in return for the withdrawal of foreign troops from Muslim lands. In them he often referred to recent events and to debates within Western media. In January 2010, for example, he released an audio-tape in which he blamed the United States and other industrialised nations for global warming and argued that world politics are not governed by reason but by 'the cruel beasts of capitalism'.[35]

Bin Laden would have undoubtedly drawn huge crowds if he had been able to hold public rallies (as well as attracting half the US Army and most of the world's intelligence agencies), but he instead had to rely on media and Internet dissemination of his tapes in order to reach his intended audiences. Modern communications technologies – from audio- and video-editing software to satellite television and the Internet – meant that he could reach an audience of many millions. The tape of 29 October 2004 was the first video message from bin Laden for a year (although three audio-tapes had been released), but Al-Jazeera only broadcast excerpts from the tape and did not make the full English transcript available until a few days later. Various translations of the original Arabic are in circulation, from Al-Jazeera, CNN and the Middle East Media Research Institute, though the Al-Jazeera version is probably the most accurate (and is the one reproduced in the following pages).

In the video, bin Laden used skilful rhetoric and reasonable language to talk directly to the American people: 'People of America, this talk of mine is for you and concerns the ideal way to prevent another Manhattan, and deals with the war and its causes and results.'

It was the first time bin Laden had admitted responsibility for 9/11 and he claimed his inspiration for the attacks came from watching the destruction of high-rise buildings during Israel's US-backed invasion of Lebanon in 1982. In his mind it showed that 'oppression and the intentional killing of innocent women and children is a deliberate American policy'. He reminded them that 'for every action, there is a reaction' and, in an echo of the Party's antithetical slogans in George Orwell's classic novel *Nineteen Eighty-Four* (War is Peace, Freedom is Slavery, Ignorance is Strength), he declared: 'Destruction is freedom and democracy, while resistance is terrorism and intolerance.'[36] Throughout his message, bin Laden returned several times to the issue of security: 'No one except a dumb thief plays with the security of others and then makes himself believe he will be secure.' And: 'the events of September 11th came as a reply to those great wrongs, should a man be blamed for defending his sanctuary?' In conclusion, he told Americans that 'your security is not in the hands of Kerry, nor Bush, nor al-Qaida. Your security is in your own hands.'

The history of bin Laden's influence in the world of Islamic militancy is complicated and often misunderstood and overstated. He was born in 1957 in Riyadh, Saudi Arabia, to a Yemeni father and Syrian mother. His father Mohammed bin Laden was a wealthy and influential businessman who had built up his construction company through profitable and high-profile government contracts, thanks to his friendship with Saudi Arabia's founding monarch, Abdul Aziz Al-Saud. When his father died in a helicopter crash in 1967, bin Laden inherited a share of the family business (which he was divested of in 1994), and from 1970 until 1994 he likely received about $1 million per year from his family (a large sum, but not the $300 million personal fortune he is often said to have inherited).[37] A soft-spoken, austere and deeply religious young man, bin Laden was first exposed to the thinking of Syed Qutb and other radical Islamists while at university in Jeddah.

When, in 1979, the Soviet Union invaded Afghanistan in support of the communist Afghan government, bin Laden made frequent trips to Afghanistan and neighbouring Pakistan to provide logistical support to Arab volunteers (the so-called Afghan Arabs) and helped to channel foreign assistance and financing to the Afghan mujahedin fighting the

Soviets. By the mid-1980s he was himself involved in heavy fighting near the border with Pakistan.[38] The Soviets finally withdrew in early 1989 and within a few years the Soviet Union had collapsed, causing bin Laden and the other Afghan Arabs to believe they had brought down the superpower by overextending it militarily and financially (something they would later hope to repeat with America). It was during this time that bin Laden and Ayman al-Zawahiri (the leader of Egyptian Islamic Jihad) formed what would become known as al-Qaida, in order to extend jihad to other parts of the world. Based for some years in Sudan during the early 1990s, bin Laden and the al-Qaida leadership made their base in Taliban-controlled Afghanistan from 1996 onwards, and it was from here that Khalid Sheikh Mohammed and others planned the 9/11 attacks that would kill nearly three thousand people.

It is important to understand that al-Qaida is not an organisation as such but rather a diverse movement. It is more helpful to view it as a consortium: a network of networks, sharing a radical world view but with individual member groups and associates working for different local objectives, independently of the al-Qaida leadership. Even the name *al-Qaida* has generated much confusion – its Arabic root can mean base or foundation but also principle, rule or method, and so can be thought of as referring both to a revolutionary vanguard and to a tactic.[39] Only in Afghanistan between 1996 and 2001 did anything approaching the commonly understood notion of al-Qaida exist, but even then it was not a structured terrorist organisation. The British journalist Jason Burke has argued convincingly that it instead represented a three-part phenomenon: a core group consisting of bin Laden and a dozen of his closest associates and around a hundred experienced militants; a wider network of co-opted or associated paramilitary groups around the world; and a world view or ideology about freeing Muslim lands and cleansing a corrupt world through violence.[40]

It is the last element – the ideology – that survived and flourished following the 2001 US-led invasion of Afghanistan (although the other two elements – the core group and the franchised network – have experienced some resurgence in recent years, particularly in Pakistan, northeast Africa and Yemen). The common characterisation of those who share the al-Qaida world view as simply hating Western freedoms is a gross misunderstanding and something bin Laden himself denied: 'I say to you that security is an indispensable pillar of human life and that free men do not forfeit their security, contrary to Bush's claim that we hate freedom.' Watch the video messages left behind by suicide bombers in London; read the postings on jihadist websites and Internet forums; read the media interviews with Taliban commanders in Afghanistan and Pakistan; listen to the recordings of sermons by radical clerics that circulate in the backstreets of Sana'a or Riyadh; or watch the jihadi DVDs for sale in the markets of Peshawar or Baghdad. Running through all of these you will find a discourse of discontent and anger at the injustices perpetrated against the Muslim world, often rooted in specific local contexts. Where al-Qaida differs from most other radical Islamist movements is in its desire to bring about the end of the Western system and sweep away its legacies in a violent revolution.[41] For many in Washington, London and elsewhere, the al-Qaida movement has been dismissed as promoting nothing but this violent ideology. However, the broad political aims of the movement can be clearly identified as the expulsion of foreign troops from the Middle East, the removal of the House of Saud and other elitist and pro-Western regimes across the region, the destruction of Israel and the creation of a Palestinian state, and support for insurgencies across the Muslim world.[42]

Bin Laden was on the FBI's most wanted fugitives list from June 1999 (for his part in the 1998 US embassy bombings).[43] However, in the build-up to the 2001 US-led invasion of Afghanistan, the Taliban leader Mohammed Omar had agreed a deal that would see bin Laden handed over to the Pakistanis and placed under house arrest in Peshawar while evidence of his involvement in 9/11 was considered by an international tribunal. The plan was blocked by the Pakistani President, Pervez Musharraf, who claimed he could not guarantee bin Laden's safety. Then the Taliban offered to detain bin Laden themselves and try him under Islamic law if the United States presented them with evidence of his involvement in the 9/11 attacks. Another offer was made a week later when the Taliban proposed handing over bin Laden for trial in a country other than the United States in return for a halt to the bombing of Afghanistan. These opportunities for a negotiated detention were rejected and war was once again brought to the people of Afghanistan.

As the air and ground offensives progressed, Northern Alliance, US and British forces pushed the Taliban first out of Mazar-i Sharif, Kabul and Kunduz and then Kandahar in December 2001. By then al-Qaida had concentrated their remaining forces in the Tora Bora cave complex on the border with Pakistan. Bin Laden was with them but, fearing high casualties, the Pentagon failed to commit enough US ground troops to the offensive on the caves – relying instead on Afghan militias – and he was able to escape over the mountains into the remote tribal regions of Pakistan.[44] A British special-forces team is reported to have pursued him and been as close as twenty minutes behind him at one point but were called off so that American forces could finish the task. By the time US soldiers arrived several hours later bin Laden had again escaped.[45] Like the opportunities for a negotiated detention, these chances to capture bin Laden were wasted. Little solid intelligence on him then came to light for nearly a decade.

Confidence in bin Laden declined over the years among Muslims in the Middle East and North Africa, and those that support suicide bombings and other attacks on civilians are in a small, decreasing minority (despite Western misconceptions to the contrary).[46] However, he remained al-Qaida's ideological figurehead and an important counter-cultural symbol with cult status – a new Che Guevara – representing a discourse of dissent for some alienated young Muslims.[47] He was one of the world's most hunted men but it was always unlikely that he would ever stand trial for his role in 9/11 and the other terrorist attacks he had helped orchestrate.[48] Bin Laden's location was unknown for years, but despite constant rumours of his ill health or death he was believed to be alive and probably hiding in Waziristan, a semi-autonomous tribal area along Pakistan's border with Afghanistan. However, in May 2011 intelligence led a US special-forces team to a compound in Abbottabad, about 35 miles north of Islamabad, where they shot and killed him. Like the earlier opportunities in Afghanistan, this final chance to capture bin Laden alive was squandered.

Waziristan, Pakistan

29 OCTOBER 2004

Praise be to Allah who created the creation for his worship and commanded them to be just and permitted the wronged one to retaliate against the oppressor in kind. To proceed:

Peace be upon he who follows the guidance.

People of America this talk of mine is for you and concerns the ideal way to prevent another Manhattan, and deals with the war and its causes and results.

Before I begin, I say to you that security is an indispensable pillar of human life and that free men do not forfeit their security, contrary to Bush's claim that we hate freedom.

If so, then let him explain to us why we don't strike for example – Sweden? And we know that freedom-haters don't possess defiant spirits like those of the nineteen – may Allah have mercy on them.*

No, we fight because we are free men who don't sleep under oppression. We want to restore freedom to our nation. Just as you lay waste to our nation, so shall we lay waste to yours.

No one except a dumb thief plays with the security of others and then makes himself believe he will be secure. Whereas thinking people, when disaster strikes, make it their priority to look for its causes, in order to prevent it happening again.

But I am amazed at you. Even though we are in the fourth year after the events of September 11th, Bush is still engaged in distortion, deception and hiding from you the real causes. And thus, the reasons are still there for a repeat of what occurred.

So I shall talk to you about the story behind those events and shall tell you truthfully about the moments in which the decision was taken, for you to consider.

I say to you, Allah knows that it had never occurred to us to strike the towers. But after it became unbearable and we witnessed the oppression and tyranny of the American/Israeli coalition against our people in Palestine and Lebanon, it came to my mind.

---

* The 9/11 attacks were carried out by nineteen hijackers, all but four of whom were from Saudi Arabia.

66 we **fight** because we are
free men who don't sleep
under oppression. 99

The events that affected my soul in a direct way started in 1982 when America permitted the Israelis to invade Lebanon and the American Sixth Fleet helped them in that. This bombardment began and many were killed and injured and others were terrorised and displaced.

I couldn't forget those moving scenes, blood and severed limbs, women and children sprawled everywhere. Houses destroyed along with their occupants and high-rises demolished over their residents, rockets raining down on our home without mercy.

The situation was like a crocodile meeting a helpless child, powerless except for his screams. Does the crocodile understand a conversation that doesn't include a weapon? And the whole world saw and heard but it didn't respond.

In those difficult moments many hard-to-describe ideas bubbled in my soul, but in the end they produced an intense feeling of rejection of tyranny, and gave birth to a strong resolve to punish the oppressors.

And as I looked at those demolished towers in Lebanon, it entered my mind that we should punish the oppressor in kind and that we should destroy towers in America in order that they taste some of what we tasted and so that they be deterred from killing our women and children.

And that day, it was confirmed to me that oppression and the intentional killing of innocent women and children is a deliberate American policy. Destruction is freedom and democracy, while resistance is terrorism and intolerance.

This means the oppressing and embargoing to death of millions as Bush Sr. did in Iraq in the greatest mass slaughter of children mankind has ever known, and it means the throwing of millions of pounds of bombs and explosives at millions of children – also in Iraq – as Bush Jr. did, in order to remove an old agent and replace him with a new puppet to assist in the pilfering of Iraq's oil and other outrages.

So with these images and their like as their background, the events of

September 11th came as a reply to those great wrongs, should a man be blamed for defending his sanctuary?

Is defending oneself and punishing the aggressor in kind, objectionable terrorism? If it is such, then it is unavoidable for us.

This is the message which I sought to communicate to you in word and deed, repeatedly, for years before September 11th.

And you can read this, if you wish, in my interview with Scott in *Time* magazine in 1996, or with Peter Arnett on CNN in 1997, or my meeting with John Weiner in 1998.

You can observe it practically, if you wish, in Kenya and Tanzania and in Aden. And you can read it in my interview with Abdul Bari Atwan, as well as my interviews with Robert Fisk.*

The latter is one of your compatriots and co-religionists and I consider him to be neutral. So are the pretenders of freedom at the White House and the channels controlled by them able to run an interview with him? So that he may relay to the American people what he has understood from us to be the reasons for our fight against you?

If you were to avoid these reasons, you will have taken the correct path that will lead America to the security that it was in before September 11th. This concerned the causes of the war.

As for its results, they have been, by the grace of Allah, positive and enormous, and have, by all standards, exceeded all expectations. This is due to many factors, chief among them, that we have found it difficult to deal with the Bush administration in light of the resemblance it bears to the regimes in our countries, half of which are ruled by the military and the other half of which are ruled by the sons of kings and presidents.

Our experience with them is lengthy, and both types are replete with those who are characterised by pride, arrogance, greed and misappropriation of wealth. This resemblance began after the visits of Bush Sr. to the region.

At a time when some of our compatriots were dazzled by America and hoping that these visits would have an effect on our countries, all of a sudden he was affected by those monarchies and military regimes, and became envious of their remaining decades in their positions, to embezzle the public wealth of the nation without supervision or accounting.

---

* Robert Fisk is the award-winning Middle East correspondent for *The Independent* and interviewed bin Laden three times during the 1990s.

So he took dictatorship and suppression of freedoms to his son and they named it the PATRIOT Act, under the pretence of fighting terrorism. In addition, Bush sanctioned the installing of sons as state governors, and didn't forget to import expertise in election fraud from the region's presidents to Florida to be made use of in moments of difficulty.

All that we have mentioned has made it easy for us to provoke and bait this administration. All that we have to do is to send two mujahedin to the furthest point east to raise a piece of cloth on which is written al-Qaida, in order to make the generals race there to cause America to suffer human, economic, and political losses without their achieving for it anything of note other than some benefits for their private companies.

This is in addition to our having experience in using guerrilla warfare and the war of attrition to fight tyrannical superpowers, as we, alongside the mujahedin, bled Russia for ten years, until it went bankrupt and was forced to withdraw in defeat.

All Praise is due to Allah.

So we are continuing this policy in bleeding America to the point of bankruptcy. Allah willing, and nothing is too great for Allah.

That being said, those who say that al-Qaida has won against the administration in the White House or that the administration has lost in this war have not been precise, because when one scrutinises the results, one cannot say that al-Qaida is the sole factor in achieving those spectacular gains.

Rather, the policy of the White House that demands the opening of war fronts to keep busy their various corporations – whether they be working in the field of arms or oil or reconstruction – has helped al-Qaida to achieve these enormous results.

And so it has appeared to some analysts and diplomats that the White House and we are playing as one team towards the economic goals of the United States, even if the intentions differ.

And it was to these sorts of notions and their like that the British diplomat and others were referring in their lectures at the Royal Institute of International Affairs.* When they pointed out that, for example, al-Qaida spent $500,000 on the event, while America, in the incident and its aftermath, lost – according to the lowest estimate – more than $500 billion.

Meaning that every dollar of al-Qaida defeated a million dollars by the

---

* The Royal Institute of International Affairs (now known as Chatham House) is a think tank based in London.

permission of Allah, besides the loss of a huge number of jobs.

As for the size of the economic deficit, it has reached record astronomical numbers estimated to total more than a trillion dollars.

And even more dangerous and bitter for America is that the mujahedin recently forced Bush to resort to emergency funds to continue the fight in Afghanistan and Iraq, which is evidence of the success of the bleed-until-bankruptcy plan – with Allah's permission.

It is true that this shows that al-Qaida has gained, but on the other hand, it shows that the Bush administration has also gained, something of which anyone who looks at the size of the contracts acquired by the shady Bush administration-linked mega-corporations, like Halliburton and its kind, will be convinced. And it all shows that the real loser is you.

It is the American people and their economy. And for the record, we had agreed with the commander General Muhammad Ataa, Allah have mercy on him, that all the operations should be carried out within twenty minutes, before Bush and his administration notice.

It never occurred to us that the commander-in-chief of the American armed forces would abandon fifty thousand of his citizens in the Twin Towers to face those great horrors alone, the time when they most needed him.

But because it seemed to him that occupying himself by talking to the little girl about the goat and its butting was more important than occupying himself with the planes and their butting of the skyscrapers, we were given three times the period required to execute the operations – all praise is due to Allah.*

And it's no secret to you that the thinkers and perceptive ones from among the Americans warned Bush before the war and told him: 'All that you want for securing America and removing the weapons of mass destruction – assuming they exist – is available to you, and the nations of the world are with you in the inspections, and it is in the interest of America that it not be thrust into an unjustified war with an unknown outcome.'

But the darkness of the black gold blurred his vision and insight, and he gave priority to private interests over the public interests of America.

---

* On the morning of 11 September 2001, Bush was at an elementary school in Sarasota, Florida, listening to children reading a story called *The Pet Goat*. As they started reading, the White House chief of staff whispered in Bush's ear that a second plane had hit the World Trade Center; however, he continued to listen to the children read for several minutes before leaving the room.

❝ It never occurred to us that the commander-in-chief of the American armed forces would abandon 50,000 of his citizens in the Twin Towers to face those great horrors alone ❞

So the war went ahead, the death toll rose, the American economy bled, and Bush became embroiled in the swamps of Iraq that threaten his future. He fits the saying: 'like the naughty she-goat who used her hoof to dig up a knife from under the earth.'

So I say to you, over fifteen thousand of our people have been killed and tens of thousands injured, while more than a thousand of you have been killed and more than ten thousand injured. And Bush's hands are stained with the blood of all those killed from both sides, all for the sake of oil and keeping their private companies in business.

Be aware that it is the nation who punishes the weak man when he causes the killing of one of its citizens for money, while letting the powerful one get off, when he causes the killing of more than a thousand of its sons, also for money.

And the same goes for your allies in Palestine. They terrorise the women and children, and kill and capture the men as they lie sleeping with their families on the mattresses, that you may recall that for every action, there is a reaction.

Finally, it behoves you to reflect on the last wills and testaments of the thousands who left you on the 11th as they gestured in despair. They are important testaments, which should be studied and researched.

Among the most important of what I read in them was some prose in their gestures before the collapse, where they say: 'How mistaken we were to have allowed the White House to implement its aggressive foreign policies against the weak without supervision.'

It is as if they were telling you, the people of America: 'Hold to account those who have caused us to be killed, and happy is he who learns from others' mistakes.'

And among that which I read in their gestures is a verse of poetry: 'Injustice chases its people, and how unhealthy the bed of tyranny.'

As has been said: 'An ounce of prevention is better than a pound of cure.'

And know that: 'It is better to return to the truth than persist in error.' And that the wise man doesn't squander his security, wealth and children for the sake of the liar in the White House.

In conclusion, I tell you in truth, that your security is not in the hands of Kerry, nor Bush, nor al-Qaida. No.

Your security is in your own hands. And every state that doesn't play with our security has automatically guaranteed its own security.

And Allah is our Guardian and Helper, while you have no Guardian or Helper.

All peace be upon he who follows the Guidance.

The Case for
Climate Security

– MARGARET BECKETT –

One of the best hopes we have for securing a safer future is to understand and address the factors that will drive insecurity and conflict around the world over the coming decades. Despite the emphasis placed on the danger posed by al-Qaida and the like, these factors will not on the whole take the form of either terrorist or conventional military threats to state security. They will instead include a range of political, economic, environmental and social issues. Important trends will include: increased competition for scarcer resources such as food, water and energy; the greater economic and socio-political marginalisation of the majority of the world's population; and the increased use of military force as an instrument of policy and the spread of new military technologies and weapons of mass destruction.[49] However, perhaps the single most significant driver of insecurity and division over the course of this century will be climate change. Together with the other interconnected trends mentioned above, climate change will affect the whole of humanity – causing instability and devastation of a magnitude unmatched by other potential threats. We will need to overcome this threat together, but human nature and current security orthodoxy threaten to turn us against one another once more and focus instead on securing resources overseas and creating fortress states at home.

This is something that Margaret Beckett clearly understood during her short time as British Foreign Secretary. On 10 May 2007 – just seven weeks before she was moved from the Foreign Office to the back benches – she gave a keynote address at the Royal United Services Institute, a military think tank in London. In her speech she declared,

'I simply do not believe that we will solve the security issues of the day unless we address the global insecurities that underlie and exacerbate them. And I do not think that I would be doing my job properly if I considered it enough simply to respond to each crisis as it occurs: the foreign policy that I will pursue is one that looks down the line at how we can prevent such crises from happening at all.' At the top of her list was climate change and its potential impact on security.

As she spoke to the audience of serving and retired military personnel, the argument for climate change to be considered a security issue had by no means yet been won. Although some significant earlier work had been carried out, the most influential report until then had been published only a month earlier. The CNA Corporation, an American non-profit research organisation, had brought together eleven retired generals and admirals from across the US military to assess the impact of climate change on national security. Their influential report, which Beckett mentioned in her speech, established the concept of climate change acting as a threat multiplier, exacerbating other trends and increasing instability in some of the most volatile regions of the world.[50] But it went further and concluded that climate change posed a threat to America's national security (a view echoed a year later by a US intelligence community National Security Assessment).[51]

The day after the CNA report was published, the UN Security Council held its first ever debate on the impact of climate change on international peace and security. This was a British initiative and the debate was chaired by Beckett. While most representatives welcomed the meeting, several developing countries were unhappy with the Security Council debating the subject, as they considered climate change to be an issue of sustainable development not security. But the UN Secretary-General Ban Ki-moon made it clear that 'issues of energy and climate change can have implications for peace and security' and Singapore's representative Vanu Gopala Menon said, 'it seems obvious to all but the wilfully blind that climate change must, if not now then eventually, have some impact on international peace and security'.[52]

The rise in interest in climate change as a security issue can be linked to three key trends that have influenced the political landscape in recent years. The first of these is the widespread acceptance of the scientific evidence that climate change is real, that it is caused by human activity and that it will have devastating consequences for all countries, including rich industrialised nations. The second trend relates to the importance of energy security and the fact that both developed and rapidly industrialising nations are becoming increasingly dependent on imported oil and gas, often reliant on supplies from already unstable parts of the world. Thirdly, there is a growing awareness in the post-9/11 world of the non-traditional threats to security arising from various social, environmental and economic factors that do not necessarily fall under conventional notions of defence.[53]

The debate at that time was still in the early stages and lacked the detailed understanding that comes from long-term research. Discussion within government often focused on the issue of energy security or on hard security issues, including an assumption that climate change would somehow lead to an increase in international terrorism. Although there were some notable exceptions, studies from think tanks were often little better: focusing on climate change, with security simply tagged onto the end. And while the analysis from the academic community was usually more advanced, it was all too often divorced from policy. What Beckett was trying to do in her speech was move the debate forward by settling the issue of whether climate change should be considered by the security community – the detail could then follow. Subsequent work has confirmed that she was right to push the issue up the security agenda and it was without doubt her most successful initiative as Foreign Secretary.[54] This is because it is clear that the environmental effects of climate change will have significant knock-on socio-economic impacts, which in turn could produce serious security consequences that will present new challenges.[55]

Climate change in this context refers to the interaction between a warming planet and the other environmental changes this is bringing about (together with related social, political and economic crises). Put simply, human activity is creating an increased concentration of greenhouse gases in the Earth's atmosphere, particularly carbon dioxide from fossil-fuel use (as Beckett pointed out: 'The threat to our climate security comes not from outside but from within: we are all our own enemies.') As these gases stop more and more of the sun's energy being radiated back into space, it is likely that there will be a global average temperature increase of between two and four degrees centigrade by the end of the century (this increase could be as much as six degrees centigrade if the worst-case scenario is realised).[56] As the oceans absorb more of this heat, seawater expands and causes a rise in sea levels. Once the full effects of glacial and ice sheet melting are also taken into account, the average rise in sea levels could be as high as a metre or more by the end of century. Other effects of climate change that are already occurring include: more frequent extreme weather events, such as floods, tropical storms, heatwaves and droughts; changes in rainfall patterns, leading to declines in crop yields and reduced water availability; an increased risk of plant and animal extinctions; the loss of coral reefs and areas of tropical rainforest; and changes in the distribution of vector-borne diseases, such as malaria.[57]

There will be significant regional variations and many of the most damaging consequences will be associated with the extremes. For example, a global average temperature increase of 4 degrees centigrade may mean temperatures at northern latitudes actually rise by 10 degrees centigrade or more, threatening the Greenland ice sheet and risking a long-term global sea-level rise of up to seven metres.[58] Another serious concern is that temperature increases may set off processes that create positive feedback in the climate system and lead to further increases in temperature. For example, the thawing of the Arctic permafrost could release the large amounts of methane currently trapped in the frozen soil. Changes such as this result in the irreversible release of large volumes of greenhouse gases into the atmosphere, leading to further temperature rises and potentially crossing a threshold that brings about abrupt climatic changes.[59]

While devastating in their own right, it is when these climatic changes and associated extreme weather events – such as intense tropical storms and storm surges – impact on human habitats that they will result in the socio-economic damage that is so concerning. This will include loss of infrastructure (including damage to ports and communication, transport and energy supply networks), resource scarcity (particularly food and water) and the mass displacement of peoples. The global population is expected to increase from today's six and a half billion to over nine billion by 2050. It is almost certain that drought, food shortages and flooding will lead to the mass movement of peoples, with perhaps up to two hundred million environmental refugees by the middle of the century.[60] Such refugees may bring the total number displaced due to natural disasters, conflict and large development projects to one billion people by 2050.[61]

These factors will interact with each other and with existing tensions to generate serious security risks. This could include civil unrest, inter-communal violence and international instability. Climate-change-related issues also have the potential to cause international legal disputes as the world map is redrawn. As coastlines retreat due to erosion and flooding, maritime borders and the associated exclusive economic zones might also have to change, as a country's ocean territory is legally determined by its land territory. Another possibility is that the evacuation or even physical disappearance of low-lying small island states – such as Tuvalu in the South Pacific – could result in challenges to sovereignty as the current qualifications defining the existence of a state include a permanent population and a defined territory. Further disputes might also be expected as ice melting opens up viable shipping routes through the Arctic, such as the Northwest Passage.[62]

Climate change is, therefore, becoming an increasingly important part of international relations. However, one problem is the (perhaps justified) resentment that those who will be worst affected by climate change feel towards the industrialised nations that have been responsible for the vast majority of greenhouse-gas emissions to date. As Beckett pointed out, on several occasions the Ugandan President, Yoweri Museveni, has called climate change an act of aggression by the rich against the poor. Other related problems may arise as emerging powers such as China and India are put under increasing pressure to cut back on emissions by Western countries, whose economies have already been able to develop while being high emitters. Furthermore, many of the countries that will be worst affected by the physical effects of climate change are weak and fragile states. By their very nature, these countries have a reduced capacity to respond effectively, meaning that they are also likely to be greatly affected by the resulting socio-economic and security consequences. The knock-on deterioration of state capacities and functions could, in extreme cases, lead to state failure.

There is genuine concern over whether the international governance system will be able to cope with these new geopolitical challenges, particularly if national governments are being undermined at the same time. If international institutions, such as the United Nations, are weakened or fail, then countries under pressure may turn away from the norms of diplomacy and resort to armed conflict to settle such disputes.[63] This led Beckett to conclude that 'The truth is that in a globalising world of interdependent states, which is already bursting at the seams, climate change is a global threat with global consequences.' However, the response should be 'not to defend a way of life but to change it'. As Beckett recognised, 'What we are seeking to do is nothing less than to shift the foundations upon which the global economy is built . . . There is only one possible answer. And that is to de-couple growth from emissions.'

Beckett was the first woman to hold the post of Foreign Secretary and only the second woman, after Margaret Thatcher, to hold one of the four great offices of state in the UK. Her appointment to the Foreign Office in May 2006 surprised many – including Beckett herself – given her relative lack of international experience. Her previous cabinet post had been as head of the Department for Environment, Food and Rural Affairs (Defra), where she had taken a leading role in the government's work on climate change – something the Prime Minister, Tony Blair, asked her to continue while Foreign Secretary. Though at times criticised, Beckett's thirteen months as Foreign Secretary were hugely important in pushing climate change up the security agenda. David Miliband, Beckett's successor at both Defra and then the Foreign Office, picked up her mantle and climate change is now widely accepted as a major security issue.

Beckett understood that the security implications of climate change will affect us all. She argued that 'what is at stake is not the narrow national security of individual states but our collective security in an interdependent world'. Our future depends on whether we recognise and build upon our interdependencies or foolishly focus on competition and narrow national interests. Unfortunately, effective international agreements are proving difficult to negotiate, as the 2009 Copenhagen summit demonstrated. We cannot, therefore, wait for such agreements. Instead, countries must immediately move to make massive unilateral emissions cuts, while pursuing bilateral agreements (for example, between China and the United States) and multilateral agreements (for example, within the EU) on cuts and adaptation funding for the developing world (while still working hard to reach binding international settlements, particularly in relation to issues such as deforestation).

In many ways, though, this is far too important to be left to the politicians alone, who have proved themselves woefully inadequate to the task. Each and every one of us can introduce our own personal emissions cuts, reducing our carbon footprint and individual impact on the environment to a minimum. We can support those non-governmental organisations working to find ways to prevent and mitigate climate change. We can prepare for the local impacts of climate change and help others to do so elsewhere. We can apply unprecedented pressure on our politicians to stop their petty squabbling. As Beckett said at the end of her speech: 'Climate change can bring us together if we are wise enough not to let it drive us apart.' This will be our greatest test.

Royal United Services Institute, London, England

10 May 2007

Good afternoon.

May I begin by thanking RUSI for organising this special event and indeed for the on-going – and ground-breaking work – they are doing in helping us to understand better the links between climate, energy and security.

There was a very powerful moment during the recent UN Security Council debate on climate security last month. The Ghanaian representative, L. K. Christian, spoke of growing evidence that nomadic Fulani cattle herdsmen were arming themselves with sophisticated assault rifles. They were doing so in order to confront local farming communities, who in turn were threatening their cattle herds. And the cause that he gave for that increasing tension: climate change expanding the Sahara desert.

The resonance in that Council chamber – as I am sure it is here today –

could hardly be stronger. Only the day before the Security Council had been discussing the crisis in Darfur.* That is a conflict in which two hundred thousand people have already died. And it is a conflict in which there has been that same struggle between nomadic and pastoral communities for resources made more scarce through a changing climate.

In making these links between natural resources and climate on the one hand and in conflict on the other, we are not saying anything particularly new or controversial. Here's a passage from Albert Hourani's seminal work *A History of the Arab Peoples*. In it, he describes the early years of the Islamic empire, roughly our eighth and ninth centuries AD:

'The symbiosis between cultivators and pastoralists', he writes, 'was a fragile one. When that symbiosis was strongly disturbed it was not because of a perpetual state of warfare between the two kinds of society but for other reasons: change in climate and water supply, for example, and the progressive desiccation of the Sahara region.'

Resource-based conflicts are not new – they are literally as old as the hills. But in climate change we have a new and potentially disastrous dynamic.

The good news is that we have the knowledge and ability to do something about it. Our forebears did not really understand the environmental changes that were happening to them and had little power to control those changes. We do and we can. Science has shown us a clearly identifiable process that is changing our climate and our world. We can predict the consequences of that change and we have the means to take action against it.

The bad news is the catastrophic and global nature of the threat we face. Again, it is the countries that are already experiencing the damage of an unstable climate that have described that best. As the representative from the Congo said during that Security Council debate: 'This will not be the first time people have fought over land, water and resources – but this time it will be on a scale that dwarfs the conflicts of the past.'

That then was the motivation behind my decision to use our presidency of the Security Council to highlight the threat of an unstable climate. And it is the reason why I have made climate security such a priority of my first year as Foreign Secretary.

* In 2003 a civil war broke out between black African rebel groups in Darfur and the Sudanese military and their Arab Janjaweed allies. The conflict involved widespread human-rights abuses and resulted in a humanitarian disaster and many tens of thousands of civilian deaths.

❝ I simply do not believe that we will **solve** the **security issues** of the day unless we **address** the **global** insecurities that **underlie** and **exacerbate** them. **❞**

In doing that, I know full well that there are some who suggest that I would be better off concentrating instead on the 'real' security problems in the world.

They could not be more wrong.

I am as focused on and as determined to address the so-called 'hard' security agenda as any Foreign Secretary. It takes up a large part of each and every working day. What has changed is not my priorities – they are resolutely foreign policy priorities not purely environmental ones – but the way in which I believe those priorities can be best pursued.

I simply do not believe that we will solve the security issues of the day unless we address the global insecurities that underlie and exacerbate them. And I do not think that I would be doing my job properly if I considered it enough simply to respond to each crisis as it occurs: the foreign policy that I will pursue is one that looks down the line at how we can prevent such crises from happening at all.

In other words, I attach no less importance to the hard security agenda but I am looking for the broadest and deepest possible understanding of what drives that agenda and what tools we can employ – going way beyond the purely military – to get the results that we want.

Take the Middle East as an example – a classic hard security issue, and one that occupies a lot of my time as it must the time of many in this room. Indeed I have just returned from a meeting of the Iraq Neighbours Group. That meeting was held in Sharm El-Sheik, in Egypt – a country that has been a relative force for stability in the region and played a positive role in building consensus both within the region and beyond.

So we should all be worried about what the science is telling us could happen to Egypt in the next few decades if we do nothing about climate change. From the south, drastic loss of Nile flow – perhaps up to 80 per cent less than there is now. From the north, rising sea levels destroying the low-lying ground on the banks of the Nile which is currently Egypt's agricultural heartland. One study suggests that a sea-level rise of just fifty centimetres – well within current estimates – would displace two million people from the delta.

What the precise security ramifications of that kind of change would be are impossible to predict in forensic detail. But make two million people in one of the most fragile regions of the world homeless in a short period of time and there will be an impact – not least on Egypt's internal stability. Reduce the total amount of Nile water supply so drastically and you risk exacerbating tensions between Egypt and her southern neighbours. Egypt has already warned off those countries upstream of it from diverting the Nile water – how much more strongly will it feel when there is far less of that water to go round.

And that pattern is going to be repeated across the Middle East – a region which contains 5 per cent of the world's population but only 1 per cent of the world's water. Climate change will make that ratio even more unfavourable. Saudi Arabia, Iran and Iraq – all countries pivotal to the regional security agenda – will see some of the biggest reductions in rainfall. Disagreements over water-access issues along the Jordan basin have on several occasions been a major driver of tension between Israel and its Arab neighbours, notably in the years leading up to the 1967 war. The water in that basin has already been overused and climate change could cause further, severe depletion.

There are, of course, many ways in which we can and must analyse the security situation in the Middle East – national, religious, economic. But my argument is that to deliberately choose to ignore a process of the magnitude of climate change – a process that threatens to raise tensions between states, that has the potential to cause widespread political instability, that might swell further the ranks of the dislocated and disaffected – would be wilfully to restrict our understanding of the challenges we face and to hamper our ability to meet those challenges in good time.

And here the Middle East is not a special case – that same set of pressures will build in other potential trouble spots around the world, most notably in South Asia where one billion may be affected by increased water stress and in Africa where vulnerable societies among the least capable of adapting will be hit first and hit hardest. President Museveni of Uganda was the first African leader to call climate change an act of aggression by the rich against the poor. I fear he will not be the last.

The truth is that in a globalising world of interdependent states, which is already bursting at the seams, climate change is a global threat with global consequences.

That was the stark warning contained in the report published last year by the former chief economist of the World Bank, Sir Nicholas Stern. That report, which the Nobel Prize winner Joseph Stiglitz described as 'the most thorough and rigorous analysis to date of the costs and risks of climate change', estimated that the costs of unabated climate change – based on the science available in 2001 and on a narrow range of effects – would be at least 5 per cent of global GDP. Taking on board more recent scientific evidence and the economic effects on human life and the environment, he estimates that the global economy could take a hit equivalent to 20 per cent of GDP or more.

If there is one resounding thing that we have learnt in the past hundred and fifty years – and in the first half of the last century in particular – it is that there is a complex and deadly link between the global economy, economic nationalism and increased global tensions. Anyone who doesn't see climate change as a security issue today will be treading in the footsteps of those who didn't see reparations as a security issue in the 1920s.

I am optimistic that the wind is already beginning to change. Two years ago the debate about the science of climate change was still going on. Today that debate – as it relates to the main findings of human-induced global warming – is effectively over.

A year ago, when I became Foreign Secretary, the idea of 'climate security' was an alien one – to many inside the FCO as well as to those outside.* Now, we have a group of the most senior retired US generals and admirals, including former Chief of Staff of the US Army General Sullivan and former Commander in Chief of CENTCOM,‡ General Zinni, putting out a report that begins with the recommendation, and I quote: 'The national security consequence of climate change should be fully integrated into national security and national defence strategies.'

The logical path that brought them to that conclusion is the same one that I have laid before you today. In their words again: 'Climate change can

* FCO: British Foreign & Commonwealth Office.
‡ CENTCOM: US Central Command.

❝ What we are seeking to do is nothing less than to shift the foundations upon which the global economy is built. ❞

act as a threat multiplier for instability in some of the most volatile regions in the world.'

And that is the motivation, of course, behind the current bills going through the US senate and Congress that will require the administration to produce a national security estimate on climate change.

But though this conceptual change is starting to happen, it is not happening fast enough. Just as 'energy security' is now an accepted and central part of the hard security discourse, so too must be 'climate security' – not least indeed, as I will come to later, because of the very close links between those two agendas.

But talking about it is only the first step. We must take action too. So what are the choices that we have to make? What can we do – specifically what can the security community, the people in this room do – to reinforce that climate security?

I believe that it requires a whole new approach to how we analyse and act on security. The threat to our climate security comes not from outside but from within: we are all our own enemies. And what is at stake is not the narrow national security of individual states but our collective security in an interdependent world.

So while an unstable climate has obvious hard security implications, the traditional tools of hard security – in simple terms, bombs and bullets – are not going to be able to solve that problem.

Instead we are going to have to think a lot more imaginatively and a lot more broadly about how we can act together to guarantee that kind of security. And that will mean much greater understanding of and commitment to non-military options: to international diplomacy; to leveraging international finance and markets; to building coalitions between governments, business and consumers. In other words, we are going to have to get a lot more hard-headed about soft power.

In the past, I have likened the task we face to the one that many of us here faced during the Cold War. Part of the response to that threat was military. But the Cold War was fought and won on many more fronts than the one that stretched from Finland to the Balkans. It was a diplomatic, economic, political and even cultural campaign. The objective was to defend the intellectual and moral integrity of our way of life in the face of what we say was an aggressive ideology.

The objective in the fight against climate change is just as clear – and no less difficult. It is not to defend a way of life but to change it. And once again we will need to assemble the broadest possible consensus – a coalition of all the talents – if we are to succeed.

What we are seeking to do is nothing less than to shift the foundations upon which the global economy is built.

We have to do so because it is the only way to resolve the shared dilemma presented to us by climate change.

We all, developed and developing countries alike, benefit from global growth, from strong economies, from the forces of globalisation that have lifted hundreds of millions out of poverty in the last decade alone.

But that growth has been reliant upon the burning of fossil fuels. We should not and cannot call a halt to that growth. But nor can we carry on as we are. Because if we do we will worsen climate change and undermine the very basis of our future prosperity and security. The dilemma then is that carbon-dependent growth, the very process that is improving the lives of millions around the world today, is also destroying their tomorrow.

There is only one possible answer. And that is to de-couple growth from emissions. And that requires a fundamental change in the way we produce and consume energy. The IEA estimates that the world will invest some 21 trillion in the energy sector between now and 2030.* The bulk of that money has to flow in the direction of low-carbon and energy-efficient investments.

Governments can't do this on their own. Nor can the private sector. Nor can individuals. We all have to play a part. Governments putting in place the long-term frameworks of goals, regulations and incentives. Business having the confidence to take and follow that lead and to start switching investment. Consumers making the right choices and keeping up the

* IEA: International Energy Agency. The figure cited is in US dollars.

pressure on others to do the same. In short, we are looking at nothing less than the greatest public–private partnership of all time.

And it is worth pointing out that if we get this right – if we diversify supply, use more renewables, improve our energy efficiency – we will also be greatly enhancing our energy security: helping to cure what President Bush famously termed our 'addiction to oil'.

Next week, for example, I am going to China and Japan. Japan is one of the most energy-efficient countries in the world. It consumes electricity ten times more efficiently than does China, twice as efficiently as does the United States. So for those who worry about the security impact of a scramble for energy resources in Africa or about the concentration of world oil and gas supplies in a few, sometimes unstable, hands then the answer lies as much in cutting-edge light bulbs as it does in high-tech weaponry.

That might not seem to be the kind of conversations that security experts are used to. You might ask, what point or value is there in the people in this room – schooled in the world of hard security – in getting involved in discussions about carbon price, wind power and energy white papers?

The answer is a great deal. Because the reality is that – globally – there is a gap between what science and good sense is telling us must be done and what we are actually doing.

And it is my contention that the reason that the political will is still lacking to close that gap is because, despite all the evidence, despite all the warnings, the understanding of the full range and scale of the threat we face is still not there.

Bringing in the security community into this debate has two distinct advantages.

The first is that when people talk about security problems they do so in terms qualitatively different from any other type of problem. Security is

❝ despite all the evidence, despite all the warnings, the understanding of the full range and scale of the threat we face is still not there ❞

seen as an imperative not an option. People don't obsess over cost–benefit analyses or about opportunity cost: they get on with what has to be done because they understand that security goes right to the heart of the basic contract between state and citizen.

In the same vein, when it comes to security you prepare for the worst-case scenario, you don't sit around and hope for the best. As General Sullivan is quoted as saying in that report I mentioned a little earlier: 'If you wait until you have 100 per cent certainty on the battlefield, something bad is going to happen.' And if we wait to act on climate change, I can promise you that something very bad indeed is going to happen.

So understanding and flagging up the security aspects of climate change has a role in galvanising those governments who have yet to act. And, for all of us, it has a role in setting the level of ambition – the political and financial commitment – that is needed.

Second, the security community has a very direct role to play. The analytical frameworks – the scenario-building – that business uses for its long-term planning was developed right here in the security community and borrowed from it. And it is still the security community – the people in this room – that does it best.

On a problem with the complexity of climate change, that ability to construct a vision of the future and to draw the links between a wide variety of physical impacts and possible consequences to our security is invaluable.

Having raised the issue of climate security up the agenda and having put it on the table at the UN Security Council, we now need to go to the next stage. We have reached a broad political conclusion as to the hard-security implications of climate change. But to make sure that we take the right action we need to have a more exact and more detailed understanding of that threat, using the expertise of everyone with an interest in this problem.

That is why, as a first step, I will host a seminar with key stakeholders to discuss the precise consequences that an unstable climate will have on our ability as a country to meet the international priorities that are set out in the FCO's strategy white paper.

Conclusion

I have spoken a lot today about the threat we face from climate change. I have no doubt that if we bury our heads in the sand we risk our world being engulfed. But if we work now to understand that threat and use that under-standing to plan and decide how we will meet and overcome it, then we can forge an opportunity. Not just an economic opportunity but an opportunity to renew our faith in humanity's ability to strive in common cause. Climate change can bring us together if we are wise enough not to let it drive us apart. And I call on the people in this room to be a part of that shared endeavour.

PART III

Might is Right

"War is not a mere act of policy
but a true political instrument,
a continuation of political activity
by other means."

General Carl von Clausewitz,
On War
(1832)

The principles of legitimate warfare originated with the classical Greek and Roman philosophers. Later, in the Christian tradition, it was St Augustine (354–430) and St Thomas Aquinas (1225–74) who laid the modern foundations of 'just war' theory. This approach argues that war can only be warranted as a last resort and only when it is both justified and conducted in an ethical manner. Traditionally, the only just causes were in response to an armed attack or to redress a grave wrong. It is arguable whether 'just war' theory has ever been fully adhered to and its tenets have certainly been rejected in more recent times in favour of treating war as politics – as a valid extension of political activity.

Closely aligned with this rejection is the concept of 'might is right': that it is natural and just for the strong to dominate the weak; that superior strength gives one the right to enforce one's will. This has been debated through history, from the ancient Greeks onwards. Along the way, it absorbed the notion of the survival of the fittest espoused by Herbert Spencer, Charles Darwin and others in the nineteenth century. It has since found its modern incarnations in, for example, American neo-conservatives, Israeli hawks and military dictators.

In combination, these two developments – war as politics and might is right – have led to the frequent use and abuse of military power (exacerbated by our tendency to divide the world into 'them and us', which was examined in Part II). This is explored in the chapters that follow, which focus primarily on wars: the politicians that start them, the soldiers that must fight them and the ordinary people whose lives are torn apart by them.

The first chapter examines a speech that Winston Churchill gave in the House of Commons on 4 June 1940, less than a month after becoming the British Prime Minister. The outlook at the time looked bleak: the fight against the advancing armies of Nazi Germany appeared all but lost, the British Expeditionary Force had only just been rescued from destruction around Dunkirk and the Battle of Britain was about to begin. For Churchill, though, there was to be no surrender and so, in many ways, his speech is about war at its most extreme: total war until victory or complete defeat. World War II involved a series of overlapping conflicts, alliances and empires, yet the history written by the victorious Allies overlooked many of the nuances of the war and painted it as a conflict of 'good' versus 'evil' – a dichotomy that would be used throughout the Cold War and again during the war on terror.

The situation at the end of World War II set the geopolitical landscape for much of the rest of the century. As the Cold War between the United States and the Soviet Union developed, many Third World countries became embroiled in proxy wars between the superpowers or were the victims of *coups d'état* backed by the Americans or the Soviets. One of the most contemptible of these *coups* was against Salvador Allende, the democratically elected President of Chile. The second chapter discusses Allende's final radio address, delivered on 11 September 1973 as soldiers attacked the presidential palace. The *coup* ushered in nearly two decades of dictatorship under General Augusto Pinochet and showed the military at its absolute worst.

The political nature of war is clearly demonstrated in the events explored in the third and fourth chapters. The third chapter examines a speech the British Prime Minister, Margaret Thatcher, gave to a Conservative Party rally on 3 July 1982. Two months earlier, Argentina's ruling junta had ordered the invasion of the Falkland Islands – a British territory in the South Atlantic that Argentina claimed and still claims sovereignty over. The invasion was largely intended to appeal to Argentine patriotism and shore up support for the unpopular regime of General Leopoldo Galtieri. Thatcher's military response also had a political dimension, allowing her to recover from extremely low opinion-poll ratings and paving the way for a more robust British foreign policy. Thatcher believed that the successful Falklands campaign had revealed the best in the British people – what she called the Falklands factor – and in her speech she expressed the hope that this would continue in peacetime as it had during war.

Those who see the world as divided into good and evil often believe they have a responsibility to use force to make the world a safer place. All too often, this goes hand in hand with other ideological or economic interests. As such, war continues to be seen as a viable instrument of foreign policy. This is explored in the fourth chapter, which looks at a speech the British Prime Minister, Tony Blair, gave at the Economic Club of Chicago on 22 April 1999. Blair used this speech to set out his doctrine of the international community and make the case for military intervention on humanitarian grounds. Humanitarian interventions are, on the face of it, one of the more justifiable uses of military force. However, in reality, the situation is often complicated by the ulterior motives of the intervening state and disagreements within the international community. Blair's speech was delivered at the time of NATO's bombing campaign against Slobodan Milošević's military apparatus in Yugoslavia – the second of the five conflicts Blair would be involved in during his premiership. The most controversial of these was the 2003 invasion and occupation of Iraq and it was his actions in the build-up to this conflict that confirmed the adage that the first casualty of war is truth.

Though war surely represents the absolute failings of humanity, when people are forced into conflict it can occasionally reveal the best, not just the worst, in human nature. The men and women of the armed forces make huge sacrifices, including, for some, the ultimate sacrifice. Although the military is an instrument of government policy, once the politicians have committed troops to war it is down to the commanding officers to prepare the men and women under their command for the dangers that lie ahead. This is explored in the last chapter, through an eve-of-battle speech delivered by Lieutenant-Colonel Tim Collins on 19 March 2003 to soldiers of the 1st Battalion the Royal Irish Regiment as they prepared for the imminent invasion of Iraq. His speech showed the military at its best: professional and restrained even under extremely difficult circumstances. Nevertheless, the effect of the invasion on Iraqi civilians has been devastating, as ever in war, and not all members of the coalition forces can be said to have acquitted themselves with honour.

Soldiers rarely fight for ideology or abstractions such as freedom or democracy (although sometimes they do). Once combat starts, they usually fight for their comrades, their friends – the man or woman beside them. The importance of this social cohesion in combat is recognised on war memorials across Britain and elsewhere with a Bible verse that reads: 'Greater love hath no man than this, that a man lay down his life for his friends.' (John 15:13.) Politicians abuse this instinct by sending young men and women to die in unnecessary or unjustified wars. The oft-used platitude that we fight in order to secure peace simply hides the truth that too much of war is about promoting economic or political interests at the expense of others' lives, both civilian and military.

We Shall Fight
on the Beaches

– WINSTON CHURCHILL –

ontrary to what Pinewood Studios and Hollywood would have us believe, World War II was not a war between Britain and Germany in Europe and the United States and Japan in the Pacific. It was a series of interlocking conflicts that started in the late 1930s in Europe with the expansion of Nazi Germany, drew in the British Empire and the Soviet Union and spread to North Africa. With the entrance of the United States into the war at the end of 1941, it grew to include the conflict in Asia and the Pacific that had begun between Japan and China but expanded to include the Axis powers and the Allies.

World War II was primarily fought between these two large military alliances: the Axis powers and the Allies. The Axis was created on 27 September 1940, when Germany, Italy and Japan signed the Tripartite Pact, recognising each other's spheres of interest and offering political, economic and military assistance should one of them be attacked. By mid-1941, the Pact had expanded to include Hungary, Romania, Slovakia, Bulgaria, Yugoslavia and Croatia (the revised Anti-Comintern Pact of 25 November 1941 also brought China, Denmark, Finland, Manchukuo and Spain into alliance with the Axis powers in opposition to the Soviet Union). Against them stood the Allies, led at first by Britain and France, supported by most of the independent dominions of the British Commonwealth – Canada, Australia, New Zealand and South Africa – and India and other territories of the British Empire. They were joined in the European conflict by the Soviet Union in June 1941 and the United States nearly six months later. The Allies were led by the

United States in the Pacific campaign, in which Britain and the Commonwealth and, in the final weeks, the Soviet Union also fought (together with China, who had been at war with Japan since 1937).

However, in the beginning it was very much a European conflict. Once Adolf Hitler had consolidated his power in Germany in 1934, he began a period of German rearmament and expansion, regaining control of the Saar (1935), Rhineland (1936) and Memelland (1939) and annexing Austria and the Sudetenland (1938). In this way, he sought to redress some of the perceived wrongs imposed upon Germany through the Treaty of Versailles at the end of World War I. Prior to Germany's expansion, Japan had invaded the Chinese province of Manchuria (1931) and Italy had invaded Ethiopia (1935) and in doing so had demonstrated the almost complete ineffectiveness of the League of Nations. The League was the post-World War I forerunner to the United Nations and was built on the principles of collective security and international disarmament – both of which failed in the 1930s. Neville Chamberlain became Prime Minister of Britain in 1937 and pursued a policy of appeasement in relation to Hitler's ambitions, sacrificing Czechoslovakia along the way, but obtaining a peace treaty from Germany and erroneously declaring he had secured 'peace for our time'.[1] It was only after the invasion of Poland on 1 September 1939 that Britain and France declared war on Germany, signalling the start of World War II. The Soviet Union invaded eastern Poland two weeks later, as agreed between Hitler and Joseph Stalin, but the United States remained neutral. There followed a period of relative calm in what was called the Phoney War (although there were some naval clashes and the Soviet Union attacked Finland in November 1939 and Germany invaded Denmark and Norway in April 1940).

This is the point at which Winston Churchill came to the fore and on 10 May 1940 he replaced Chamberlain as Prime Minister. He formed a coalition government and told the House of Commons: 'I have nothing to offer but blood, toil, tears and sweat.'[2] The day that Churchill became Prime Minister, Germany began its invasion of Western Europe – attacking Belgium, the Netherlands and Luxembourg. Within days the German army was in France and the situation looked desperate as the French defences were overwhelmed by the force and speed of the German blitzkrieg.

Churchill had been warning against the dangers of a strengthened Germany since Hitler first came to power. In 1934, six years before the Blitz, he warned parliament that 'the crash of bombs exploding in London and the cataracts of masonry and fire and smoke will apprise us of any inadequacy which has been permitted in our aerial defences'.[3] However, political blunders and unpopular views had left Churchill in the political wilderness in the 1930s. His warnings about the rise of Hitler and calls for Britain to rearm were thus labelled nothing more than scaremongering. When war broke out, though, public opinion demanded the return to the cabinet of this complex figure. He was bombastic, uncharismatic, dependent on alcohol and often rude to his staff. He also struggled with depression throughout his life (what he called his 'black dog'). But he was an inspirational leader: his stubborn courage and rousing speeches set the narrative for the war and steadied the collective nerve of the country. By the end of the war Churchill was a national hero and, despite his 1945 electoral defeat, his place in history as arguably the greatest British Prime Minister of the twentieth century was secure.[4]

His 4 June 1940 speech came at a crucial point in the war. Belgium had surrendered a week earlier, exposing the flank of the British Expeditionary Force (BEF) and, although not known at the time, France was about to fall to German occupation. The BEF and part of the French and Belgian armies were trapped by the German army in northern France and western Belgium and disaster looked so certain that the British government declared 26 May as a day of national prayer for the soldiers 'in dire peril'.[5] However, on 24 May Hitler ordered a surprise halt to the German advance, inadvertently giving the Allies a three-day window of opportunity to prepare an evacuation. The Royal Navy had been moving destroyers and transport ships to the English Channel and together with a flotilla of hundreds of civilian-crewed merchant navy ships, lifeboats, fishing boats, pleasure cruisers and yachts they undertook the rescue of thousands of trapped soldiers as the German air force, the Luftwaffe, strafed the beaches and attacked the ships. In what Churchill described as a 'miracle of deliverance', over three hundred thousand Allied soldiers were evacuated 'out of the jaws of death and shame' in Dunkirk and the surrounding beaches between 26 May and 4 June 1940.[6] However,

Churchill made it clear that 'We must be very careful not to assign to this deliverance the attributes of a victory. Wars are not won by evacuations.' He warned that the success of the Dunkirk evacuation 'must not blind us to the fact that what has happened in France and Belgium is a colossal military disaster'. Thousands of Allied troops had been killed or captured, including the French rearguard that had remained to protect the evacuation, and all the heavy equipment and vehicles of the BEF had to be abandoned.

Nine days after Churchill's speech, Paris was declared an open city and the French government fled in an attempt to spare the city from total destruction. On 22 June, France surrendered and signed an armistice with Germany. This left Britain isolated and facing the might of the German war machine, the Wehrmacht, over the English Channel. Though Britain still had the support of troops and pilots from the Commonwealth and the British Empire, as well as the French, Polish and other European armed forces in exile, Churchill might have admitted defeat and attempted to negotiate an agreement with Hitler whereby Britain avoided occupation and kept its Empire – but this would have meant accepting a Europe united under Nazi rule and he was not prepared to do that. Churchill refused to capitulate to Hitler, despite serious opposition from some in the cabinet and parliament. As he had told the House of Commons on 4 June, 'we shall not flag or fail. We shall go on to the end. We shall fight in France, we shall fight on the seas and oceans, we shall fight with growing confidence and growing strength in the air, we shall defend our island, whatever the cost may be.' He then delivered some of the most stirring lines in history: 'We shall fight on the beaches, we shall fight on the landing grounds, we shall fight in the fields and in the streets, we shall fight in the hills; we shall never surrender.' The Battle of France had been lost but the Battle of Britain was about to begin.

Churchill believed that if Britain did fall to the Nazis the rest of the British Empire would continue fighting, protected and supported by the Royal Navy. They would, he hoped, 'carry on the struggle, until, in God's good time, the new world, with all its power and might, steps forth to the rescue and the liberation of the old'. The new world he spoke of was the United States, and Churchill's 4 June speech was, in part, a frank appeal to President Franklin D. Roosevelt for the United States to enter the war and rescue the old world of Europe. The United States had been supporting Britain and France with arms transfers and active naval patrols in the western Atlantic and had deployed troops to defend Iceland, relieving the British garrison there. However, the United States did not enter the war in Europe until Germany and Italy declared war on it on 11 December 1941, three days after the United States had itself declared war on Japan following the attack on the US Pacific Fleet at Pearl Harbor, Hawaii (a prelude to Japan's plans to seize the US-controlled Philippines, British Malaya and the Dutch East Indies). The Allies now faced Germany and Italy in Europe and North Africa, and Japan in the Pacific.

The crucial role the United States played has given rise to a mistaken belief that it won the war. It is true that the United States was the key player in the war against Japan. The United States was also essential to the success of the D-Day landings of 6 June 1944 and the liberation of Western Europe. However, the armies of Europe had fought the invading German army all the way to the English Channel and, once occupied, implemented guerrilla resistance campaigns against the Nazi apparatus. Britain, as an island, was able to resist and, thanks to its air force and navy, was never occupied. The entry of the United States into the war eighteen months after the fall of France undoubtedly turned the tide of the conflict and helped save Britain and others from further occupation. However, no one country can lay claim to winning the war in Europe – it was an Allied victory.

The essential role that the Soviet Union played in the victory is often overlooked in this Western-centric view of the overwhelming importance of American involvement. The Soviet Union started the war with a treaty of non-aggression with Germany but Hitler launched a surprise invasion in June 1941. The Soviets fought German forces and their allied armies on the Eastern Front for four years and launched a fierce counter-offensive that eventually saw Berlin fall to the Red Army on 2 May 1945 and the unconditional German surrender a week later. The Soviet Union thus ended the war occupying much of the territory it had liberated from the Germans. However, World War II, or the Great Patriotic War as it was known to the Soviets, cost the Soviet Union a great deal. By the end of the war, as many as twenty million Soviets had been killed – by far the largest loss of any country – and the Soviet Union had spent nearly $200 billion on the war effort, losing nearly a third of its national wealth in the process.[7] In turn, though, Soviet forces had committed gross war crimes and crimes against humanity during the war, including the murder of an estimated twenty-two thousand Polish prisoners and the rape of an estimated two million German women.[8] Their Western allies at first turned a blind eye to many of these crimes (although they were later used in anti-Soviet propaganda during the Cold War).

This raises important questions about the conduct of the Allies during World War II. Although the Axis powers were the aggressors and committed numerous atrocities, Allied soldiers are known to have mistreated civilians and prisoners of war – including incidents of rape, torture, murder and the mutilation of war dead.[9] The Allied command also deliberately targeted the civilian populations of Germany and Japan.[10] They bombed Hamburg between 24 July and 2 August 1943, killing more than fifty thousand people; fire-bombed Dresden on 13 and 14 February 1945, killing up to twenty-five thousand people; and fire-bombed Tokyo on 9 to 10 March 1945, killing around a hundred thousand people.[11] Then on 6 August 1945, the United States dropped an atomic bomb on Hiroshima, followed three days later by a nuclear detonation over Nagasaki. It is estimated that these bombings caused between a hundred and fifty and two hundred and fifty thousand deaths in the following two months.[12] The description of World War II as 'the last good war' is thus something of a misnomer, at least when applied to its conduct (and even when compared to the Korean and Vietnam Wars that would follow). Might is not always right; human dignity is shown little respect in total war and, at times, the line between right and wrong is blurred beyond recognition. But when history is written by the victors, it is often only their heroic deeds that are recorded.

World War II ended with the formal surrenders of Germany on 8 May 1945, following the fall of Berlin, and Japan on 2 September 1945, following the American bombing of Hiroshima and Nagasaki and the Soviet invasion of Manchuria. Italy had already signed an armistice with the Allies in September 1943, Romania and Bulgaria had done the same with the Soviet Union in September 1944 and Hungary had fallen to the Soviets in April 1945. World War II had been the deadliest in history, costing the lives of at least fifty million people. The true scale of Nazi Germany's crimes became clear by the end of the war, when it was discovered that the Nazi apparatus had been responsible for the systematic murder of approximately six million Jews as part of the horrific Endlösung der Judenfrage (Final Solution to the Jewish Question).

The geopolitical map was completely redrawn and the power dynamic at the end of the war shaped the rest of the century. The United Nations was formed in the hope of preventing another world conflict and officially came into existence in October 1945 with fifty-one founding members – all of whom had stood against the Axis powers by the end of the war. Its principal organ, the UN Security Council, was made up of the United States, the United Kingdom, France, the Soviet Union and the Republic of China – the victorious powers of World War II. The pre-war empires of Britain, France, Germany, Italy and Japan had either crumbled or were in decline. By the time Churchill died in 1965 much of the British Empire had gained independence, and the Suez crisis nine years earlier had demonstrated that Britain would find it difficult to act on the international stage without US approval (the United States had used political and financial pressure on Britain to end the joint British, French and Israeli military attack on Egypt following its nationalisation of the Suez Canal). The wars of national liberation and the process of decolonisation were largely complete by the mid-1970s, signalling the end to five hundred years of European empire-building and leaving the United States and the Soviet Union as the world's only superpowers.

House of Commons, London, England

4 JUNE 1940

From the moment that the French defences at Sedan and on the Meuse were broken at the end of the second week of May, only a rapid retreat to Amiens and the south could have saved the British and French armies who had entered Belgium at the appeal of the Belgian king, but this strategic fact was not immediately realised. The French high command hoped they would be able to close the gap, and the armies of the north were under their orders. Moreover, a retirement of this kind would have involved almost certainly the destruction of the fine Belgian army of over twenty divisions and the abandonment of the whole of Belgium. Therefore, when the force and scope of the German penetration were realised and when a new French generalissimo, General Weygand, assumed command in place of General Gamelin, an effort was made by the French and British armies in Belgium to keep on holding the right hand of the Belgians and to give their own right hand to a newly created French army which was to have advanced across the Somme in great strength to grasp it.

However, the German eruption swept like a sharp scythe around the right and rear of the armies of the north. Eight or nine armoured divisions, each of about four hundred armoured vehicles of different kinds, but carefully assorted to be complementary and divisible into small self-contained units, cut off all communications between us and the main French armies. It severed our own communications for food and ammunition, which ran first to Amiens and afterwards through Abbeville, and it shore its way up the coast to Boulogne and Calais, and almost to Dunkirk. Behind this armoured and mechanised onslaught came a number of German divisions in lorries, and behind them again there plodded comparatively slowly the dull brute mass of the ordinary German army and German people, always so ready to be led to the trampling down in other lands of liberties and comforts which they have never known in their own.

I have said this armoured scythe-stroke almost reached Dunkirk – almost but not quite. Boulogne and Calais were the scenes of desperate fighting. The Guards defended Boulogne for a while and were then withdrawn by orders from this country. The Rifle Brigade, the 60th Rifles, and the Queen Victoria's Rifles, with a battalion of British tanks and a thousand Frenchmen, in all about four thousand strong, defended Calais to the last. The British brigadier was given an hour to surrender. He spurned the offer, and four days of intense street fighting passed before silence reigned over Calais, which marked the end of a memorable resistance. Only thirty unwounded survivors were brought off by the navy and we do not know the fate of their comrades. Their sacrifice, however, was not in vain. At least two armoured divisions, which otherwise would have been turned against the British Expeditionary Force, had to be sent for to overcome them. They have added another page to the glories of the Light Division, and the time gained enabled the Graveline waterlines to be flooded and to be held by the French troops.

Thus it was that the port of Dunkirk was kept open. When it was found impossible for the armies of the north to reopen their communications to Amiens with the main French armies, only one choice remained. It seemed, indeed, forlorn. The Belgian, British and French armies were almost surrounded. Their sole line of retreat was to a single port and to its neighbouring beaches. They were pressed on every side by heavy attacks and far outnumbered in the air.

When a week ago today I asked the House to fix this afternoon as the occasion for a statement, I feared it would be my hard lot to announce the greatest military disaster in our long history. I thought – and some good judges agreed with me – that perhaps twenty thousand or thirty thousand men might be re-embarked. But it certainly seemed that the whole of the French First Army and the whole of the British Expeditionary Force north of the Amiens–Abbeville gap would be broken up in the open field or else would have to capitulate for lack of food and ammunition. These were the hard and heavy tidings for which I called upon the House and the nation to prepare themselves a week ago. The whole root and core and brain of the British army, on which and around which we were to build, and are to build, the great British armies in the later years of the war, seemed about to perish upon the field or to be led into an ignominious and starving captivity.

That was the prospect a week ago. But another blow which might well have proved final was yet to fall upon us. The King of the Belgians had called upon us to come to his aid. Had not this ruler and his government severed themselves from the Allies, who rescued their country from extinction in the late war, and had they not sought refuge in what has proved to be a fatal neutrality, the French and British armies might well at the outset have saved not only Belgium but perhaps even Poland. Yet at the last moment, when Belgium was already invaded, King Leopold called upon us to come to his aid, and even at the last moment we came. He and his brave, efficient army, nearly half a million strong, guarded our eastern flank and thus kept open our only line of retreat to the sea. Suddenly, without prior consultation, with the least possible notice, without the advice of his ministers and upon his own personal act, he sent a plenipotentiary to the German command, surrendered his army and exposed our whole flank and means of retreat.

I asked the House a week ago to suspend its judgement because the facts were not clear, but I do not feel that any reason now exists why we should not form our own opinions upon this pitiful episode. The surrender of the Belgian army compelled the British at the shortest notice to cover a flank to the sea more than thirty miles in length. Otherwise all would have been cut off, and all would have shared the fate to which King Leopold had condemned the finest army his country had ever formed. So in doing this and in exposing this flank, as anyone who followed the operations on the map will see, contact was lost between the British and two out of the three corps forming the First French Army, who were still further from the coast than we were, and it seemed impossible that any large number of Allied troops could reach the coast.

The enemy attacked on all sides with great strength and fierceness, and their main power, the power of their far more numerous air force, was thrown into the battle or else concentrated upon Dunkirk and the beaches. Pressing in upon the narrow exit, both from the east and from the west, the enemy began to fire with cannon upon the beaches by which alone the shipping could approach or depart. They sowed magnetic mines in the channels and seas; they sent repeated waves of hostile aircraft, sometimes more than a hundred strong in one formation, to cast their bombs upon the single pier that remained, and upon the sand dunes upon which the troops had their eyes for shelter. Their U-boats, one of which was sunk, and their motor launches took their toll of the vast traffic which now began. For four or five days an intense struggle reigned. All their armoured divisions – or what was left of them – together with great masses of German infantry and artillery, hurled themselves in vain upon the ever-narrowing, ever-contracting appendix within which the British and French armies fought.

Meanwhile, the Royal Navy, with the willing help of countless merchant seamen, strained every nerve to embark the British and Allied troops. Two hundred and twenty light warships and six hundred and fifty other vessels were engaged. They had to operate upon the difficult coast, often in adverse weather, under an almost ceaseless hail of bombs and an increasing concentration of artillery fire. Nor were the seas, as I have said, themselves free from mines and torpedoes. It was in conditions such as these that our men carried on, with little or no rest, for days and nights on end, making trip after trip across the dangerous waters, bringing with them always men whom they had rescued. The numbers they have brought back are the measure of their devotion and their courage. The hospital ships, which brought off many thousands of British and French wounded, being so plainly marked were a special target for Nazi bombs; but the men and women on board them never faltered in their duty.

Meanwhile, the Royal Air Force, which had already been intervening in the battle, so far as its range would allow, from home bases, now used part of its main metropolitan fighter strength, and struck at the German bombers, and at the fighters which in large numbers protected them. This struggle was protracted and fierce. Suddenly the scene has cleared, the crash and thunder has for the moment – but only for the moment – died away. A miracle of deliverance, achieved by valour, by perseverance, by perfect discipline, by faultless service, by resource, by skill, by unconquerable fidelity, is manifest to us all. The enemy was hurled back by the retreating British and French troops. He was so roughly handled that he did not harry their departure seriously. The Royal Air Force engaged the main strength of the German air force, and inflicted upon them losses of at least four to one; and the navy, using nearly a thousand ships of all kinds, carried over three hundred and thirty-five thousand men, French and British, out of the jaws of death and shame, to their native land and to the tasks which lie immediately ahead. We must be very careful not to assign to this deliverance the attributes of a victory. Wars are not won by evacuations. But there was a victory inside this deliverance, which should be noted. It was gained by the air force. Many of our soldiers coming back have not seen the air force at work; they saw only the bombers which escaped its protective attack. They underrate its achievements. I have heard much talk of this; that is why I go out of my way to say this. I will tell you about it.

This was a great trial of strength between the British and German air forces. Can you conceive a greater objective for the Germans in the air than to make evacuation from these beaches impossible, and to sink all these ships which were displayed, almost to the extent of thousands? Could there have been an objective of greater military importance and significance for the whole purpose of the war than this? They tried hard, and they were beaten back; they were frustrated in their task. We got the army away; and they have paid fourfold for any losses which they have inflicted. Very large formations of German aeroplanes – and we know that they are a very brave race – have turned on several occasions from the attack of one-quarter of their number of the Royal Air Force, and have dispersed in different directions. Twelve aeroplanes have been hunted by two. One aeroplane was driven into the water and cast away, by the mere charge of a British aeroplane, which had no more ammunition. All of our types – the Hurricane, the Spitfire and the new Defiant – and all our pilots have been vindicated as superior to what they have at present to face.

When we consider how much greater would be our advantage in defending the air above this island against an overseas attack, I must say that I find in these facts a sure basis upon which practical and reassuring thoughts may rest. I will pay my tribute to these young airmen. The great French army was very largely, for the time being, cast back and disturbed by the onrush of a few thousands of armoured vehicles. May it not also be that the cause of civilisation itself will be defended by the skill and devotion of a few thousand airmen? There never has been, I suppose, in all the world, in all the history of war, such an opportunity for youth. The Knights of the Round Table, the Crusaders, all fall back into a prosaic past: not only distant but prosaic; but these young men, going forth every morn to guard their native land and all that we stand for, holding in their hands these instruments of colossal and shattering power, of whom it may be said that 'When every morning brought a noble chance,' 'And every chance brought out a noble knight,' deserve our gratitude, as do all of the brave men who, in so many ways and on so many occasions, are ready, and continue ready, to give life and all for their native land.

❝ May it not also be that the cause of civilisation itself will be defended by the skill and devotion of a few thousand airmen? ❞

I return to the army. In the long series of very fierce battles, now on this front, now on that, fighting on three fronts at once, battles fought by two or three divisions against an equal or somewhat larger number of the enemy, and fought fiercely on some of the old grounds that so many of us knew so well, in these battles our losses in men have exceeded thirty thousand killed, wounded and missing. I take occasion to express the sympathy of the House to all who have suffered bereavement or who are still anxious. The President of the Board of Trade is not here today. His son has been killed, and many in the House have felt the pangs of affliction in the sharpest form. But I will say this about the missing. We have had a large number of wounded come home safely to this country – the greater part – but I would say about the missing that there may be very many reported missing who will come back home, some day, in one way or another. In the confusion of this fight it is inevitable that many have been left in positions where honour required no further resistance from them.

Against this loss of over thirty thousand men, we can set a far heavier loss certainly inflicted upon the enemy. But our losses in material are enormous. We have perhaps lost one-third of the men we lost in the opening days of the battle of 21 March 1918, but we have lost nearly as many guns – nearly one thousand guns – and all our transport, all the armoured vehicles that were with the army in the north.* This loss will impose a further delay on the expansion of our military strength. That expansion had not been proceeding as fast as we had hoped. The best of all we had to give had gone to the British Expeditionary Force, and although they had not the numbers of tanks and some articles of equipment which were desirable, they were a very well and finely equipped army. They had the first fruits of all that our industry had to give, and that is gone. And now here is this further delay. How long it will be, how long it will last, depends upon the exertions which we make in this island. An effort the like of which has never been seen in our records is now being made. Work is proceeding everywhere, night and day, Sundays and week days. Capital and labour have cast aside their interests, rights, and customs and put them into the common stock. Already the flow of munitions has leapt forward. There is no reason why we should not in a few months overtake the sudden and serious loss that has come upon us, without retarding the development of our general programme.

* The Second Battle of the Somme lasted from 21 March to 4 April 1918 during World War I. This German offensive on the Western Front pushed the British lines back and resulted in 177,739 British casualties.

❝ our **thankfulness** at the **escape** of **our army** and so many men … must **not blind** us to the **fact** that what has happened in France and Belgium is a **colossal military disaster**. ❞

Nevertheless, our thankfulness at the escape of our army and so many men, whose loved ones have passed through an agonising week, must not blind us to the fact that what has happened in France and Belgium is a colossal military disaster. The French army has been weakened, the Belgian army has been lost, a large part of those fortified lines upon which so much faith had been reposed is gone, many valuable mining districts and factories have passed into the enemy's possession, the whole of the Channel ports are in his hands, with all the tragic consequences that follow from that, and we must expect another blow to be struck almost immediately at us or at France. We are told that Herr Hitler has a plan for invading the British Isles. This has often been thought of before. When Napoleon lay at Boulogne for a year with his flat-bottomed boats and his Grand Army, he was told by someone, 'There are bitter weeds in England.' There are certainly a great many more of them since the British Expeditionary Force returned.

The whole question of home defence against invasion is, of course, powerfully affected by the fact that we have for the time being in this island incomparably more powerful military forces than we have ever had at any moment in this war or the last. But this will not continue. We shall not be content with a defensive war. We have our duty to our ally. We have to recon-stitute and build up the British Expeditionary Force once again, under its gallant commander-in-chief, Lord Gort. All this is in train; but in the interval we must put our defences in this island into such a high state of organisation that the fewest possible numbers will be required to give effective security and that the largest possible potential of offensive effort may be realised. On this we are now engaged. It will be very convenient, if it be the desire of the House, to enter upon this subject in a secret session. Not that the government would necessarily be able to reveal in very great detail military secrets, but we like to have our discussions free, without the restraint imposed by the fact that they will be read the next day by the enemy, and the government would benefit by views freely expressed in all parts of the House by members with their knowledge of so many different parts of the country. I understand that some request is to be made upon this subject, which will be readily acceded to by His Majesty's Government.

We have found it necessary to take measures of increasing stringency, not only against enemy aliens and suspicious characters of other nationalities, but also against British subjects who may become a danger or a nuisance should the war be transported to the United Kingdom. I know there are a great many people affected by the orders which we have made who are the passionate enemies of Nazi Germany. I am very sorry for them, but we cannot, at the present time and under the present stress, draw all the distinctions which we should like to do. If parachute landings were attempted and fierce fighting attendant upon them followed, these unfortunate people would be far better out of the way, for their own sakes as well as for ours. There is, however, another class, for which I feel not the slightest sympathy. Parliament has given us the powers to put down Fifth Column activities with a strong hand, and we shall use those powers, subject to the supervision and correction of the House, without the slightest hesitation until we are satisfied, and more than satisfied, that this malignancy in our midst has been effectively stamped out.*

Turning once again, and this time more generally, to the question of invasion, I would observe that there has never been a period in all these long centuries of which we boast when an absolute guarantee against invasion, still less against serious raids, could have been given to our people. In the days of Napoleon, of which I was speaking just now, the same wind which would have carried his transports across the Channel might have driven away the blockading fleet. There was always the chance, and it is that chance which has excited and befooled the imaginations of many Continental tyrants. Many are the tales that are told. We are assured that novel methods will be adopted, and when we see the originality of malice, the ingenuity of aggression, which our enemy displays, we may certainly

---

* The term 'Fifth Column' originated during the Spanish Civil War and is used to describe a subversive group who covertly undermine a larger group from within in order to aid an external enemy. During World War II it was applied to German nationals living in Britain and British Nazi sympathisers who might provide support to Germany.

prepare ourselves for every kind of novel stratagem and every kind of brutal and treacherous manoeuvre. I think that no idea is so outlandish that it should not be considered and viewed with a searching, but at the same time, I hope, with a steady eye. We must never forget the solid assurances of sea power and those which belong to air power if it can be locally exercised.

I have, myself, full confidence that if all do their duty, if nothing is neglected, and if the best arrangements are made, as they are being made, we shall prove ourselves once again able to defend our island home, to ride out the storm of war, and to outlive the menace of tyranny, if necessary for years, if necessary alone. At any rate, that is what we are going to try to do. That is the resolve of His Majesty's Government – every man of them. That is the will of parliament and the nation. The British Empire and the French Republic, linked together in their cause and in their need, will defend to the death their native soil, aiding each other like good comrades to the utmost of their strength. Even though large tracts of Europe and many old and famous states have fallen or may fall into the grip of the Gestapo and all the odious apparatus of Nazi rule, we shall not flag or fail. We shall go on to the end. We shall fight in France, we shall fight on the seas and oceans, we shall fight with growing confidence and growing strength in the air, we shall defend our island, whatever the cost may be. We shall fight on the beaches, we shall fight on the landing grounds, we shall fight in the fields and in the streets, we shall fight in the hills; we shall never surrender, and even if, which I do not for a moment believe, this island or a large part of it were subjugated and starving, then our Empire beyond the seas, armed and guarded by the British Fleet, would carry on the struggle, until, in God's good time, the new world, with all its power and might, steps forth to the rescue and the liberation of the old.

> 66 We shall fight on the beaches,
> we shall fight on the landing grounds,
> we shall fight in the fields and in the streets,
> we shall fight in the hills; we shall
> never surrender 99

This Dark and
Bitter Moment

– Salvador Allende –

S eptember 11 is an infamous date in the Americas. For the United States, it is the date of the al-Qaida attacks of 2001 and the beginning of the war on terror. But it is also Chile's 9/11: the date in 1973 that the United States backed a *coup d'état* against President Salvador Allende and ended four decades of unbroken constitutional rule. For both countries, it is a date that ushered in the erosion of civil liberties, the implementation of authoritarian policies, the use of torture, detention without trial and years of bloodshed.

The Chilean *coup* was part of the ideological Cold War that had developed between the United States and the Soviet Union as each vied to shape the world after 1945. Though initially focused on Europe, throughout the 1950s and 1960s this confrontation manifested itself in proxy wars and *coups* across Asia, Africa and Latin America. As communism grew in strength across the Third World, the United States responded by intervening in wars in Korea (1950–53), Laos (1953–75), Vietnam (1959–75), the Congo (1960–66) and Namibia and Angola (1966–89), and instigating or supporting *coups* in Iran (1953), Guatemala (1954) and Iraq (1963) and a failed *coup* in Cuba (1959). Others conflicts, such as the Malayan Emergency (1948–60), the Arab–Israeli conflict (1948 to the present) and the Suez crisis (1956), took place against the backdrop of the confrontation between the Soviet Union and the United States. As this process continued, internal unrest and conflict between left- and right-wing political groups was developing in Chile, a country with strong economic links to the United States. By the time

Allende came to power in a close-run election in 1970 as the head of the left-wing coalition Unidad Popular (Popular Unity), the Cold War confrontation meant that Chile would not be allowed to control its own destiny.

A few months before the election, Henry Kissinger, then National Security Adviser to Richard Nixon, had told the secret 40 Committee of the National Security Council: 'I don't see why we need to stand by and watch a country go communist due to the irresponsibility of its own people. The issues are much too important for the Chilean voters to be left to decide for themselves.'[13] In doing so he managed to undermine Chilean democracy and sovereignty in a single patronising statement. He also managed to secure an increase in funding for the anti-Allende campaign that the CIA was already running in Chile – a campaign that included spreading propaganda, creating anti-communist media organisations, providing financial support to opposition political parties and developing assets within the Socialist Party and senior levels of the government. In October 1970, after Allende had won the election but before he had been inaugurated, the CIA instigated an attempted military *coup* under direct instructions from Nixon that Allende should not be allowed to take power. The *coup* failed but General René Schneider, the constitutionalist head of the army, was killed resisting a kidnap attempt by one of the groups of plotters.[14]

Despite the CIA campaign against him, Allende won the election and was confirmed as President, in part thanks to Soviet financial support through the KGB.[15] It was his fourth attempt for the presidency and his success made him the world's first democratically elected Marxist leader. Although he was largely opposed by Congress, the civil service and the judiciary he embarked upon a programme of what has been called socialism by democratic means (as opposed to authoritarian bureaucracy), restructuring Chilean society along socialist lines while respecting democratic principles and the rule of law. However, his Marxist policies caused concern among Chilean conservatives and the United States was alarmed by his close ties with the Soviet Union and Cuba. After some initial success, his nationalisation of industries and wide-reaching land-reform programmes eventually led to high inflation and a drop in crop production, the effects of which were hugely worsened by American economic sanctions and CIA propaganda. As a result, discontent with Allende's regime slowly grew within certain sections of the Chilean population and in the military in particular.

The CIA's activities in Chile were not unusual in the context of US policy towards Latin America during the Cold War. Following the rise to power of Fidel Castro in Cuba in the 1950s, the United States developed a two-track approach to halting the spread of Soviet-backed communism to other countries in the region. Malnutrition, low literacy rates, unemployment and poor housing were believed to create fertile breeding grounds for communism, so America's Track I response was to hugely increase its economic and development assistance to Latin-American governments. For Chile, this meant over a billion dollars in direct aid between 1962 and 1969 – more aid per capita than any other country in the region.[16] However, the United States' second response was far more insidious. Track II involved covert action and other CIA clandestine activities and the training of Latin-American armed forces in counter-insurgency techniques. In Chile, this amounted to over thirty covert action projects between 1961 and 1974. As the US senate Church committee concluded, the United States also sought to directly influence Chilean presidential and congressional elections: 'Covert American activity was a factor in almost every major election in Chile in the decade between 1963 and 1973. In several instances the United States' intervention was massive.'[17]

The first nine months of 1973 saw strikes by miners, doctors, teachers, shopkeepers, students and truck, bus and taxi owners. In June, a rebel tank regiment entered downtown Santiago and attacked the presidential palace and defence ministry before troops loyal to the government forced it to surrender. Civil unrest increased and there were almost daily outbreaks of violence between left- and right-wing groups. On 22 August, the Council of Deputies called upon the armed forces to restore constitutional order (the Supreme Court had by that time already denounced Allende's government). The next day, General Carlos Prats resigned as the Defence Minister and head of the army and Allende named General Augusto Pinochet as the new commander-in-chief.

Then on the morning of 11 September, Pinochet, Admiral José Merino of the navy, the head of the air force General Gustavo Leigh and

General César Mendoza of the Carabineros (the national police) launched a *coup* against the government. Allende and his supporters retreated to La Moneda, the presidential palace, where together with his bodyguards they prepared to defend themselves. As tanks and infantry surrounded the palace, Allende made his final address to the nation via a telephone broadcast through the communist Radio Magallanes, the only station not under the control of the junta. He told those listening that he would not resign and would continue his constitutional duty as President even if it cost him his life. In doing so he was sure that his sacrifice would not be in vain and that it would 'be a moral lesson that will punish felony, cowardice and treason'. He recognised that 'foreign capital [and] imperialism . . . created the climate in which the armed forces broke their tradition' and accused those members of the military involved in the *coup* of betraying their oaths to protect Chile. Tanks and troops then attacked the palace. Shortly afterwards an aerial bombardment left the palace badly damaged and in flames.

Allende committed suicide a few hours after making his final address. He asked his supporters to lay down their weapons and surrender, and as fighter jets and tanks pounded La Moneda he reportedly went and sat in the Independence Hall and shot himself using an AK-47 assault rifle that had been a gift from Castro and bore the inscription: 'To my good friend Salvador from Fidel, who by different means tries to achieve the same goals.'[18] For years afterwards many refused to believe the official version of events, assuming instead that he had been killed defending La Moneda. However, it is now generally accepted that he took his own life as troops stormed the palace.[19] Around forty of his supporters were arrested at the palace, half of whom were executed two days later. In the weeks that followed, many of his remaining supporters were imprisoned or killed and his family and other associates were sent into exile. The *coup* leaders named Pinochet as permanent head of the military junta and instituted tight authoritarian controls, which included banning political parties, halting political activity, suspending the constitution and censoring the press.

CIA covert actions and contact with potential *coup* leaders within the military had continued throughout the early 1970s but no evidence has yet come to light that the United States was directly involved in formulating the successful *coup* of 1973. However, the American government did have prior knowledge of the plot and had encouraged and supported its leaders through US actions over the years.[20] Within days of the *coup*, the CIA was reporting human rights abuses by the junta.[21] None of this worried the US government, though, and in 1975 the Church committee concluded that the goal of covert action immediately following the *coup* was to 'assist the junta in gaining a more positive image, both at home and abroad' and to use CIA-controlled media outlets to present the junta 'in the most positive light for the Chilean public'.[22]

In his final address Allende said, 'Workers of my country, I have faith in Chile and its destiny. Other men will overcome this dark and bitter moment when treason seeks to prevail. Go forward knowing that, sooner rather than later, the great avenues will open again where free men will walk to build a better society.' However, it took nearly two decades for democracy to be restored to his country. Pinochet appointed himself President of Chile in December 1974 and remained in office until he stepped down in March 1990 (although he remained commander-in-chief of the army for another eight years). During his dictatorship at least three thousand people are thought to have been killed and close to thirty thousand tortured, although the actual numbers may never be known.[23] From the late 1990s onwards, Pinochet was hounded by arrest and legal proceedings in Europe and Chile, but he successfully evaded conviction and died while under house arrest on 10 December 2006, two weeks after his ninety-first birthday. During this period one of his staunchest supporters was the former British Prime Minister, Margaret Thatcher. Pinochet had provided secret assistance to the British during the 1982 Falklands War against Argentina and the two leaders greatly admired one another – a relationship that generated some controversy in the UK.[24] In the end, Pinochet was never held accountable for the serious human-rights abuses that occurred during his dictatorship – despite publicly assuming political responsibility for all that happened.[25] The American policymakers and intelligence agents who had helped lay the foundations for Pinochet's regime have also never been held accountable.

The United States is often unfairly singled out when others are equally at fault and too much of the criticism is simple anti-Americanism.

Many countries exert control over neighbouring states and regional spheres of influence for national-security purposes or maintain overseas territories for strategic or economic reasons. European states – including Spain, Portugal, Britain, France, the Netherlands, Germany and Belgium – expanded their empires through hundreds of years of colonialism; the Ottoman Empire spanned three continents and lasted over six centuries until 1923; China has intervened across its region, including in Russia, Korea and Vietnam, and continues to annex Tibet and threaten Taiwan; and during the Cold War the Soviet Union exerted influence throughout the Third World and the countries of the Eastern Bloc, and Russia continues to do so today in neighbouring countries such as Ukraine and Georgia. Interference also occurs through economic neo-colonialism and various non-state actors, from multinational corporations to international terrorist movements (as well as through potentially more benign mechanisms such as humanitarian interventions).

However, no country in recent history has interfered in the affairs of others more than the United States, and much of the criticism of this is well founded and justified. Since World War II, the US military and CIA have intervened dozens of times in countries in every region of the world, often with disastrous consequences. As the world's largest economic and military power – the single remaining superpower – the United States continues to act in its own interests, with Iraq, Afghanistan and Iran the most recent examples of its political or military interference. But with that power comes a responsibility to be a wise and restrained international player and to resist the temptation to deny other peoples their autonomy, sovereignty and, above all, dignity. Allende's thoughts on the 1973 Chilean *coup* leaders could apply just as readily to today's American political and military machine: 'They have strength and will be able to dominate us, but social processes can be arrested neither by crime nor force. History is ours, and people make history.'

Palacio de La Moneda, Santiago, Chile

My friends.

Surely this will be the last opportunity for me to address you. The air force has bombed the towers of Radio Portales and Radio Corporación.

My words do not have bitterness but disappointment. May they be a moral punishment for those who have betrayed their oath: soldiers of Chile, titular commanders in chief, Admiral Merino, who has designated himself commander of the navy, and Mr Mendoza, the despicable general who only yesterday pledged his fidelity and loyalty to the government, and who also has appointed himself chief of the Carabineros.

Given these facts, the only thing left for me is to say to workers: I am not going to resign!

Placed in a historic transition, I will pay for loyalty to the people with my life. And I say to them that I am certain that the seed which we have planted in the good conscience of thousands and thousands of Chileans will not be shrivelled forever.

They have strength and will be able to dominate us, but social processes can be arrested neither by crime nor force. History is ours, and people make history.

Workers of my country: I want to thank you for the loyalty that you always had, the confidence that you deposited in a man who was only an interpreter of great yearnings for justice, who gave his word that he would respect the constitution and the law and did just that. At this definitive moment, the last moment when I can address you, I wish you to take advantage of the lesson: foreign capital, imperialism, together with the reaction, created the climate in which the armed forces broke their tradition, the tradition taught by General Schneider and reaffirmed by Commander

❝ Placed in a historic transition, I will pay for loyalty to the people with my life. ❞

Araya, victims of the same social sector which will today be in their homes hoping, with foreign assistance, to retake power to continue defending their profits and their privileges.

I address, above all, the modest woman of our land, the *campesina* who believed in us, the worker who laboured more, the mother who knew our concern for children. I address professionals of Chile, patriotic professionals, those who days ago continued working against the sedition sponsored by professional associations, class-based associations that also defended the advantages which a capitalist society grants to a few.

I address the youth, those who sang and gave us their joy and their spirit of struggle. I address the man of Chile, the worker, the farmer, the intellectual, those who will be persecuted, because in our country fascism has been already present for many hours – in terrorist attacks, blowing up the bridges, cutting the railroad tracks, destroying the oil and gas pipelines, in the face of the silence of those who had the obligation to protect them. They were committed. History will judge them.

Surely Radio Magallanes will be silenced, and the calm metal instrument of my voice will no longer reach you. It does not matter. You will continue hearing it. I will always be next to you. At least my memory will be that of a man of dignity who was loyal to the workers.

The people must defend themselves, but they must not sacrifice themselves. The people must not let themselves be destroyed or riddled with bullets, but they cannot be humiliated either.

Workers of my country, I have faith in Chile and its destiny. Other men will overcome this dark and bitter moment when treason seeks to prevail. Go forward knowing that, sooner rather than later, the great avenues will open again where free men will walk to build a better society.

Long live Chile! Long live the people! Long live the workers!

These are my last words, and I am certain that my sacrifice will not be in vain, I am certain that, at the very least, it will be a moral lesson that will punish felony, cowardice and treason.

The Falklands Factor

– Margaret Thatcher –

'We have apparently reliable evidence that an Argentine task force could be assembling off Stanley at dawn tomorrow. You will wish to make your dispositions accordingly.'[26] This very British telegram arrived at Government House on the Falkland Islands at 3.30 p.m. on 1 April 1982. It was the only warning that Governor Rex Hunt received of an imminent Argentine invasion of the British overseas territory. By early the next morning, Hunt and Major Mike Norman had managed to mobilise a small force of around a hundred men – mostly Royal Marines, together with eleven Royal Navy sailors, a small group of civilian volunteers and two dozen members of the local volunteer Falkland Islands Defence Force. There was fierce fighting around the capital Stanley and when Argentine troops attacked the governor's residence the former RAF fighter pilot armed himself with a 9mm handgun and prepared to defend his office.[27] In the end the defenders managed to repel the attack on Government House but by then it was obvious that they could not resist the overwhelming Argentine forces. Hunt assumed military command and surrendered to the Argentinian commander at 9.30 a.m. The governor and captured Royal Marines were flown off the islands later that day and many of the local defence force members were placed under house arrest. From the Argentine perspective, Operación Rosario to liberate Las Malvinas from British occupation had been a success.

The Falkland Islands – known as Las Malvinas in Argentina – are a cold and windswept archipelago in the South Atlantic Ocean consisting of the two main islands of East and West Falkland and hundreds of smaller islands, covering a total area of 4,700 square miles. They lie three hundred miles off the east coast of southern Argentina and are today home to around three thousand people, mostly of British birth or descent.[28] The islands are a self-governing British overseas territory but have a long and complex colonial history. They were first sighted by European explorers in the sixteenth century, although the first landing did not occur until 1690 – when an English ship sailing to southern Argentina was driven off course by headwinds. From 1764 onwards, France, Spain and Britain all built settlements on the islands, claiming sovereignty over all or parts of them. In 1820, the newly independent Argentina (or the Provincias Unidas as it was called then) claimed ownership over the islands following the withdrawal of the last of the colonial powers. However, a decade later the United States destroyed the settlement at Puerto Luis and declared the islands *res nullius* (belonging to no one) after a fishing dispute with the island's Argentinian governor. Britain reasserted its sovereignty in 1833 and established settlements at Port Louis and then Stanley. The islands have been the subject of a territorial dispute between Britain and Argentina ever since.[29] On 2 April 1982, Argentina sought to finally settle the issue using military force.

The next day, the British Prime Minister, Margaret Thatcher, told parliament that a naval task force was being prepared.[30] By this time, Argentine forces had also seized control of the Falkland dependencies of South Georgia and the South Sandwich Islands. On 5 April, the first ships of the British task force set sail from Portsmouth for the South Atlantic. Over a three-week period the task force grew to include two aircraft carriers, various other warships, dozens of logistics ships and their escorts and private ships requisitioned and converted into transport and hospital ships. Warships and nuclear-powered submarines that had been on exercises near Gibraltar had already been diverted to the region as an advance group. Over a hundred ships and twenty-eight thousand personnel were eventually involved in the British campaign.[31] On 20 April, the British government ordered the retaking of the Falkland Islands and ten days later a two-hundred-mile total exclusion zone was imposed around the islands. The task force arrived in the exclusion zone at the end of April.

What followed was a particularly bloody conflict. The British lost over thirty aircraft and seven ships, including HMS *Sheffield*, which was hit by an Exocet missile, killing twenty men. The Argentinians lost nearly a hundred aircraft and at least eight ships, including the ARA *General Belgrano*, which claimed three hundred and twenty-three lives when she was sunk outside the exclusion zone by a British submarine. British and Argentine ground forces fought fierce battles at Goose Green, Mount Longdon, Wireless Ridge, Mount Tumbledown and all the way to Stanley. In the end, the Argentine forces failed to hold the islands and the seventy-four-day conflict resulted in the loss of six hundred and forty-nine Argentinian and two hundred and fifty-five British personnel (and three civilians), with nearly two thousand men wounded. It was a vicious war and stories of bayonet charges, foreign mercenaries and executed prisoners persist to this day.[32] Nonetheless, Operation Corporate to liberate the Falklands from Argentine occupation was a success.

It was, however, one of the more futile conflicts in modern times. The Argentine junta sent ill-trained and poorly equipped teenage conscripts into battle against one of the most respected professional militaries in the world. The British government in turn sent a hastily deployed expeditionary force eight thousand miles with little chance of success due to the harsh operational conditions and numerical superiority of the Argentine forces. Peaceful negotiations might have eventually reached an agreement on the islands' status. Although the British government had been holding up prior negotiations, they had been looking for a formula that would gain the support of both parliament and the islanders.[33] So why was such a costly and unnecessary war fought?

Las Malvinas are an important part of Argentine national identity and are considered an integral part of its national territory. Argentina claims to be the regional heirs to the Spanish colonial owners and argues it has been denied sovereignty over the islands since the British occupation of 1833. Although there are some grounds for such a claim, they are not overwhelming given the islands' complex history and the islanders' repeatedly expressed wish to remain British. Nonetheless, the 1982 invasion received high levels of popular support in Argentina, which is precisely what the ruling junta had hoped for. The military had first come to power in 1976 in a *coup d'état* against President Isabel Perón. Years of state-sponsored violence against left-wing dissidents followed, with the loss of thousands of lives in what has become known as Argentina's Dirty War (which overlapped with the US-backed Operation Condor carried out by right-wing governments of South America against communist influence in the region). As the economy went into further decline, the junta suspended Congress and banned political parties and unions. Torture, kidnappings, executions and other human rights violations became the norm.

In December 1981, the commander-in-chief of the army, General Leopoldo Galtieri, took over as head of a new junta and de facto President. Galtieri was deeply unpopular during his first few months in power, which saw widespread civil unrest, demonstrations against the junta and demands for a return to democracy. In April 1982, in an attempt to divert public attention, he ordered the occupation of Las Malvinas, and the initial success of the operation led to patriotic demonstrations and an outpouring of support for his regime. The defeat in Las Malvinas eventually brought about the end of military rule in Argentina, but at the time it seemed almost inconceivable to Galtieri and the Argentine military that Britain would try to retake the islands once they had been occupied. In the preceding years, Britain had decided to remove its only patrol ship stationed in the area, continued selling arms to Argentina, implemented cuts in defence spending and limited the islanders' British citizenship.[34] The junta had not, however, counted on the reaction from Thatcher or the British public.

The British government could have responded diplomatically rather than militarily. They had the immediate backing of the majority of the UN Security Council, the European Economic Community and NATO; US Secretary of State Alexander Haig was brokering negotiations while the task force was still being deployed; even once the fighting started, several peace proposals were put forward by Peru and the United Nations. Norway, France, Chile and, eventually, the United States provided the British with crucial military and intelligence support, which could just as easily have been turned to further diplomatic support. However, Thatcher wanted to show that Britain was still a military power, with a leader who would stand firm against those who threatened British interests. For her it was an opportunity to lay the foundations for a more robust foreign policy than her predecessors had pursued. Britain fought, she argued, 'to show that aggression does not pay and that the robber cannot be allowed to get away with his swag'. The influence that senior naval commanders had on the decision to use force and on subsequent debates in Thatcher's war cabinet should also not be underestimated.[35]

Additionally, there were important domestic political reasons for Thatcher sending the task force. Chief among them was the fact that by early 1982 her government was deeply unpopular and Thatcher was receiving the lowest approval ratings of any Prime Minister since polling began.[36] If the task force had failed to recapture the Falklands it is possible that Thatcher would have been forced out. Instead, her robust response played well with the British public and the Falklands success, together with a recovering economy, ensured a landslide victory for her Conservative Party in the June 1983 elections.[37] While the Falklands conflict failed to shore up Galtieri's regime, it certainly helped save Thatcher's.

The conflict has become an important part of the British national psyche, seen as either the last throes of a dead empire or living proof that Britain still rules the waves. Thatcher was clear that it was the latter. Four weeks after the Argentine surrender she gave a key speech to a Conservative rally at Cheltenham Racecourse (an extract of which is reproduced in the following pages). She used the occasion to point her finger at 'the waverers and the fainthearts. The people who thought that Britain could no longer seize the initiative for herself. The people who thought we could no longer do the great things which we once did. Those who believed that our decline was irreversible – that we could never again be what we were.' She said that these people thought that Britain was 'no longer the nation that had built an Empire and ruled a quarter of the world'. The Falklands conflict, she argued, had proved them wrong and that Britain still had 'those sterling qualities which shine through our history'.

She recognised that 'When the demands of war and the dangers to our own people call us to arms – then we British are as we have always been: competent, courageous and resolute.' This is what she called the Falklands factor. But she lamented the fact that 'it took the demands of war for every stop to be pulled out and every man and woman to do their best'. She asked 'Why does it need a war to bring out our qualities and reassert our pride?' and 'Why can't we achieve in peace what we can do so well in war?' Unsurprisingly, Thatcher did not make this argument in order to encourage people to work just as hard for peace as for war. Instead, she tried to turn the Falklands factor to her own political advantage and use it against the train drivers, NHS workers, miners and others whose strike actions threatened her programmes for economic and social reform.

Thatcher had come to power in 1979, making history as Britain's first female Prime Minister. She helped define 1980s Britain and is one of the most controversial and divisive recent Prime Ministers. Her supporters point to a remarkable political career in which she reinvigorated Britain's foreign policy and placed Britain back on the world stage, paving the way for its involvement in future conflicts (the repercussions of which are being felt in Iraq and Afghanistan today). At home, she is said to have revived the economy and reformed outdated institutions. In doing so she faced down violent miners' strikes, survived an IRA bomb attack in Brighton, provoked the poll-tax riots that nearly saw the police lose control of central London, encouraged the deregulation and growth of the financial and service sectors and managed numerous cabinet rifts and internal party differences until they finally precipitated her resignation in November 1990. By the end of her premiership, she had won three general elections and served as Prime Minister for over eleven years. To her detractors, though, the Iron Lady represents a particularly uncaring form of conservative conviction politics. On domestic issues they criticise her attacks on the welfare state, the weakening of the trade unions and privatisation of state assets, and point to the high income inequality that occurred in Britain during the 1980s. On international issues they criticise her support for Augusto Pinochet, resistance to imposing economic sanctions on apartheid South Africa, hard-line stance against the Soviet Union and close alliance with conservative US President Ronald Reagan. One of the places she remains popular, though, is the Falkland Islands.

The islands have once more attracted international attention in recent years as both Argentina and Britain seek to lay claim to areas of the seabed beyond the traditional exclusive economic zone of two hundred nautical miles. Article 76 of the UN Convention on the Law of the Sea provides the criteria by which a coastal state may establish the outer limits of its continental shelf and the UN Commission on the Limits of the Continental Shelf was established to make recommendations in this respect. In April 2009, Argentina lodged a claim with the Commission for six hundred and sixty thousand square miles of the South Atlantic seabed, including areas surrounding the Falkland Islands and other nearby British overseas territories.[38] Three weeks later, and only days before the UN deadline expired, the UK presented a counter-claim for four hundred and sixty thousand square miles of the seabed surrounding the Falklands Islands, South Georgia and the South Sandwich Islands.[39] These mutually exclusive claims are important as their resolution may help confirm ownership over the islands and, perhaps more importantly, the untapped resources in the surrounding seabed, including large oil, gas and mineral reserves.

The reformed Argentine constitution of 1994 states that the recovery of the Falklands Islands, South Georgia and the South Sandwich Islands are a 'permanent and unrelinquished goal of the Argentine people'.[40] Though it says this will be carried out in a manner 'respectful of the way of life of their inhabitants and according to the principles of international law', the continental shelf and resource issues add a further dynamic. Argentinian President Cristina Fernández de Kirchner has indicated that Argentina is prepared to assert its claimed sovereignty and protect what it sees as its natural resources.[41] For their part, it is highly unlikely that the UK government will recognise the Argentine claims to sovereignty while the Falkland islanders wish to remain British. In June 2009, the Falklands government accused Argentina of waging an economic war against the islanders by deliberately hampering their fishing, tourism and oil and gas exploration industries.[42] The issue came to the fore again in February 2010 when a British oil rig began drilling sixty miles offshore from the Falkland Islands, once more raising the diplomatic tension between Argentina and Britain.[43]

If the 1982 Falklands conflict demonstrated anything, it is that these disputes must be settled through peaceful diplomatic means. Long-drawn-out negotiations are almost always preferable to short bloody wars. This is something that another long-serving British Prime Minister, Tony Blair, would have done well to understand during the conflicts that marked his premiership.

Cheltenham Racecourse, Gloucestershire, England

3 JULY 1982

Today we meet in the aftermath of the Falklands Battle. Our country has won a great victory and we are entitled to be proud. This nation had the resolution to do what it knew had to be done – to do what it knew was right.

We fought to show that aggression does not pay and that the robber cannot be allowed to get away with his swag. We fought with the support of so many throughout the world. The Security Council, the Commonwealth, the European Community and the United States. Yet we also fought alone – for we fought for our own people and for our own sovereign territory.

Now that it is all over, things cannot be the same again for we have learned something about ourselves – a lesson which we desperately needed to learn.

When we started out, there were the waverers and the fainthearts. The people who thought that Britain could no longer seize the initiative for herself.

The people who thought we could no longer do the great things which we once did. Those who believed that our decline was irreversible – that we could never again be what we were.

There were those who would not admit it – even perhaps some here today – people who would have strenuously denied the suggestion but – in their heart of hearts – they too had their secret fears that it was true: that Britain was no longer the nation that had built an Empire and ruled a quarter of the world.

Well, they were wrong. The lesson of the Falklands is that Britain has not changed and that this nation still has those sterling qualities which shine through our history.

This generation can match their fathers and grandfathers in ability, in courage, and in resolution. We have not changed. When the demands of war and the dangers to our own people call us to arms – then we British are as we have always been: competent, courageous and resolute.

When called to arms – ah, that's the problem.

It took the battle in the South Atlantic for the shipyards to adapt ships way ahead of time; for dockyards to refit merchantmen and cruise liners, to fix helicopter platforms, to convert hospital ships – all faster than was thought possible; it took the demands of war for every stop to be pulled out and every man and woman to do their best.

British people had to be threatened by foreign soldiers and British territory invaded and then – why then – the response was incomparable. Yet why does it need a war to bring out our qualities and reassert our pride? Why do we have to be invaded before we throw aside our selfish aims and begin to work together as only we can work and achieve as only we can achieve?

That, ladies and gentlemen, really is the challenge we as a nation face today. We have to see that the spirit of the South Atlantic – the real spirit of Britain – is kindled not only by war but can now be fired by peace.

We have the first prerequisite. We know we can do it – we haven't lost the ability. That is the Falklands Factor. We have proved ourselves to ourselves. It is a lesson we must not now forget. Indeed it is a lesson which we must apply to peace just as we have learned it in war. The faltering and the self-doubt has given way to achievement and pride. We have the confidence and we must use it.

Just look at the Task Force as an object lesson. Every man had his own task to do and did it superbly. Officers and men, senior NCO and newest recruit – every one realised that his contribution was essential for the success of the whole. All were equally valuable – each was differently qualified.

By working together – each was able to do more than his best. As a team they raised the average to the level of the best and by each doing his utmost together they achieved the impossible. That's an accurate picture of Britain at war – not yet of Britain at peace. But the spirit has stirred and the nation has begun to assert itself. Things are not going to be the same again.

All over Britain, men and women are asking – why can't we achieve in peace what we can do so well in war?

> **“** When the **demands** of **war** and the **dangers to our own people call us to arms** – then we British are as we have always been: **competent, courageous** and **resolute**. **”**

And they have good reason to ask.

Look what British Aerospace workers did when their Nimrod aeroplane needed major modifications. They knew that only by mid-air refuelling could the Task Force be properly protected. They managed those complicated changes from drawing board to airworthy planes in sixteen days – one year faster than would normally have been the case.

Achievements like that, if made in peacetime, could establish us as aeroplane makers to the world.

That record performance was attained not only by superb teamwork, but by brilliant leadership in our factories at home which mirrored our forces overseas. It is one of the abiding elements of our success in the South Atlantic that our troops were superbly led. No praise is too high for the quality and expertise of our commanders in the field.

Their example, too, must be taken to heart. Now is the time for management to lift its sights and to lead with the professionalism and effectiveness it knows is possible.

If the lessons of the South Atlantic are to be learned, then they have to be learned by us all. No one can afford to be left out. Success depends upon all of us – different in qualities, but equally valuable.

During this past week, I have read again a little-known speech of Winston Churchill, made just after the last war. This is what he said:

'We must find the means and the method of working together not only in times of war, and mortal anguish, but in times of peace, with all its bewilderments and clamour and clatter of tongues.'

Thirty-six years on, perhaps we are beginning to re-learn the truth which Churchill so clearly taught us.

We saw the signs when, this week, the NUR came to understand that its strike on the railways and on the Underground just didn't fit – didn't match

> **" We know we can do it –
> we haven't lost the ability.
> That is the Falklands Factor.
> We have proved ourselves
> to ourselves. "**

the spirit of these times. And yet on Tuesday, eight men, the leaders of ASLEF, misunderstanding the new mood of the nation, set out to bring the railways to a halt.*

Ignoring the example of the NUR, the travelling public whom they are supposed to serve, and the jobs and future of their own members, this tiny group decided to use its undoubted power for what? – to delay Britain's recovery, which all our people long to see.

Yet we can remember that on Monday, nearly a quarter of the members of NUR turned up for work.

Today, we appeal to every train driver to put his family, his comrades, and his country first, by continuing to work tomorrow. That is the true solidarity which can save jobs and which stands in the proud tradition of British railwaymen.

But it is not just on the railways that we need to find the means and the method of working together. It is just as true in the NHS. All who work there are caring, in one way or another, for the sick.

To meet their needs we have already offered to the ancillary workers almost exactly what we have given to our armed forces and to our teachers, and more than our Civil Servants have accepted. All of us know that there is a limit to what every employer can afford to pay out in wages. The increases proposed for nurses and ancillary workers in the Health Service are the maximum which the government can afford to pay.

And we can't avoid one unchallengeable truth. The government has no money of its own. All that it has it takes in taxes or borrows at interest. It's all of you – everyone here – that pays.

Of course, there is another way. Instead of taking money from our people openly, in taxation or loans, we can take it surreptitiously, by subterfuge. We can print money in order to pay out of higher inflation what we dare not tax and cannot borrow.

But that disreputable method is no longer open to us. Rightly this government has abjured it. Increasingly this nation won't have it. Our people are now confident enough to face the facts of life. There is a new mood of realism in Britain.

That too is part of the Falklands Factor.

The battle of the South Atlantic was not won by ignoring the dangers or denying the risks.

* The National Union of Railwaymen (NUR) and the Associated Society of Locomotive Engineers and Firemen (ASLEF) are two of the main railway unions in Britain.

&& We faced them squarely and we were determined to **overcome**. That is increasingly the **mood** of Britain. **,,**

It was achieved by men and women who had no illusions about the difficulties. We faced them squarely and we were determined to overcome. That is increasingly the mood of Britain. And that's why the rail strike won't do.

We are no longer prepared to jeopardise our future just to defend manning practices agreed in 1919 when steam engines plied the tracks of the Grand Central Railway and the motor car had not yet taken over from the horse.

What has indeed happened is that now once again Britain is not prepared to be pushed around.

We have ceased to be a nation in retreat.

We have instead a new-found confidence – born in the economic battles at home and tested and found true eight thousand miles away.

That confidence comes from the re-discovery of ourselves, and grows with the recovery of our self-respect.

And so today, we can rejoice at our success in the Falklands and take pride in the achievement of the men and women of our Task Force.

But we do so, not as at some last flickering of a flame which must soon be dead. No – we rejoice that Britain has rekindled that spirit which has fired her for generations past and which today has begun to burn as brightly as before.

Britain found herself again in the South Atlantic and will not look back from the victory she has won.

Doctrine of the International Community

– TONY BLAIR –

T ony Blair came to power in 1997 on a wave of public optimism. His charisma and persuasive charm were the antithesis of the tired Conservative government that New Labour replaced seven years after the departure of Margaret Thatcher. At first he was considered by many to be a foreign-policy lightweight. However, by the time he left Downing Street ten years later, he had become Britain's longest-serving Labour Prime Minister and had taken the country to war five times.[44] His wars began with air strikes against Iraq in 1998, which were quickly followed by the NATO bombing of Yugoslavia during the Kosovo war a year later and the deployment of British soldiers to Sierra Leone in 2000. However, it was the post-9/11 invasions and on-going conflicts in Afghanistan from 2001 and Iraq from 2003 that caused the greatest controversy. The only factor linking these five conflicts was that they were not wars of necessity: none of the countries involved posed a direct threat to British security.

Much of the thinking behind Blair's use of military force was first laid out in a speech to the Economic Club of Chicago on 22 April 1999. This was during the NATO air strikes against Slobodan Milošević's military apparatus in Yugoslavia, and in his speech Blair argued that 'The most pressing foreign policy problem we face is to identify the circumstances in which we should get actively involved in other people's conflicts.' He characterised his thinking as a 'doctrine of the international community'. By this he meant 'the explicit recognition that today more than ever before we are mutually dependent, that national interest is to a significant extent governed by international collaboration'. It was a direct call for the United States to remain outward-looking and engaged with the world and to resist the temptation of isolationism (a theme that would remain central to Blair's dealings with the United States throughout his premiership).

This was a broad-ranging speech. It covered the globalisation of economics, politics and security and called for the reform of international institutions in order to better reflect post-Cold War realities. He addressed the aims of the NATO involvement in the Kosovo war, the Asian financial crisis of the previous year, the need to assist in reforming Russia's economy and the domestic agenda of his New Labour government. But it was the application of his doctrine to international security and humanitarian intervention that the speech is remembered for.

Blair called upon the idea of a war based on values rather than territorial ambitions. While he pointed out that the principle of non-interference in another country should not be rejected too readily, he argued that it must be qualified in certain important respects – for example, acts of genocide should never be considered purely internal matters. When deciding when and where to intervene, he proposed five considerations: Are we sure of our case? Have we exhausted all diplomatic options? Are there military operations we can sensibly and prudently undertake? Are we prepared for the long term? And do we have national interests involved?

This is actually a more fundamental change in the way that states engage with each other than it at first sounds. In making this argument he was essentially updating hundreds of years of 'just war' theory, moving beyond the notion of independent sovereign states and calling for a significant revision of the UN Charter. He was not, however, the first to do this: the French politician Bernard Kouchner made similar arguments for humanitarian intervention in the late 1980s and early 1990s. Nor was he the last: the International Commission on Intervention and State Sovereignty called for an international 'responsibility to protect' in its important 2001 report.[45]

Although it was Professor Sir Lawrence Freedman who purportedly provided the intellectual backbone of this part of the Chicago speech, it was Blair who coined the phrase 'doctrine of international community'.[46] Blair's doctrine suffered from some fundamental difficulties. First, who are the international community? All too often the 'international community' looks like nothing more than a small group of Western governments attempting to impose their will on others. Secondly, whose values are being upheld? The values should relate to those rights accorded to people under the large body of international human rights law, not those values that the so-called international community has held up, sometimes legitimately and sometimes not, as ad hoc explanations for the use of military force. The problem remained that any force with the power to intervene outside of the UN could have interests that extended beyond the cessation of genocide and the liberation of the oppressed. Not only were Blair's criteria for intervention too weak to divorce humanitarianism from imperialism (in terms of both its intention and application), but his version of intervention seemed to emphasise military intervention and then only as a reactive measure. As Blair himself recognised, there are also diplomatic and economic measures that can be used. In addition, very little attention was paid to preventing these crises in the first place, and it looked like intervention would only be exercised by the strong against the weak.[47]

Many of these dilemmas became abundantly clear when it came to the invasion of Iraq in 2003. The removal of Saddam Hussein – singled out alongside Milošević in Blair's speech – was supposed to bring freedom to the Iraqi people and make the world a safer place by destroying Iraq's weapons of mass destruction, combating terrorism and bringing greater stability to the Middle East. First, the invasion created a humanitarian disaster and led to the violent deaths of well over one hundred thousand Iraqi civilians (although the exact figure is unknown and likely to be much higher).[48] Secondly, there were no weapons of mass destruction. Thirdly, Iraq now serves as a rallying call to radicalised individuals and groups around the world and the country itself has become a combat training zone for jihadist paramilitaries. Fourthly, the invasion has greatly added to instability in the region, the repercussions of which will be felt for decades.

However, none of the publicly stated reasons for the invasion were entirely true. Nor was it simply about controlling Iraq's oil, as many suspected. The real aim was regime change: to bring about a market-based democracy in the heart of the Middle East and governed under the control of the United States, which would act as a warning to other countries in the region – particularly Iran and Syria – that might try to resist Western influence or threaten US interests. Post-invasion Iraq was to become the linchpin in neoconservative efforts to reshape the oil-rich Middle East – a beacon of democracy in an otherwise troubled region.

The invasion of Iraq failed to meet any of the five criteria for intervention that Blair had set out in his Chicago speech. Yet he is reported to have written a private letter to George Bush in July 2002 containing the opening line: 'You know, George, whatever you decide to do, I'm with you.'[49] So why did Blair stake his political future – and the lives of British soldiers – on supporting this very American strategy? Put simply, it is highly likely that he actually agreed with the strategy and, in any case, believed Saddam Hussein to be a truly evil man who had to be removed from power, whether he had weapons of mass destruction or not. Blair's thinking had shifted significantly in the years since Chicago, not least because of 9/11. His focus was no longer on intervention on humanitarian grounds but on intervention in order to counter actual or perceived threats to national and international security. He would later say that 9/11 changed 'the calculus of risk': risks and threats became conflated in his mind.[50] He was one of the first leaders to intuitively understand the true impact of 9/11 on global security and US strategy. At the Labour party conference on 2 October 2001, he declared: 'This is a moment to seize. The kaleidoscope has been shaken. The pieces are in flux. Soon they will settle again. Before they do, let us reorder this world around us.'[51] He wanted to maintain, at almost any cost, the special relationship Britain is supposed to enjoy with the United States in order to influence that reordering. Blair then later allowed himself to believe the intelligence – and increasingly his own spin – that indicated Saddam Hussein might be trying to develop weapons of mass destruction.

Blair was so firm in his conviction that removing Saddam Hussein was the right thing to do that he did not let the facts, and other people's interpretation of them, interfere with his judgement. Politicians, Foreign

Office officials, military chiefs, academics, Middle East experts and the court of public opinion were all telling him not to send British troops into Iraq. That the British public opposed the war did not matter; he thought that he could turn public opinion around – as if democracy was, in his mind, based on the persuasive skills of the Prime Minister rather than the will of the people. When he could not change their minds he eventually ignored them and instead listened to those on both sides of the Atlantic who were telling him what he wanted to hear.

It is clear that the invasion of Iraq has not made the world a safer place and has actually threatened Britain's security (as demonstrated by the suicide bombings in London on 7 July 2005 and the failed attacks two weeks later, as well as the attempted car bombings in London on 29 June 2007 and the attack on Glasgow airport the following day). For Blair it was an error of almost unforgivable magnitude and a decision of dubious legality. However, the vast majority of the cabinet, parliament, civil service and military command either supported or did not resist his strategy, in what must be one of the greatest ever failings of the British political system. In fact, many commentators consider it to have been the worst foreign-policy disaster since the Suez Crisis, over fifty years ago. While others have expressed their regret, Blair still stands by his decision to send troops to Iraq – holding firm to his belief that he did the right thing.

Towards the end of 2009, the official Iraq inquiry began hearing public evidence in London relating to the period leading up to the invasion of Iraq. The evidence confirmed many of the worst suspicions about Blair's deceit in the build-up to the war, including an early commitment to Bush that Britain would join the invasion, political interference in Ministry of Defence logistic preparations and support for regime change whether Iraq had weapons of mass destruction or not.[52] Blair attempted to recast the debate during his own evidence, telling the committee that 'this isn't about a lie or a conspiracy or a deceit or a deception, it is a decision'.[53] In other words, question his judgement but not his character. Few were convinced and Blair continues to be hounded for his actions.

On 27 June 2007, the day that he resigned as Prime Minister, Blair was appointed as the official envoy of the Quartet on the Middle East, acting on behalf of the UN, EU, the United States and Russia, in relation to various Palestinian issues. Then at the end of 2009, when the Lisbon treaty was finally ratified by all twenty-seven EU member states, he initially looked set to become the first permanent President of Europe. Although in the end he proved to be too divisive a figure for the role, Blair looks likely to remain on the international stage for some time to come. However, his doctrine of the international community has been left in tatters by his own actions. The invasion of Iraq has ensured that it will be some time before the issue of military intervention for purely humanitarian ends can be sensibly discussed again. In the meantime, those people in need of help may be left waiting.

Economic Club of Chicago, United States

22 APRIL 1999

It is a great pleasure to be here in Chicago this evening and addressing the Economic Club. My thanks to your chairman, Phil Rooney, and your President, Grace Barry. My thanks too to Mayor Daley for your kindness in welcoming me here.

I must start this evening by saying, on behalf of the British people, how saddened we are by the tragic events in Littleton on Tuesday.* For us it brings back sad memories of a school tragedy of our own on 13 March 1996 in a small town called Dunblane in Scotland when sixteen children and a teacher died in a hail of bullets. From us in Britain to you here in the United States: we offer you our deepest sympathy, our thoughts and our prayers.

I am absolutely delighted to be the first serving British Prime Minister to visit Chicago. I wanted to come here to the heart of this great country. To a great cosmopolitan city and the capital of middle America.

Despite the absence of prime ministerial visits, there is a long British history with Chicago. We set up our Consulate here in 1855.

---

* On 20 April 1999, Dylan Klebold and Eric Harris, two high-school seniors, killed thirteen people at Columbine High School near Littleton, Colorado, before committing suicide.

Marshall Field opened their first overseas buying office in Manchester in 1870. One of Field's shop assistants subsequently opened his own store in London in 1909. His name was Harry Selfridge. He employed the same architect who designed your City Hall to build Selfridges, the landmark store on London's Oxford Street.

That sort of interchange goes on today too. Chicagoland is the headquarters of some of Britain's most important inward investors: Motorola, Sara Lee, RR Donnelly. Nearly half the $124 billion US firms spent on foreign acquisitions last year went on British companies. We would like it to be even more.

Nor is the traffic all one way. British investment in Illinois generates some forty-six thousand jobs, making us the biggest foreign investor in the state. And the London Futures Exchange is working alongside your Board of Trade and Mercantile Exchange to lead the revolution in electronic trading. The London Futures Exchange looks forward to receiving early CFTC approval for its system to be installed here.[*]

Kosovo

While we meet here in Chicago this evening, unspeakable things are happening in Europe. Awful crimes that we never thought we would see again have reappeared – ethnic cleansing, systematic rape, mass murder.

I want to speak to you this evening about events in Kosovo. But I want to put these events in a wider context – economic, political and security – because I do not believe Kosovo can be seen in isolation.

No one in the West who has seen what is happening in Kosovo can doubt that NATO's military action is justified. Bismarck famously said the Balkans were not worth the bones of one Pomeranian grenadier. Anyone who has seen the tear-stained faces of the hundreds of thousands of refugees streaming across the border, heard their heart-rending tales of cruelty or contemplated the unknown fates of those left behind knows that Bismarck was wrong.

This is a just war, based not on any territorial ambitions but on values. We cannot let the evil of ethnic cleansing stand. We must not rest until it is reversed. We have learned twice before in this century that appeasement does not work. If we let an evil dictator range unchallenged, we will have to spill infinitely more blood and treasure to stop him later.

But people want to know not only that we are right to take this action but

---

[*] CFTC: The US Commodity Futures Trading Commission.

66 This is a just war, based not on any territorial ambitions but on values. 99

also that we have clear objectives and that we are going to succeed.

We have five objectives: a verifiable cessation of all combat activities and killings; the withdrawal of Serb military, police and paramilitary forces from Kosovo; the deployment of an international military force; the return of all refugees and unimpeded access for humanitarian aid; and a political framework for Kosovo building on the Rambouillet accords.* We will not negotiate on these aims. Milošević must accept them.

Through the air campaign, we have destroyed the greater part of Milošević's operational air force; a quarter of his SAM radar systems – the rest do not operate for fear of being destroyed; his oil refineries and the lines of communication into Kosovo; his military infrastructure including his means of command and communication; and a good part of his ammunition dumps. The morale of the Yugoslav army is beginning to crack. And the KLA is now larger and has more support than when Milošević started his campaign. ‡

We have always made clear this campaign will take time. We will not have succeeded until an international force has entered Kosovo and allowed the refugees to return to their homes. Milošević will have no veto on the entry of this international force.

Just as I believe there was no alternative to military action, now it has started I am convinced there is no alternative to continuing until we succeed. On its fiftieth birthday NATO must prevail. Milošević had, I believe, convinced himself that the alliance would crack. But I am certain that this weekend's Summit in Washington under President Clinton's leadership will make our unity and our absolute resolve clear for all to see. Success is the only exit strategy I am prepared to consider.

We need to begin work now on what comes after our success in Kosovo. We will need a new Marshall plan for Kosovo, Montenegro, Macedonia, Albania and Serbia too if it turns to democracy. We need a new framework for the security of the whole of the Balkans. And we will need to assist the

* The Rambouillet accords formed an interim agreement over Kosovo that NATO attempted to impose on Yugoslavia.
‡ KLA: Kosovo Liberation Army (Ushtria Çlirimtare e Kosovës).

war crimes tribunal in its work to bring to justice those who have committed these appalling crimes.

This evening I want to step back and look at what is happening in Kosovo in a wider context.

Global Interdependence

Twenty years ago we would not have been fighting in Kosovo. We would have turned our backs on it. The fact that we are engaged is the result of a wide range of changes – the end of the Cold War; changing technology; the spread of democracy. But it is bigger than that.

I believe the world has changed in a more fundamental way. Globalisation has transformed our economies and our working practices. But globalisation is not just economic – it is also a political and security phenomenon.

We live in a world where isolationism has ceased to have a reason to exist. By necessity we have to cooperate with each other across nations.

Many of our domestic problems are caused on the other side of the world. Financial instability in Asia destroys jobs in Chicago and in my own constituency in County Durham. Poverty in the Caribbean means more drugs on the streets in Washington and London. Conflict in the Balkans causes more refugees in Germany and here in the US. These problems can only be addressed by international cooperation.

We are all internationalists now, whether we like it or not. We cannot refuse to participate in global markets if we want to prosper. We cannot ignore new political ideas in other countries if we want to innovate. We cannot turn our backs on conflicts and the violation of human rights within other countries if we want still to be secure.

On the eve of a new millennium we are now in a new world. We need new rules for international cooperation and new ways of organising our international institutions.

After World War II, we developed a series of international institutions to cope with the strains of rebuilding a devastated world: Bretton Woods, the United Nations, NATO, the EU.* Even then, it was clear that the world was

---

* In July 1944, delegates from the Allied countries met in Bretton Woods, New Hampshire, to agree a system of rules and institutions to regulate commercial and financial relations among the world's industrialised countries. This included establishing the International Bank for Reconstruction and Development (which became part of the World Bank) and the International Monetary Fund.

" We are all internationalists now,
whether we like it or not. "

becoming increasingly interdependent. The doctrine of isolationism had been a casualty of a world war, where the United States and others finally realised standing aside was not an option.

Today the impulse towards interdependence is immeasurably greater. We are witnessing the beginnings of a new doctrine of international community. By this I mean the explicit recognition that today more than ever before we are mutually dependent, that national interest is to a significant extent governed by international collaboration and that we need a clear and coherent debate as to the direction this doctrine takes us in each field of international endeavour. Just as within domestic politics, the notion of community – the belief that partnership and cooperation are essential to advance self-interest – is coming into its own; so it needs to find its own international echo. Global financial markets, the global environment, global security and disarmament issues: none of these can he solved without intense international cooperation.

As yet, however, our approach tends towards being ad hoc. There is a global financial crisis: we react, it fades; our reaction becomes less urgent. Kyoto can stimulate our conscience about environmental degradation but we need constant reminders to refocus on it. We are continually fending off the danger of letting wherever CNN roves be the cattle prod to take a global conflict seriously.

We need to focus in a serious and sustained way on the principles of the doctrine of international community and on the institutions that deliver them. This means:

1. In global finance, a thorough, far-reaching overhaul and reform of the system of international financial regulation. We should begin it at the G7 at Cologne.
2. A new push on free trade in the WTO with the new round beginning in Seattle this autumn.
3. A reconsideration of the role, workings and decision-making process of the UN, and in particular the UN Security Council.

4. For NATO, once Kosovo is successfully concluded, a critical examination of the lessons to be learnt, and the changes we need to make in organisation and structure.
5. In respect of Kyoto and the environment, far closer working between the main industrial nations and the developing world as to how the Kyoto targets can be met and the practical measures necessary to slow down and stop global warming, and
6. A serious examination of the issue of Third World debt, again beginning at Cologne.

In addition, the EU and US should prepare to make real step-change in working more closely together. Recent trade disputes have been a bad omen in this regard. We really are failing to see the bigger picture with disputes over the banana regime or hushkits or whatever else.* There are huge issues at stake in our cooperation. The EU and the US need each other and need to put that relationship above arguments that are ultimately not fundamental.

Now is the time to begin work in earnest on these issues. I know President Clinton will stand ready to give a lead on many of them. In Kosovo but on many other occasions, I have had occasion to be truly thankful that the United States has a president with his vision and steadfastness.

Globalisation

Globalisation is most obvious in the economic sphere. We live in a completely new world. Every day about one trillion dollars moves across the foreign exchanges, most of it in London. Here in Chicago the Mercantile Exchange and the Chicago Board of Trade contract is worth more than $1.2 billion per day.

Any government that thinks it can go it alone is wrong. If the markets don't like your policies they will punish you.

The same is true of trade. Protectionism is the swiftest road to poverty.

---

* In April 1999, the EU sought to reduce aircraft noise levels at regional airports by adopting a regulation imposing restrictions on the use of re-engineered or muffled aircraft registered in or flying into Europe. The United States argued that the technology and equipment primarily affected by the regulation – including 'hushkits', which are used to muffle noise on older aircraft – were largely produced by American companies and in retaliation the US Congress threatened to ban Concorde from US airspace.

Only by competing internationally can our companies and our economics grow and succeed. But it has to be an international system based on rules. That means accepting the judgements of international organisations even when you do not like them. And it means using the new trade round to be launched at Seattle to extend free trade.

The international financial system is not working as it should. The Asian financial crisis of last year, and the knock-on impact on Brazil demonstrate that.

The fact is that the Bretton Woods machinery was set up for the post-war world. The world has moved on. And we need to modernise the international financial architecture to make it appropriate for the new world.

The lesson of the Asian crisis is above all that it is better to invest in countries where you have openness, independent central banks, properly functioning financial systems and independent courts, where you do not have to bribe or rely on favours from those in power.

We have therefore proposed that we should make greater transparency the keystone of reform. Transparency about individual countries' economic policies through adherence to new codes of conduct on monetary and fiscal policy; about individual companies' financial positions through new internationally agreed accounting standards and a new code of corporate governance; and greater openness too about IMF and World Bank discussions and policies.

We also need improved financial supervision both in individual countries through stronger and more effective peer group reviews, and internationally through the foundation of a new Financial Stability Forum. And we need more effective ways of resolving crises, like that in Brazil. The new contingent credit line at the IMF will assist countries pursuing sensible economic reforms and prevent damaging contagion. But we should also think creatively about how the private sector can help to resolve short-term financial crises.

Secretary Rubin and Chancellor Gordon Brown both put forward ideas yesterday. They highlighted the progress already made on improving transparency and in developing internationally agreed standards, particularly for the financial sector. But both identified the key challenges going forward, including how to involve the private sector in the prevention and resolution of crises. G7 Finance Ministers will be discussing these issues next week. I want to see agreement on the key outstanding questions reached by the Cologne Summit.

I hope the Summit will go further too in the case of Russia. We simply cannot stand back and watch that great nation teeter on the brink of ruin. If it slides into the abyss, it will affect all of us. A democratic, outward-looking, prosperous Russia is of key importance to the West. We must not let our current differences set us on a route towards the mutual hostility and suspicion which has too often characterised our relationship in the past.

I very much hope that Russia and the IMF can reach an early agreement on a new programme to provide macro-economic stability, avoid hyper-inflation and encourage Russian companies and savers to keep their own money in the country. This however will only be a first step. I want to see a wider dialogue between Russia and the G7 focusing on all of the structural and legal reforms that are needed to improve the economic prospects for ordinary Russians. Russia is a unique economy with its own special problems and its own unique potential. We all need to build on the lessons of the last few years and develop a long-term strategy for reform that respects Russia's history, her culture and her aspirations. If Russia is prepared, with our understanding and cooperation, to take the difficult economic action it needs to reform its economy – to build a sound and well-regulated financial system, to restructure and close down bankrupt enterprises to develop and enforce a clear and fair legal system and to reduce the damage caused by nuclear waste – the G7 must be prepared to think imaginatively about how it can best support these efforts.

We will be putting forward concrete ideas on how to do this at the Cologne Summit – by opening up our markets to Russian products, by providing technical advice and sharing our expertise with the Russians, and by providing support both bilaterally and through the IMF, the World Bank and the other IEIs and the Paris Club for the Russian reform efforts.*

I believe passionately that we will all benefit hugely from a thriving Russia making use of its immense natural resources, its huge internal market and its talented and well-educated people. Russia's past has been as a world power that we felt confronted by. We must work with her to make her future as a world power with whom we cooperate in trust and to mutual benefit.

International Security
The principles of international community apply also to international security.

---

* IEIs: international economic institutions.

We now have a decade of experience since the end of the Cold War. It has certainly been a less easy time than many hoped in the euphoria that followed the collapse of the Berlin Wall. Our armed forces have been busier than ever – delivering humanitarian aid, deterring attacks on defenceless people, backing up UN resolutions and occasionally engaging in major wars as we did in the Gulf in 1991 and are currently doing in the Balkans.

Have the difficulties of the past decade simply been the aftershocks of the end of the Cold War? Will things soon settle down, or does it represent a pattern that will extend into the future?

Many of our problems have been caused by two dangerous and ruthless men – Saddam Hussein and Slobodan Milošević . Both have been prepared to wage vicious campaigns against sections of their own community. As a result of these destructive policies both have brought calamity on their own peoples. Instead of enjoying its oil wealth Iraq has been reduced to poverty, with political life stultified through fear. Milošević took over a substantial, ethnically diverse state, well placed to take advantage of new economic opportunities. His drive for ethnic concentration has left him with something much smaller, a ruined economy and soon a totally ruined military machine.

One of the reasons why it is now so important to win the conflict is to ensure that others do not make the same mistake in the future. That in itself will be a major step to ensuring that the next decade and the next century will not be as difficult as the past. If NATO fails in Kosovo, the next dictator to be threatened with military force may well not believe our resolve to carry the threat through.

At the end of this century the US has emerged as by far the strongest state. It has no dreams of world conquest and is not seeking colonies. If anything Americans are too ready to see no need to get involved in affairs of the rest of the world. America's allies are always both relieved and gratified by its continuing readiness to shoulder burdens and responsibilities that come with its sole superpower status. We understand that this is something that we have no right to take for granted, and must match with our own efforts. That is the basis for the recent initiative I took with President Chirac of France to improve Europe's own defence capabilities.

As we address these problems at this weekend's NATO Summit we may be tempted to think back to the clarity and simplicity of the Cold War. But now we have to establish a new framework. No longer is our existence as states under threat. Now our actions are guided by a more subtle blend of mutual self-interest and moral purpose in defending the values we cherish.

In the end values and interests merge. If we can establish and spread the values of liberty, the rule of law, human rights and an open society then that is in our national interests too. The spread of our values makes us safer. As John Kennedy put it: 'Freedom is indivisible and when one man is enslaved who is free?'

The most pressing foreign-policy problem we face is to identify the circumstances in which we should get actively involved in other people's conflicts. Non-interference has long been considered an important principle of international order. And it is not one we would want to jettison too readily. One state should not feel it has the right to change the political system of another or foment subversion or seize pieces of territory to which it feels it should have some claim. But the principle of non-interference must be qualified in important respects. Acts of genocide can never be a purely internal matter. When oppression produces massive flows of refugees which unsettle neighbouring countries then they can properly be described as 'threats to international peace and security'. When regimes are based on minority rule they lose legitimacy – look at South Africa.

Looking around the world there are many regimes that are undemocratic and engaged in barbarous acts. If we wanted to right every wrong that we see in the modern world then we would do little else than intervene in the affairs of other countries. We would not be able to cope.

So how do we decide when and whether to intervene. I think we need to bear in mind five major considerations.

First, are we sure of our case? War is an imperfect instrument for righting humanitarian distress; but armed force is sometimes the only means of dealing with dictators. Second, have we exhausted all diplomatic options? We should always give peace every chance, as we have in the case of

" The most pressing foreign-policy problem we face is to identify the circumstances in which we should get actively involved in other people's conflicts."

Kosovo. Third, on the basis of a practical assessment of the situation, are there military operations we can sensibly and prudently undertake? Fourth, are we prepared for the long term? In the past we talked too much of exit strategies. But having made a commitment we cannot simply walk away once the fight is over; better to stay with moderate numbers of troops than return for repeat performances with large numbers. And finally, do we have national interests involved? The mass expulsion of ethnic Albanians from Kosovo demanded the notice of the rest of the world. But it does make a difference that this is taking place in such a combustible part of Europe.

I am not suggesting that these are absolute tests. But they are the kind of issues we need to think about in deciding in the future when and whether we will intervene.

Any new rules however will only work if we have reformed international institutions with which to apply them.

If we want a world ruled by law and by international cooperation then we have to support the UN as its central pillar. But we need to find a new way to make the UN and its Security Council work if we are not to return to the deadlock that undermined the effectiveness of the Security Council during the Cold War. This should be a task for members of the Permanent Five to consider once the Kosovo conflict is complete.

Politics

This speech has been dedicated to the cause of internationalism and against isolationism. On Sunday, along with other nations' leaders, including President Clinton, I shall take part in a discussion of political ideas. It is loosely based around the notion of the Third Way, an attempt by centre and centre-left governments to re-define a political programme that is neither old left nor 1980s right. In the field of politics, too, ideas are becoming globalised. As problems become global – competitivity, changes in technology, crime, drugs, family breakdown – so the search for solutions becomes global too. What amazes me, talking to other countries' leaders, is not the differences but the points in common. We are all coping with the same issues: achieving prosperity in a world of rapid economic and techno-logical change; social stability in the face of changing family and community mores; a role for government in an era where we have learnt Big Government doesn't work, but no government works even less.

Certain key ideas and principles are emerging. Britain is following them. It is one of the things that often makes it difficult for commentators to define the New Labour government. We are parodied as either being Mrs Thatcher with a smile instead of a handbag; or as really old-style socialists in drag, desperate to conceal our true identity. In reality, we are neither. The political debates of the twentieth century – the massive ideological battleground between left and right – are over. Echoes remain, but they mislead as much as they illuminate.

Let me summarise the new political agenda we stand for:

1. Financial prudence as the foundation of economic success. In Britain, we have eliminated the massive budget deficit we inherited; put in new fiscal rules; granted Bank of England independence – and we're proud of it.

2. On top of that foundation, there is a new economic role for government. We don't believe in laissez-faire. But the role is not picking winners, heavy-handed intervention, old-style corporatism, but: education, skills, technology, small-business entrepreneurship. Of these, education is recognised now as much for its economic as its social necessity. It is our top priority as a government.

3. We are reforming welfare systems and public services. In Britain, we are introducing measures to tackle failing schools and reform the teaching profession that would have been unthinkable by any government even a few years ago. Plus big changes to the NHS. For the first two years of this government, welfare bills have fallen for the first time in two decades.

4. We are all tough on crime, tough on the causes of crime. The debate between 'liberals' and 'hard-liners' is over. No one disputes the causes of crime. In particular social exclusion – a hard core of society outside its mainstream – needs a special focus. We won't solve it just by general economic success. But we don't excuse crime either. Criminals get punished. That's justice. Fairness.

5. We are reinventing or reforming government itself. The government machine is being overhauled. Here, Al Gore has led the way. But the whole basis of how we deliver government services is being altered.

For Britain there is a special dimension to this.

We are modernising our constitution. We have devolved power to a new parliament in Scotland and a new assembly in Wales. We are handing power back to local government, because we believe that power should be exercised as close as possible to the people it affects. We have introduced the concept of elected mayors which, strange as it may seem to you here in Chicago, has not existed in the past in Britain. The first election for a Mayor of London will take place next year. And we are removing the constitutional anomalies from the past, like hereditary peers voting on legislation, that have proved too difficult to tackle previously.

We also want to change the way in which Northern Ireland is governed, and let me say something on this.

We have made great progress in bringing peace to Northern Ireland. The Good Friday Agreement last year was a breakthrough. We have to make one last heave to get over the one remaining obstacle, so that we can establish the executive and the North/South bodies and hand over power to the elected assembly. The stand-off on decommissioning cannot be allowed to derail the process when we have come so far. Bertie Ahern, the Irish Taoiseach, and I are determined to find a way through. The people will never forgive the politicians unless we resolve it.

And I would like to thank President Clinton and the Irish American community in the US for the great contribution they have made to coming this far. I know you will assist us again in the final straight.

And the final thing we all have in common, the new centre, centre-left governments, is we are internationalists and that returns me to my original theme.

For Britain, the biggest decision we face in the next couple of decades is our relationship with Europe. For far too long British ambivalence to Europe has made us irrelevant in Europe, and consequently of less importance to the United States. We have finally done away with the false proposition that we must choose between two diverging paths – the transatlantic relationship or Europe. For the first time in the last three decades we have a government that is both pro-Europe and pro-American. I firmly believe that it is in Britain's interest, but it is also in the interests of the US and of Europe.

Being pro-Europe does not mean that we are content with the way it is. We believe it needs radical reform. And I believe we are winning the battle for economic reform within the EU. Two weeks ago the Conservative Spanish Prime Minister and I issued a joint declaration on economic reform.

📝 those nations which have the power, have the responsibility 📝

Shortly, the German Social Democratic Chancellor Schroeder and I will be issuing a declaration on the same subject. We all understand the need to ensure flexible labour markets, to remove regulatory burdens and to untie the hands of business if we are going to succeed. The tide of Euro-sclerosis has begun to turn: the Third Way in Europe as much as in Britain.

As to Britain and the euro, we will make our decision not on political grounds but on the basis of our national economic interests. We must however ensure that we are ready to enter if we make the decision to do so. And the government has put a national changeover plan in place to convert sterling that will make that possible if we decide to do so.

I also pledge that we will prevent the European Union becoming a closed fortress. Europe must be a force for openness and free trade. Indeed it is fundamental to my whole thesis tonight that we can only survive in a global world if we remove barriers and improve cooperation.

Conclusion

This has been a very broad-ranging speech, but maybe the time is right for that. One final word on the USA itself: you are the most powerful country in the world, and the richest. You are a great nation. You have so much to give and to teach the world; and I know you would say, in all modesty, a little to learn from it too. It must be difficult and occasionally irritating to find yourselves the recipient of every demand, to be called upon in every crisis, to be expected always and everywhere to do what needs to be done. The cry 'What's it got to do with us' must be regularly heard on the lips of your people and be the staple of many a politician running for office.

Yet just as with the parable of the individuals and the talents, so those nations which have the power, have the responsibility. We need you engaged. We need the dialogue with you. Europe over time will become stronger and stronger; but its time is some way off.

I say to you: never fall again for the doctrine of isolationism. The world cannot afford it. Stay a country, outward-looking, with the vision and imagination that is in your nature. And realise that in Britain you have a friend and an ally that will stand with you, work with you, fashion with you the design of a future built on peace and prosperity for all, which is the only dream that makes humanity worth preserving.

The Mark
of Cain

– TIM COLLINS –

When politicians send troops into war it is down to the commanding officers to cut through the politics and speak to their soldiers to prepare them for the dangerous tasks ahead. It is rare for these eve-of-battle speeches to be remembered outside the military – not since World War II and Generals Montgomery and Patton has that really happened. One speech that captured the public imagination, though, was the address given by Lieutenant-Colonel Tim Collins to soldiers of the 1st Battalion the Royal Irish Regiment on 19 March 2003 as they prepared to enter Iraq from Kuwait as part of the coalition invasion to topple Saddam Hussein.

No recording, film or proper transcript exists. Collins spoke with no notes and apparently little preparation, saying later that it came 'partly from the head, partly from the heart and mostly from the shoulder'.[54] Only three journalists were present; one – Sarah Oliver, an embedded reporter from the *Mail on Sunday* – took shorthand notes and filed a pooled report that is the only record available.[55] The report generated huge media interest and was one of the few positive moments in what had already become a deeply divisive war well before the first bullet had been fired. While millions of people had marched in cities around the world to demonstrate their opposition to the war (with over a million people marching in London on 15 February), many still believed that Saddam Hussein had to be removed by force.

Collins's speech stood in stark contrast to the horse-trading, manipulation and deceit that had characterised the political build-up to the war. It was dignified and thoughtful, respectful towards the Iraqi people and firm in reminding the soldiers of their responsibilities. It allowed newspapers to rally around the troops – supporting 'our boys' while remaining sceptical about the actual war – and gave some pride back to a British public that had seen its country characterised as a lapdog to the United States.

The soldiers gathered around Collins knew that this was an unpopular and controversial war, and no doubt were looking to their commanding officer for reassurance. Collins kept it simple, ignoring the politics and telling them they went to 'liberate, not to conquer' and they must 'leave Iraq a better place for us having been there'. A large part of Collins's address was given over to the need for the soldiers to respect Iraq and its people. He also reminded them that enemy soldiers had the right under international law to surrender and be treated humanely. He impressed upon them to 'bring shame on neither our uniforms nor our nation' by 'over-enthusiasm in killing, or cowardice' because 'your deeds will follow you down through history'. He implored them to not treat the Iraqi people as refugees in their own country and told them that as they had not come to conquer 'the only flag that will be flown in that ancient land will be their own'.

At one point Collins made reference to Cain of the Old Testament, who killed his brother Abel and was cursed by God: 'I know of men who have taken life needlessly in other conflicts. I can assure you that they live with the mark of Cain upon them.' He also referred to Iraq as 'the site of the Garden of Eden, of the Great Flood and the birthplace of Abraham', adding even more biblical weight to what he was saying. His speech had hints of both Winston Churchill and William Shakespeare in its tone (something not lost on the BBC, who cast veteran thespian Kenneth Branagh in the lead role in a television adaptation of the speech). He told those present that 'The enemy should be in no doubt that we are his nemesis and we are bringing about his rightful destruction', but reminded them that if 'you are ferocious in battle, remember to be magnanimous in victory'.

The man himself was an instant media hit: his trademark Ray-Ban sunglasses and Cuban cigars made him seem far more exciting and 'American' than the other British officers. His time in special forces and even his nickname 'Nails' implied that, although he might be eloquent, he was a real soldier and therefore someone to be respected. Born in Belfast in 1960, Collins joined the British army after university and served in the Royal Signals, the Royal Irish Rangers, the SAS and the Royal Irish Regiment in a military career that spanned nearly twenty-three years (plus his earlier time in the Combined Cadet Force and the Territorial Army).

Collins's speech attracted some high-profile admirers. The Prince of Wales sent him a personal letter telling him he had been profoundly moved by his 'extraordinarily stirring, civilised and humane words'.[56] George Bush is also reported to have requested a copy of the transcript for the wall of the Oval Office. However, controversy has followed him since the speech made him famous. He was investigated following accusations by a US Army reservist major that he had mistreated Iraqi civilians and prisoners of war. The investigation cleared Collins of any wrongdoing but left him with the bitter feeling that he had been targeted by the army leadership and abandoned by the Ministry of Defence. He later won substantial undisclosed libel damages against two national newspapers that had made allegations about his conduct during the war.[57]

Questions have also been raised, perhaps unfairly, about the effect such a sombre speech had on the soldiers in his battalion.[58] Reminding them as it did on the eve of battle of their own mortality and the considerable dangers they faced, the effect may have been a little more sobering than Collins had intended. But, true to his word, he brought every one of his men home from Iraq (although one hundred and seventy-nine British personnel lost their lives in the conflict).

After his tour in Iraq, Collins was promoted to full colonel and on 7 April 2004 he was awarded an OBE for his role in Operation Telic, the British contribution to the invasion. He left the army on the same day and has since been an outspoken critic of military bureaucracy and the wars in Iraq and Afghanistan, particularly questioning the lack of planning for the aftermath of the invasion of Iraq.[59] He has been a regular, and sometimes controversial, media commentator and public speaker, presented several television documentaries and written numerous newspaper articles and a bestselling autobiography. The

Conservatives and the Ulster Unionists approached him at one point to run for parliament and he would no doubt prove to be a popular candidate if he ever chose to enter politics. For now, though, he remains the chief executive of New Century, a private military company he established in 2007 that works closely with the US Defense Department in Iraq and Afghanistan.[60]

Collins's pleas for Iraqis to be shown respect were not heeded by all: in the years that followed there were many cases of abuse, torture or murder by British and American soldiers or private contractors. Some of the most horrific incidents were exposed in 2004 when it became clear that there had been regular torture and sexual abuse of prisoners – including rape and sodomy – at the Abu Ghraib detention facility near Baghdad and that some of it may have been linked to a strategy encouraged by senior civilian figures in the Pentagon.[61] Equally, Collins's hope that Iraqis would not be treated as refugees in their own country was not realised. In January 2009, the UN High Commissioner for Refugees estimated that nearly five million Iraqis had been forced to leave their homes, with two million of these having left Iraq for neighbouring countries, predominantly Syria and Jordan, creating a desperate humanitarian situation.[62]

Collins's worst fears have surely come true. Although British combat operations in Iraq finally came to an end in April 2009 and Iraqis may no longer suffer under Saddam Hussein, they now live in a country repeatedly on the brink of civil war and where violence and corruption are still a part of everyday life. Much of the population lives in poverty, food shortages and malnutrition are increasing and unemployment is rising rapidly. The water, sanitation and electricity infrastructure are close to collapse and medical facilities are in an alarming state. History will judge whether Iraq has been left a better place for Collins and others like him having been sent there.

Fort Blair Mayne, Kuwait

19 MARCH 2003

We are going to Iraq to liberate and not to conquer. We will not fly our flags in their country. We are entering Iraq to free a people and the only flag that will be flown in that ancient land will be their own. Show respect for them.

The enemy knows this moment is coming too. Some have resolved to fight and others wish to survive. Be sure to distinguish between them. There are some who are alive at this moment who will not be alive shortly. Those who do not wish to go on that journey, we will not send; as for the others, I expect you to rock their world. Wipe them out if that is what they choose. But if you are ferocious in battle, remember to be magnanimous in victory.

Iraq is steeped in history; it is the site of the Garden of Eden, of the Great Flood and the birthplace of Abraham. Tread lightly there.

In the near future you will see things that no man could pay to see – and you will have to go a long way to find a more decent, generous and upright people than the Iraqis. You will be embarrassed by the hospitality they offer you, even though they have nothing. Don't treat them as refugees for they are in their own country. Their children will be poor, in years to come they will know that the light of liberation in their lives was brought by you.

If there are casualties of war, then remember that when they got up this morning and got dressed they did not plan to die this day. Allow them dignity in death. Bury them with due reverence and properly mark their graves.

It is my foremost intention to bring every single one of you out alive. But there may be those among us who will not see the end of this campaign. We will put them in their sleeping bags and send them back. There will be no time for sorrow.

The enemy should be in no doubt that we are his nemesis and we are bringing about his rightful destruction. There are many regional commanders who have stains on their souls and they are stoking the fires of hell for Saddam. He and his forces will be destroyed for what they have done to their people. As they die, they will know that it is their deeds that have brought them to this place. Show them no pity. It is a big step to take another human life. It is not to be done lightly. I know of men who have taken life needlessly in other conflicts. I can assure you that they live with the mark of Cain upon them.

If someone surrenders to you, remember they have that right in

> 66 I know of men who have **taken life needlessly** in other conflicts. I can assure you that **they live with** the **mark of Cain** upon them. 99

international law and ensure that one day they go home to their family. The ones who wish to fight, well, we aim to please. Remember, however, if you harm your regiment or its history by over-enthusiasm in killing, or cowardice, know it is your family who will suffer. You will be shunned unless your conduct is of the highest, for your deeds will follow you down through history. We will bring shame on neither our uniforms nor our nation.

As for chemical and biological weapons, I believe the threat is very real. We know that the order to use these weapons has been delegated down to regional commanders. That means he has already taken the decision to use them. Therefore it is not a question of if, it is a question of when they attempt this.* If we survive the first strike, we will survive the attack.

As for ourselves, let's bring everyone home safely and leave Iraq a better place for us having been there. Our business now is north. Good luck.

---

* Chemical and biological weapons were not used by the Iraqi army against the coalition forces and no production facilities for or stockpiles of these weapons were found following the invasion of Iraq. It is now thought that Saddam Hussein had abandoned Iraq's weapons of mass destruction programmes by the mid-1990s.

PART IV

Give Peace
a Chance

"Peace is not only better than war,
but infinitely more arduous."

George Bernard Shaw,
Heartbreak House
(1919)

We live in predominantly martial societies. The founding myths of many nations and countries are rooted in war; the statues in most country's capitals are those of their greatest military leaders; film and television glamorise war and normalise killing; joining the armed forces is seen as a chance for education, travel and adventure. Despite this, there are those in politics, religion and everyday life who strive to create a culture of peace. They recognise that war is the ultimate betrayal of our common humanity and that conflict often only leads to further violence. They believe that the only sustainable way forward is through dialogue, respect and understanding wherever possible. Not all these people would describe themselves as pacifist – though many clearly are – but what they share in common is a desire to achieve a better world, just not via the barrel of a gun.

There are some positive signs they can point to. Since the end of the Cold War there has been a steady decline in the numbers of armed conflicts and combat deaths around the world. There is a growing recognition that addressing conflict through peaceful means is usually far cheaper and more effective than using military force. There is a greater understanding of the factors that may lead to conflict, and there are slowly improving international institutions that are designed to intervene in the early stages of conflict. There is also now a real understanding of the power of non-violence in resisting repression and hostility. These issues and other aspects of peace and how to achieve it are discussed in the chapters that follow (in contrast to Part III, which dealt with war and its place in politics).

The first chapter focuses on the non-violent resistance promoted by Mohandas Gandhi during the Indian struggle for independence from Britain. One of the key moments in this struggle was the Dandi Salt March of 1930, which marked the beginning of a campaign of civil disobedience that Gandhi built around breaking the British salt-tax laws. On 11 March 1930, the night before Gandhi and his followers left Ahmedabad for Dandi, he addressed a crowd of thousands on the banks of the Sabarmati River. He explained the various ways that people could break the British salt monopoly and went on to outline other methods of civil disobedience and non-cooperation. Gandhi showed that non-violent resistance is much more than the simple absence of violence; it is the effective application of peaceful methods of opposition, communication and persuasion in order to bring about social or political change – a lesson which has been followed by many others since and still holds true today.

For peace and security to be maintained at the international level, we must be aware of the vested interests that might encourage war. In his farewell address to the nation on 17 January 1961, the US President, Dwight D. Eisenhower, warned of the danger posed by one such group of people: those in the military–industrial complex. This network was originally formulated as the military–industrial–congressional complex, which is a more accurate description. This triangle consists of elites in the military, industry and government who exert significant influence on the civilian policymaking and military procurement processes, yet act largely outside of effective democratic control. The relationship between the three groups is not equal and the interests of privately owned arms companies and defence contractors may sometimes run counter to the national interest. Eisenhower argued that an alert and knowledgeable electorate is needed to help counter the insidious nature of the military and industrial machineries and to promote peaceful methods and goals.

While Eisenhower focused on the military and industrial aspects of the elite triangle, the government element can be just as powerful a factor in the drive to war. This is discussed in relation to the resignation speech that Robin Cook, a senior British MP, gave in the House of Commons on 17 March 2003. The British government, led by Tony Blair, was rushing to join the US-led invasion of Iraq, despite serious concerns that this would be disastrous. Cook and others had managed to secure the right of parliament to vote on whether troops should be committed to the war and Cook intended to vote against the government. He therefore resigned from the cabinet and delivered one of the most dignified and powerful resignation speeches that the Commons had ever heard, succinctly and powerfully dismantling the government's case for war. In the end, though, parliament voted over-whelmingly to support Blair's commitment to war: one of the greatest ever failings of the British political system.

The British involvement in the invasion and occupation of Iraq lasted six years and contributed to the deaths of well over one hundred thou-sand Iraqi civilians as insurgency, inter-communal violence and criminality turned the country into a state of bloody chaos. It also provoked angry reactions from Britain's diverse Muslim community. While the overwhelming majority of British Muslims oppose terrorism, a small handful have sought violent outlets for their anger and alienation. One such group of young men targeted the London transport system on 7 July 2005, detonating homemade bombs on three underground trains and a bus, killing fifty-two people. Marie Fatayi-Williams was the mother of one of the dead and she flew from Nigeria to London desperately seeking information about her son. On 11 July she gave an emotional press conference near the site of the bus bombing where her son was thought to have died. Almost overcome with emotion, she still managed to show compassion and resilience. She urged people to turn away from hatred, fear and violence, citing Nelson Mandela, Martin Luther King and Gandhi as positive role models. She has since become a powerful campaigner for peace and forgiveness despite her personal pain.

Al-Qaida-inspired terrorism and the US-led war on terror have created huge divisions between the Muslim world and the West – divisions which if not healed will inevitably lead to further conflict. Barack Obama understood this well and five months after becoming the US President he fulfilled a pre-election promise to deliver a major address to Muslims from a Muslim capital during his first few months in office. On 4 June 2009 he gave a speech at Cairo University in Egypt in which he specifically addressed some of the grievances of the Muslim world. He spoke a great deal about the need for understanding and peace between different peoples and his desire for a new beginning between the Western and Muslim worlds. One of the most important issues he touched upon was Israel–Palestine and the wider Arab–Israeli conflict. Resolving these interrelated conflicts is the key to securing regional peace and will deny radical Islamic groups an important recruitment and propaganda tool.

History is taught as if it were made up of a series of wars and conflicts, with peace only what happened in between. But peace is so much more than the simple absence of war. This positive definition is better reflected in the Arabic and Hebrew words for peace, *salām* and *shalóm* respectively, which come from the same Semitic root, meaning safety, welfare and completeness. At the national level peace is the presence of healthy inter-communal relationships and proper social, political and economic equality and security. At the international level it is the presence of effective political institutions and norms of cooperation and diplomacy. Achieving and maintaining peace means overcoming the human tendency for division, suspicion and retaliation and instead focusing on collaboration, trust and forgiveness. Peace, therefore, exists only where it is worked for – only where people strive to achieve it. The absence of war is not enough.

Let No One Commit a Wrong in Anger

– MOHANDAS GANDHI –

Mohandas Karamchand Gandhi is rightly regarded as one of history's greatest proponents of non-violence. His life was his message and he embodied non-violence in action, thought and spirit. He explained at his 1922 trial for sedition, 'Non-violence is the first article of my faith. It is also the last article of my creed.'[1] Gandhi showed that non-violent resistance is much more than the simple absence of violence: it is the effective application of peaceful methods of opposition, communication and persuasion in order to bring about social or political change. It involves resisting iniquity with good, rather than further evil, and so demands patience and self-sacrifice.[2]

Non-violent resistance proved to be an important weapon in the struggle against British colonial rule in India. The British had been a trading presence in India since the early 1600s and the East India Company had maintained de facto rule over many Indian states for a hundred years, from the Battle of Plassey in 1757 to the Sepoy Mutiny of 1857. In 1858, the Crown assumed direct administration over the Company's territories in India, ushering in ninety years of the British Raj – the jewel in the Empire's crown.

Gandhi was born in Porbandar on 2 October 1869 and grew up in the state of Gujarat in western India. He studied law in London and practised for a while in India before sailing for the British colony of Natal and a job at an Indian law firm in Durban. He arrived in what is today South Africa in May 1893 and was immediately shocked by the lack of respect shown to Indians. In little over a year he had established the

Natal Indian Congress to redress grievances and protest against discrim-
inatory legislation. He read widely throughout his time in southern
Africa and was particularly influenced by Ralph Waldo Emerson's defence
of non-conformity in *Self-Reliance* (1841); the individual resistance
espoused by Henry Thoreau in *On the Duty of Civil Disobedience* (1849)
and the self-reliance described in his *Walden; or, Life in the Woods* (1854);
the critique of capitalism given by John Ruskin in *Unto This Last* (1862);
and the concepts of non-resistance, Christian pacifism and anarchy
central to Leo Tolstoy's *The Kingdom of God is Within You* (1894).[3] He also
exchanged a series of letters with his friend Shrimad Rajchandra, a Jain
philosopher whose attainment of renunciation and self-realisation greatly
influenced his approach to religion. All these ideas, taken from East and
West, reflected and shaped his own thinking on non-violent resistance,
which was further determined by his experiences fighting discrimination
in South Africa.

Gandhi returned to India in 1915, by which time war had broken out
in Europe. He supported the British during World War I in the hope that
it would hasten India's freedom from colonial rule. He had organised an
ambulance corps in South Africa during the Second Boer War of 1899 to
1902 and the Zulu Rebellion of 1906 and he once again helped recruit
stretcher-bearers for the British in the early years of World War I. In
1918, he went further and personally encouraged Indians to enlist as
soldiers – a controversial recruitment campaign that seemed to be at odds
with his promotion of non-violence in other contexts.[4] The Indian Army
was cannon fodder for the British war machine, fighting first the
Germans on the Western Front and then the Ottomans in Mesopotamia
and Palestine. They acquitted themselves well but suffered heavy losses –
with over a hundred and twenty thousand men killed, wounded or
missing by the end of the war.[5] In return, Indians expected substantial
concessions on independence from the British.

While Britain did grant some moderate political reforms, they also
extended emergency measures enacted to control civil unrest and deal
with revolutionary activity in India. A climate of dissatisfaction and
violence spread throughout the country, particularly in Punjab. Then
on 13 April 1919, in defiance of martial law, thousands of people
gathered in the Jallianwala Bagh in Amritsar to celebrate Baisakhi day,

an important Sikh festival. In an attempt to crush what was mistakenly viewed as the beginnings of a rebellion, Brigadier-General Reginald Dyer ordered the men under his command to open fire on the crowd without warning and to continue firing until they had run out of ammunition. Hundreds were killed and at least a thousand injured.[6]

The Jallianwala Bagh massacre was an important catalyst for the Indian independence movement, paving the way for Gandhi and others. One of the leading parties in the movement was the Indian National Congress, established in 1885 and with a membership numbering in the millions. Gandhi became leader of the Congress in 1921 and it adopted his programme of non-violent non-cooperation, or *satyagraha* (holding to the truth), in the struggle for an independent India. There were three pillars to Gandhi's *satyagraha*: it did not allow violence under any circumstances (*ahimsa*), it always insisted upon the truth and it was a weapon of the strong not the weak.[7] This was the method through which he sought to obtain decentralised self-governance (*swaraj*) in India at every level (individual, community and national), free from both British rule and unnecessary state control. Despite repeated outbreaks of violence and occasional armed revolts, which led him at times to withdraw from the Congress and announce the failure of his civil-disobedience campaigns, he became increasingly influential in the Indian national movement throughout the 1920s and into the 1930s.

One of the key moments in the fight for Indian independence was the Dandi Salt March of 1930. Fifty years earlier, the British had instituted a salt-tax law in India that essentially made the processing of salt illegal unless through official government salt depots. These laws thus maintained a British monopoly over something that could otherwise have been collected for free from the low-lying coastal regions. Gandhi called this 'the most inhuman poll tax the ingenuity of man can devise' and built a campaign of civil disobedience around breaking the salt laws.[8] The start of the campaign involved a two-hundred-and-forty-mile march from Gandhi's ashram on the outskirts of Ahmedabad to the coastal village of Dandi. On 11 March 1930, the night before Gandhi and his followers left Ahmedabad, he addressed a crowd of thousands on the banks of the Sabarmati River. He explained the various ways that people could break the salt monopoly and went on to outline other methods of civil disobedience, including picketing foreign shops, refusing to pay taxes, boycotting the courts and with-drawing children from school. He called upon lawyers to stop practising and government officials to resign. In short, he called upon 'all who are cooperating with the government in one way or another' to 'withdraw their cooperation in all or as many ways as possible'. He knew that he faced imprisonment or worse during the campaign that was to come, but asked that 'there be not a semblance of breach of peace even after all of us have been arrested. We have resolved to utilise all our resources in the pursuit of an exclusively non-violent struggle.'

Gandhi and his followers reached Dandi on 5 April and the next day broke the salt laws by extracting salt from saline mud and auction-ing it that evening. The salt *satyagraha* campaign spread and continued for nearly a year, with tens of thousands of protesters arrested – including Gandhi – as millions broke the salt-tax laws and committed other acts of civil disobedience.

George Orwell warned in his 1949 essay on Gandhi that 'Saints should always be judged guilty until they are proved innocent.'[9] Although Gandhi came to be known by the epithet Mahatma (Great Soul), he was not a saint; he was a politician, complete with all the prejudices, contradictions, hypocrisies and other human flaws that this would suggest. But where Gandhi's greatness lay, according to his biog-rapher Louis Fischer, was in doing what everyone else could have done but did not.[10] The Dandi Salt March was one such act. Despite being unsuccessful in getting the salt laws repealed, it did force the British to negotiate with Gandhi as an equal. It also raised awareness of India's cause across the world: America's *Time* magazine featured Gandhi on its front cover for 31 March 1930 and later named him Man of the Year.[11]

The salt *satyagraha* campaign helped to create a mass movement across India that would eventually lay the foundations for independ-ence from Britain in the aftermath of World War II. Unlike in earlier wars, Gandhi did not offer his full support to the British during World War II but instead in 1942 launched the Quit India movement demanding immediate independence. Gandhi and the leadership of the Indian National Congress were arrested and demonstrations across the country were crushed by the police and army. While the movement failed to secure immediate independence, it succeeded in reinforcing nationalist sentiment and made full independence a non-negotiable goal. It took the economic ravages of war and growing mutiny within the Indian armed forces to finally force Britain to grant independence to India in 1947.

Gandhi's plea before the salt march that 'no one commit a wrong in anger' was not heeded over the years: violence on a massive scale was unleashed at the very point when his dream for a free India was realised. He was opposed to the partitioning of British India into separate Muslim- and Hindu-majority states but the Muslim League and, eventually, the Congress leadership thought it was the only way to avoid a civil war, and Gandhi gave his reluctant endorsement to the proposal. The Dominion of Pakistan (later the Islamic Republic of Pakistan) and the Union of India (later the Republic of India) officially came into existence on 14 and 15 August 1947 respectively. Massive population exchanges of at least fourteen million people occurred between the two states in the months and years that followed. The rioting and dislocation associated with the partition led to horrendous inter-communal violence between Sikhs, Hindus and Muslims, with the deaths of between two hundred thousand and one million people. Since then, India and Pakistan have gone to war three times over control of the Kashmir region (1947, 1965 and 1999) and once over East Pakistan's (now Bangladesh) secession from Pakistan (1971). Tensions between the two nuclear-armed countries remain high and further conflict is always a possibility – a situation exacerbated by fundamentalists on both sides.

Gandhi did not live to see most of this. On 30 January 1948 he was shot and killed by Nathuram Godse, a Hindu nationalist who held him responsible for weakening India. Against all that Gandhi stood for, Godse was executed for the murder, and anti-Brahmin riots caused the deaths of a number of people (Godse was a member of the Brahmin caste). Although Gandhi is honoured in India as the Father of the Nation, his teachings have had little meaningful impact on Indian politics since his death. Successive governments have in reality rejected many of his ideas, instead pursuing the Western economic model at the cost of great social and economic disparities and building up large armed forces for use externally against Pakistan and internally against the rural Naxalite–Maoist insurgency. India today does not reflect the *swaraj* Gandhi fought so hard to create.

It is one of history's bitter ironies that the man who made peace such a central part of his life should have had his final years marred by such violence. However, his legacy has lived on and inspired many of those fighting injustice. There is now a real understanding of the power of non-violence. It has been put into practice time and time again since Gandhi's death: by the Dalai Lama in response to China's annexation of Tibet; by Martin Luther King in the struggle for African-American civil rights; by Desmond Tutu in apartheid South Africa; by demonstrators during Czechoslovakia's Velvet Revolution; by an unknown Chinese protester against tanks near Tiananmen Square; by Aung San Suu Kyi in the face of oppression by the Burmese junta; and by activists and campaigners working on a wide range of peace, human-rights and environmental issues across the world. Even among some politicians and policymakers there is a growing recognition that addressing conflict through peaceful means is usually far cheaper and more effective than using military force.[12]

Throughout his struggle, Gandhi understood that he could not win India's independence by fighting fire with fire but that the British had to be turned with patience and sympathy. He also recognised that in facing an opponent who was prepared to kill, he had to be prepared to die. As he told those gathered to hear him before the Dandi March: 'In all probability this will be my last speech to you . . . Possibly these may be the last words of my life here.' However, he clearly showed that someone who is prepared to die for their cause can be victorious over those who are prepared to kill for theirs. In holding to the truth and working patiently and peacefully, non-violence becomes a tool of the strong not the weak.

Sabarmati Ashram, Ahmedabad, India

11 MARCH 1930

In all probability this will be my last speech to you. Even if the government allow me to march tomorrow morning, this will be my last speech on the sacred banks of the Sabarmati. Possibly these may be the last words of my life here.

I have already told you yesterday what I had to say. Today I shall confine myself to what you should do after my companions and I are arrested. The programme of the march to Jalalpur must be fulfilled as originally settled. The enlistment of volunteers for this purpose should be confined to Gujarat only. From what I have seen and heard during the last fortnight, I am inclined to believe that the stream of civil resisters will flow unbroken.

But let there be not a semblance of breach of peace even after all of us have been arrested. We have resolved to utilise all our resources in the pursuit of an exclusively non-violent struggle. Let no one commit a wrong in anger. This is my hope and prayer. I wish these words of mine reached every nook and corner of the land. My task shall be done if I perish and so do my comrades. It will then be for the Working Committee of the Congress to show you the way and it will be up to you to follow its lead. So long as I have reached Jalalpur, let nothing be done in contravention of the authority vested in me by the Congress. But once I am arrested, the whole responsibility shifts to the Congress. No one who believes in non-violence, as a creed, need, therefore, sit still. My compact with the Congress ends as soon as I am arrested. In that case, volunteers, wherever possible civil disobedience of salt laws should be started. These laws can be violated in three ways. It is an offence to manufacture salt wherever there are facilities for doing so. The possession and sale of contraband salt, which includes natural salt or salt earth, is also an offence. The purchasers of such salt will be equally guilty. To carry away the natural salt deposits on the seashore is likewise violation of law. So is the hawking of such salt. In short, you may choose any one or all of these devices to break the salt monopoly.

We are, however, not to be content with this alone. There is no ban by the Congress and wherever the local workers have self-confidence other suitable measures may be adopted. I stress only one condition, namely, let our pledge of truth and non-violence as the only means for the attainment of *swaraj* be faithfully kept. For the rest, every one has a free hand. But that does not give a licence to all and sundry to carry on their own responsibility. Wherever there are local leaders, their orders should be obeyed by the people. Where there are no leaders and only a handful of men have faith in the programme, they may do what they can, if they have enough self-confidence. They have a right, nay it is their duty, to do so. History is full of instances of men who rose to leadership by sheer force of self-confidence, bravery and tenacity. We too, if we sincerely aspire to *swaraj* and are impatient to attain it, should have similar self-confidence. Our ranks will swell and our hearts strengthen, as the number of our arrests by the government increases.

Much can be done in many other ways besides these. The liquor and foreign-cloth shops can be picketed. We can refuse to pay taxes if we have the requisite strength. The lawyers can give up practice. The public can boycott the law courts by refraining from litigation. Government servants can resign their posts. In the midst of the despair raining all round, people quake with fear of losing employment. Such men are unfit for *swaraj*. But why this despair? The number of government servants in the country does not exceed a few hundred thousand. What about the rest? Where are they to go? Even free India will not be able to accommodate a greater number of public servants. A collector then will not need the number of servants he has got today. He will be his own servant. Our starving millions can by no means afford this enormous expenditure. If, therefore, we are sensible enough, let us bid goodbye to government employment, no matter if it is the post of a judge or a peon. Let all who are cooperating with the government in one way or another, be it by paying taxes, keeping titles, or sending children to official schools, et cetera, withdraw their cooperation in all or as many ways as possible. Then there are women who can stand shoulder to shoulder with men in this struggle.

You may take it as my will. It was the message that I desired to impart to you before starting on the march or for the jail. I wish that there should be no suspension or abandonment of the war that commences tomorrow

66 I have faith in the
righteousness of our cause
and the **purity** of our **weapons.** 99

morning, or earlier if I am arrested before that time. I shall eagerly await the news that ten batches are ready as soon as my batch is arrested. I believe there are men in India to complete the work begun by me. I have faith in the righteousness of our cause and the purity of our weapons. And where the means are clean, there God is undoubtedly present with His blessings. And where these three combine, there defeat is an impossibility. A *satyagrahi*, whether free or incarcerated, is ever victorious. He is vanquished only when he forsakes truth and non-violence and turns a deaf ear to the inner voice. If, therefore, there is such a thing as defeat for even a *satyagrahi*, he alone is the cause of it. God bless you all and keep off all obstacles from the path in the struggle that begins tomorrow.

> **Let no one commit a wrong in anger. This is my hope and prayer. I wish these words of mine reached every nook and corner of the land. My task shall be done if I perish and so do my comrades.**

The Military–
Industrial Complex

– DWIGHT D. EISENHOWER –

In December 1959, US President Dwight D. Eisenhower visited India as part of a nineteen-day goodwill tour of eleven European, Asian and North African countries. On his arrival in New Delhi he placed a wreath on Mohandas Gandhi's tomb and at a civic reception three days later he told a massive crowd, 'America's right, our obligations, for that matter, to maintain a respectable establishment for defence – our duty to join in company with like-thinking peoples for mutual self-defence – would, I am sure, be recognised and upheld by the most saintly men.' Eisenhower's invocation of Gandhi drew loud cheers from the crowd and according to the Indian Prime Minister, Jawaharlal Nehru, he left India with a piece of their heart.[13]

Eisenhower's presidency came to an end a little over a year later. On 17 January 1961, as is tradition, he gave a televised farewell address to the nation. He ended his address with the words: 'To all the peoples of the world, I once more give expression to America's prayerful and continuing aspiration . . . that the scourges of poverty, disease and ignorance will be made to disappear from the earth; and that in the goodness of time, all peoples will come to live together in a peace guaranteed by the binding force of mutual respect and love.' It seems like a remarkable statement, sounding more like Gandhi than a US President. However, it is not Eisenhower's desire for peace for which his address has been remembered. In those fifteen minutes he articulated a powerful concept that holds just as true today as it did nearly fifty years ago: that of the military–industrial complex.

Eisenhower – or Ike as he was known – was a complicated figure, capable of great diplomacy but also great harm. He had been a five-star general in the US Army and the supreme Allied commander in Europe during World War II. His support for the Allied re-designation of German prisoners of war as 'disarmed enemy forces' denied them the protection of the Geneva Conventions and the Red Cross (much as George Bush's classification of 'enemy combatants' would do during the war on terror). His recognised leadership ability and organisational and administrative skills, rather than any direct combat experience, took him to the very top of the army hierarchy before he retired from active service in 1952. Not long after leaving the army he won the Republican nomination for the presidency and then, at the age of sixty-two, became the 34th President of the United States on 20 January 1953. Despite, or perhaps because of, his long military career Eisenhower was no hawk. In 1946, he told an audience at the Canadian Club of Ottawa, 'I hate war as only a soldier who has lived it can, only as one who has seen its brutality, its futility, its stupidity.'[14] This was borne out through his two terms of office as he worked to reduce Cold War tensions with a post-Stalin Soviet Union. He also played a central role in finalising the armistice ending hostilities in the Korean War and halted further British, French and Israeli action during the Suez crisis.

At the same time, however, Eisenhower ordered US operations overseas to combat supposed Soviet influence. He continued his predecessor's financial assistance to the French fighting Hồ Chí Minh's forces in Indochina and extended US Navy, Air Force and CIA support (although he decided against direct military intervention). In 1953, wrongly fearing communist control of Iran, he ordered the CIA to work with British intelligence in organising a *coup d'état* against Iranian Prime Minister Mohammad Mosaddeq, who had earlier nationalised the Anglo-Iranian Oil Company. Eisenhower also continued US interventions in Latin American politics under the guise of the Cold War. In 1954, for example, he authorised CIA operations to support a *coup* against the democratically elected Guatemalan President Jacobo Guzmán Arbenz because Arbenz's land-reform programme threatened US corporate interests and he was suspected of communist sympathies. Eisenhower went on to support anti-communist measures across Latin America and oversaw large amounts of military aid and training for US allies in the region, including military regimes and dictators.[15] In July 1958, Eisenhower once again intervened in the Middle East, sending US troops to bolster the pro-Western Lebanese government of Camille Chamoun. Many of these interventions laid the foundations for an anti-Americanism that still has repercussions today.

However, in his final address to the nation, it was not the Soviet Union or the spread of communism that Eisenhower chose to warn the country about. He was so concerned by one particular influence on American politics that he told those listening, 'We have been compelled to create a permanent armaments industry of vast proportions. Added to this, three and a half million men and women are directly engaged in the defence establishment. We annually spend on military security alone more than the net income of all United States corporations.' Explaining that 'this conjunction of an immense military establishment and a large arms industry is new in the American experience. The total influence – economic, political, even spiritual – is felt in every city, every statehouse, every office of the federal government.' And he warned, 'In the councils of government, we must guard against the acquisition of unwarranted influence, whether sought or unsought, by the military–industrial complex.'

The original phrase as drafted by his speechwriters was the 'military–industrial–congressional complex' but at the last minute Eisenhower removed 'congressional' to avoid upsetting fellow politicians.[16] However, the military–industrial–congressional complex better describes the 'iron triangle' that exists between the military, industry and government. This group of military, business and political leaders – what the sociologist C. Wright Mills called 'the power elite' – exert significant influence on the civilian policymaking and military procurement processes, yet act largely outside of effective democratic control in pursuit of their interests.[17] In some countries the military–industrial–political triangle is much smaller: the military is the government and the arms companies are state-owned. Strangely, this situation is less insidious than in democratic countries (where the overlaps are less obvious and the interests of the three parties are often less aligned). In a democracy, the interests of privately owned arms companies and defence contractors – including financial gain from actual or potential conflict – may sometimes run counter to the national interest, which usually involves the peaceful resolution of conflict.

The relationship between the military, business and politics is not, therefore, an equal one and the economic interests of the arms companies often seem to supersede what should be the priorities of government or the actual procurement needs of the military. The relationship is not entirely one-way, though, and each side of the triangle benefits. Arms deals can sometimes help facilitate political or military interests – for example, acting as a sweetener for the building of US bases in the Middle East. The government needs the military for obvious national security and defence reasons but also, increasingly, to act as an instrument of its foreign policy or to garner regional influence. And the military needs an active arms industry to meet its genuine procurement needs and to help encourage ever-larger defence budgets. In the majority world, the military may also occasionally take the upper hand and attempt to seize control of the government. The military is the only constant political power in many developing countries – able to impose its will on government and the people, through force if necessary. As such, there have been over five hundred successful or attempted *coups* documented worldwide since World War II (predominantly in sub-Saharan Africa and the Americas).[18] The only protection politicians may have against such *coups* is to try to ensure the continuing loyalty of the senior military leadership through political concessions or economic incentives.

It was the influence of the arms companies that worried Eisenhower the most in 1960s America. He was concerned that his inexperienced successor, John F. Kennedy, would not be able to withstand the pressure for increased funding that the arms industry would demand.[19] So he warned, 'Only an alert and knowledgeable citizenry can compel the proper meshing of the huge industrial and military machinery of defence with our peaceful methods and goals, so that security and liberty may prosper together.' Unfortunately, it is debatable whether many countries today benefit from such an alert and knowledgeable citizenry and, instead, the power elite maintain their control.

Defence companies receive government support in the form of tax breaks, research and development funding, export subsidies, loan guarantees and assistance from senior officials in securing foreign contracts. Some, such as Halliburton and its subsidiaries in Iraq, have been able to rely on direct political support in the awarding of government contracts and military outsourcing. They can also count on the protection of their governments in the name of national interest. For example, in 2006 Britain's attorney-general controversially blocked a corruption investigation into a BAE Systems arms deal with Saudi Arabia, citing national security as the reason. BAE is one of the world's largest defence companies and has also been investigated for using bribery to secure contracts in Chile, the Czech Republic, Romania, South Africa, Tanzania and Qatar. In February 2010 the company admitted accounting irregularities and the following month pleaded guilty to conspiring to defraud the US government by making false statements in connection with foreign arms deals.[20] This sort of duplicitous behaviour is unfortunately nothing new in the arms trade. In 1936, the Nye Committee of the US senate concluded:

> Almost without exception, the American munitions companies investigated have at times resorted to such unusual approaches, questionable favours and commissions, and methods of 'doing the needful' as to constitute, in effect, a form of bribery of foreign governmental officials or of their close friends in order to secure business. These business methods carried within themselves the seeds of disturbance to the peace and stability of those nations in which they take place.[21]

Defence spending is on such a massive scale that its corruptive influence is hardly surprising. The total world military expenditure for 2008 was $1,464 billion. The top military spenders were the United States, China, France, the United Kingdom and Russia, in that order. However, the United States was by far the largest spender, accounting for 42 per cent of world military expenditure that year (over $600 billion). During the eight years George Bush was in office, the war on terror and the conflicts in Afghanistan and Iraq pushed US military spending to the highest level in real terms since World War II, contributing to major budget deficits. Arms procurement accounted for the second largest increase in America's military spending during this time (after military construction).[22]

The United States is also the world's largest supplier of arms, making $38 billion of arms-transfer agreements in 2008 alone. In the eight years up to and including 2008, the largest suppliers of arms were the United States, Russia, France, the United Kingdom and China – the five permanent members of the UN Security Council. Developing countries are the primary market for these suppliers, accounting for the vast majority of arms-transfer agreements (nearly 80 per cent in 2008).[23] These transfers are draining developing countries' limited budgets, fuelling conflict and often arming human rights abusers and dictators. To put this all in context, in 2008 the world's governments spent ten times more on their militaries than they did on foreign aid ($1,464 billion on military expenditure compared to only $145 billion on overseas development assistance).[24] As Eisenhower said in a speech to the American Society of Newspaper Editors shortly after he became President: 'Every gun that is made, every warship launched, every rocket fired signifies, in the final sense, a theft from those who hunger and are not fed, those who are cold and are not clothed.'[25]

In addition to the military–industrial complex, Eisenhower referred in his farewell address to a related 'scientific–technological elite'. The dominance of this elite in American political and military thinking began with the Manhattan Project and the development of the atomic bomb, and reached new levels in the early days of the space race, during which the United States lost out to faster developments by the Soviet Union.[26] This saw the Soviets launch the world's first artificial satellite (the Sputnik 1 in 1957) and the first spacecraft to reach the moon's surface (the Luna 2 in 1959). Then on 12 April 1961, three months after Eisenhower's farewell address, the Soviets put the first person into space. The following years saw a number of other space firsts from the Soviet Union – including sending the first woman into space and undertaking the first spacewalk. Then on 20 July 1969, the Americans finally landed on the moon and Neil Armstrong took 'one small step for man, one giant leap for mankind'. That was the pinnacle of the unofficial space race, although both sides claimed victory – one for putting the first man in space, the other for landing the first man on the moon.

Throughout this entire period the desire to develop space for military purposes was never far behind the civilian scientific efforts. As the Cold War progressed, this included military communication, navigation and early warning systems and developed into Ronald Reagan's much-criticised proposal for a 'Star Wars' system to defend against strategic nuclear missiles. In the twenty-first century, the next development in the militarisation of space may be the deployment of space-based weapons. The United States is determined to retain its dominance of space, resisting any arms-control agreements and working to deny other countries space capabilities deemed hostile to US interests.[27] A US Air Force annual report caused alarm in 2003 by outlining the possible development of anti-satellite missiles and space-based directed energy weapons.[28] Although more recent reports have looked at predominantly passive or reversible ways of protecting US space assets, the goal is still to maintain American military dominance of space – through weaponisation if necessary.

Sometimes a new weapon system is so advanced that the edge it gives on the battlefield becomes a provocative and destabilising factor in geopolitics: a military weapon becomes a political one. Nuclear weapons are one such case. Their huge destructive power means they actually have limited military use but were a key factor in the Cold War and remain a dangerous and destabilising force today. Space-based weapons may be another such case. States such as China and Russia will not accept a situation where the United States has the unique combination of overwhelming conventional military forces, advanced nuclear forces, effective missile defence systems and near-complete military control of space. Such a situation would represent a revolution in warfare and geopolitics that would be fiercely resisted by other countries.[29] In the resulting arms race, the only winners would once again be those in the military–industrial complex, which we were warned about fifty years ago. Instead, as Eisenhower implored, 'Disarmament, with mutual honour and confidence, is a continuing imperative. Together we must learn how to compose differences, not with arms, but with intellect and decent purpose.'

The White House, Washington DC, United States

Good evening, my fellow Americans.

First, I should like to express my gratitude to the radio and television networks for the opportunities they have given me over the years to bring reports and messages to our nation. My special thanks go to them for the opportunity of addressing you this evening.

Three days from now, after a half-century in the service of our country, I shall lay down the responsibilities of office as, in traditional and solemn ceremony, the authority of the presidency is vested in my successor. This evening, I come to you with a message of leave-taking and farewell, and to share a few final thoughts with you, my countrymen.

Like every other citizen, I wish the new President, and all who will labour with him, Godspeed. I pray that the coming years will be blessed with peace and prosperity for all.

Our people expect their President and the Congress to find essential agreement on issues of great moment, the wise resolution of which will better shape the future of the nation. My own relations with the Congress, which began on a remote and tenuous basis when, long ago, a member of the senate appointed me to West Point, have since ranged to the intimate during the war and immediate post-war period, and finally to the mutually interdependent during these past eight years. In this final relationship, the Congress and the administration have, on most vital issues, cooperated well, to serve the national good, rather than mere partisanship, and so have assured that the business of the nation should go forward. So, my official relationship with the Congress ends in a feeling – on my part – of gratitude that we have been able to do so much together.

We now stand ten years past the midpoint of a century that has witnessed four major wars among great nations. Three of these involved our own country. Despite these holocausts, America is today the strongest, the most influential, and most productive nation in the world. Understandably proud of this pre-eminence, we yet realise that America's leadership and prestige depend, not merely upon our unmatched material progress, riches, and military strength, but on how we use our power in the interests of world peace and human betterment.

Throughout America's adventure in free government, our basic purposes have been to keep the peace, to foster progress in human achievement, and to enhance liberty, dignity, and integrity among peoples and among nations. To strive for less would be unworthy of a free and religious people. Any failure traceable to arrogance, or our lack of comprehension, or readiness to sacrifice would inflict upon us grievous hurt, both at home and abroad.

Progress toward these noble goals is persistently threatened by the conflict now engulfing the world. It commands our whole attention, absorbs our very beings. We face a hostile ideology global in scope, atheistic in character, ruthless in purpose, and insidious in method. Unhappily, the danger it poses promises to be of indefinite duration. To meet it successfully, there is called for, not so much the emotional and transitory sacrifices of crisis, but rather those which enable us to carry forward steadily, surely, and without complaint the burdens of a prolonged and complex struggle with liberty the stake. Only thus shall we remain, despite every provocation, on our charted course toward permanent peace and human betterment.

Crises there will continue to be. In meeting them, whether foreign or domestic, great or small, there is a recurring temptation to feel that some spectacular and costly action could become the miraculous solution to all current difficulties. A huge increase in newer elements of our defences; development of unrealistic programmes to cure every ill in agriculture; a dramatic expansion in basic and applied research – these and many other possibilities, each possibly promising in itself, may be suggested as the only way to the road we wish to travel.

But each proposal must be weighed in the light of a broader consideration: the need to maintain balance in and among national programmes, balance between the private and the public economy, balance between the cost and hoped for advantages, balance between the clearly necessary and the comfortably desirable, balance between our essential requirements as a nation and the duties imposed by the nation upon the individual, balance between actions of the moment and the national welfare of the future. Good judgement seeks balance and progress. Lack of it eventually finds imbalance and frustration. The record of many decades stands as proof that our people and their government have, in the main, understood these truths and have responded to them well, in the face of threat and stress.

But threats, new in kind or degree, constantly arise. Of these, I mention two only.

A vital element in keeping the peace is our military establishment. Our arms must be mighty, ready for instant action, so that no potential aggressor may be tempted to risk his own destruction. Our military organisation today bears little relation to that known of any of my predecessors in peacetime, or, indeed, by the fighting men of World War II or Korea.

Until the latest of our world conflicts, the United States had no armaments industry. American makers of ploughshares could, with time and as required, make swords as well. But we can no longer risk emergency improvisation of national defence. We have been compelled to create a permanent armaments industry of vast proportions. Added to this, three and a half million men and women are directly engaged in the defence establishment. We annually spend on military security alone more than the net income of all United States corporations.

Now this conjunction of an immense military establishment and a large arms industry is new in the American experience. The total influence – economic, political, even spiritual – is felt in every city, every statehouse, every office of the federal government. We recognise the imperative need for this development. Yet, we must not fail to comprehend its grave implications. Our toil, resources, and livelihood are all involved. So is the very structure of our society.

In the councils of government, we must guard against the acquisition of unwarranted influence, whether sought or unsought, by the military–industrial complex. The potential for the disastrous rise of misplaced power exists and will persist. We must never let the weight of this combination endanger our liberties or democratic processes. We should take nothing for granted. Only an alert and knowledgeable citizenry can compel the proper meshing of the huge industrial and military machinery of defence with our peaceful methods and goals, so that security and liberty may prosper together.

Akin to, and largely responsible for, the sweeping changes in our industrial–military posture, has been the technological revolution during recent decades. In this revolution, research has become central; it also becomes more formalised, complex and costly. A steadily increasing share is conducted for, by, or at the direction of, the federal government.

Today, the solitary inventor, tinkering in his shop, has been overshadowed by task forces of scientists in laboratories and testing fields. In the same fashion, the free university, historically the fountainhead of free ideas and scientific discovery, has experienced a revolution in the conduct of research. Partly because of the huge costs involved, a government contract becomes virtually a substitute for intellectual curiosity. For every old blackboard there are now hundreds of new electronic computers. The prospect of domination of the nation's scholars by federal employment, project allocations, and the power of money is ever present – and is gravely to be regarded.

Yet, in holding scientific research and discovery in respect, as we should, we must also be alert to the equal and opposite danger that public policy could itself become the captive of a scientific–technological elite.

It is the task of statesmanship to mould, to balance, and to integrate these and other forces, new and old, within the principles of our democratic system – ever aiming toward the supreme goals of our free society.

Another factor in maintaining balance involves the element of time. As we peer into society's future, we – you and I, and our government – must avoid the impulse to live only for today, plundering for our own ease and convenience the precious resources of tomorrow. We cannot mortgage the material assets of our grandchildren without risking the loss also of their political and spiritual heritage. We want democracy to survive for all generations to come, not to become the insolvent phantom of tomorrow.

Down the long lane of the history yet to be written, America knows that this world of ours, ever growing smaller, must avoid becoming a community of dreadful fear and hate, and be, instead, a proud confederation of mutual trust and respect. Such a confederation must be one of equals. The weakest must come to the conference table with the same confidence as do we, protected as we are by our moral, economic, and military strength. That table, though scarred by many past frustrations, cannot be abandoned for the certain agony of the battlefield.

Disarmament, with mutual honour and confidence, is a continuing imperative. Together we must learn how to compose differences, not with

❝ In the councils of government, we must guard against the acquisition of unwarranted influence, whether sought or unsought, by the military–industrial complex. ❞

arms, but with intellect and decent purpose. Because this need is so sharp and apparent, I confess that I lay down my official responsibilities in this field with a definite sense of disappointment. As one who has witnessed the horror and the lingering sadness of war, as one who knows that another war could utterly destroy this civilisation which has been so slowly and painfully built over thousands of years, I wish I could say tonight that a lasting peace is in sight.

Happily, I can say that war has been avoided. Steady progress toward our ultimate goal has been made. But so much remains to be done. As a private citizen, I shall never cease to do what little I can to help the world advance along that road.

So, in this, my last good night to you as your President, I thank you for the many opportunities you have given me for public service in war and in peace. I trust in that service you find some things worthy. As for the rest of it, I know you will find ways to improve performance in the future.

You and I, my fellow citizens, need to be strong in our faith that all nations, under God, will reach the goal of peace with justice. May we be ever unswerving in devotion to principle, confident but humble with power, diligent in pursuit of the nation's great goals.

To all the peoples of the world, I once more give expression to America's prayerful and continuing aspiration: we pray that peoples of all faiths, all races, all nations may have their great human needs satisfied; that those now denied opportunity shall come to enjoy it to the full; that all who yearn for freedom may experience its few spiritual blessings. Those who have freedom will understand, also, its heavy responsibility; that all who are insensitive to the needs of others will learn charity; and that the scourges of poverty, disease, and ignorance will be made to disappear from the earth; and that in the goodness of time, all peoples will come to live together in a peace guaranteed by the binding force of mutual respect and love.

Now, on Friday noon, I am to become a private citizen. I am proud to do so. I look forward to it.

Thank you, and good night.

With a
Heavy Heart

– ROBIN COOK –

The House of Commons is not the place one expects to witness a standing ovation, but that is precisely what Robin Cook received on taking his seat at the end of his resignation speech on 17 March 2003. This was an extraordinary and unprecedented response to a speech but, then again, this was no ordinary resignation; Cook was a member of the cabinet and he had just stepped down on the eve of a crucial parliamentary vote on the Iraq War, telling MPs: 'I intend to join those tomorrow night who will vote against military action'.

This was a critical juncture in the political build-up to the imminent invasion of Iraq and the role Britain was to play in it. It was an essential vote for the Prime Minister, Tony Blair, as he had already given his support to regime change in Iraq in private discussions with George Bush as far back as April 2002. If the government had lost the vote, Blair would have been forced to resign and the United States would have lost its most important junior partner in the coalition. Instead, parliament failed and voted overwhelmingly to support Blair's commitment to war – a commitment that lasted six years.

But Cook had struck two important blows. First, as Leader of the House he had helped secure the right of parliament to have such a vote. Secondly, in his speech he succinctly and powerfully dismantled the government's case for war. He made it clear just how isolated Britain would be in going ahead without EU, NATO or UN support and in direct opposition to many of its European allies. He also made it clear that Blair was, in fact, supporting a neoconservative strategy of regime change – a strategy that in reality had little to do with disarming Saddam Hussein of his alleged weapons of mass destruction. Undermining the government's position, he told MPs that 'Iraq probably has no weapons of mass destruction in the commonly understood sense of the term – namely a credible device capable of being delivered against a strategic city target.'

His words carried considerable weight, as he had been Foreign Secretary until two years previously and so privy to much of the intelligence on Iraq's weapons programmes. As the first Labour Foreign Secretary for eighteen years he had tried to introduce a new ethical dimension to Britain's foreign policy. He wanted to make Britain a force for good in the world and place human rights at the top of the political agenda. However, his approach ran into difficulties straight away when faced with the decision of whether or not to allow the sale of training aircraft, water cannons and armoured cars to Indonesia despite the Suharto regime's human-rights abuses in East Timor and elsewhere. In the end, Blair and Cook agreed to the deal but Cook's ethical foreign policy would clash time and time again with the military–industrial complex Dwight D. Eisenhower had warned of (Cook would later write that the chairman of BAE 'appeared to have the key to the garden door to No. 10').[30] Cook's idealism soon began to take a back seat to a foreign-policy agenda set by Downing Street; an agenda that saw military interventions in Kosovo in 1999 and Sierra Leone in 2000 before Cook was moved against his wishes in June 2001 to the less prestigious cabinet post of Leader of the House of Commons.

Although many members of the government were deeply unhappy with the decision to go to war with Iraq, Cook was one of only three ministers to resign in protest (the others were John Denham, a Home Office minister, and Lord Hunt, a junior health minister; six parliamentary aides also resigned). A fourth minister, Claire Short, had publicly threatened to resign but stayed on hoping to influence the reconstruction of Iraq in her role as Secretary of State for International Development. She resigned two months later – greatly reducing the impact her resignation could have had, had it been coordinated with Cook's.

Far more damaging than Short's non-resignation was the departure of Elizabeth Wilmshurst, a deputy legal adviser at the Foreign Office for thirty years, who resigned because she considered the use of force against Iraq to be illegal without UN Security Council authorisation. The government argued that authorisation already existed through previous Security Council resolutions from the 1990s and resolution 1441 from 2002 that gave Iraq 'a final opportunity to comply with its disarmament obligations'.[31] However, those involved in negotiating agreement on 1441 made it clear at the time that the resolution did not automatically authorise any state to use force if Iraq failed to disarm but that the matter would have to be referred back to the Security Council for discussion.[32] This is why Blair put so much effort into securing a second UN resolution explicitly authorising military action against Iraq and why Cook pointed out that 'the very intensity of those attempts underlines how important it was to succeed. Now that those attempts have failed, we cannot pretend that getting a second resolution was of no importance.'

Just how desperate those efforts were had become clear two weeks earlier when a translator working for GCHQ (the government's communications headquarters) leaked a memo reporting a surge in spying on UN Security Council members by the US National Security Agency and requesting British support for the surveillance operations ahead of a possible Council vote on a second resolution.[33] The whistleblower, Katharine Gun, was sacked, arrested and charged under the Official Secrets Act – charges that were later dropped, probably to save the British and American governments further embarrassment. Gun reportedly exposed the dirty tricks operation in order to prevent what she saw as an illegal war against Iraq. In any case, attempts to gain a second resolution were dropped when it became clear that the United States and Britain could not secure the majority vote needed.

The legal basis for the war had been bitterly argued and was highly dubious without a second resolution. The initial secret legal advice the Attorney-General, Lord Goldsmith, gave to Blair on 7 March 2003 stretched to thirteen pages and warned that an attack on Iraq could be in breach of international law for various reasons, including the lack of a second UN resolution, and explicitly stated that regime change could not be the objective of any military action.[34] But ten days later, in a short statement to the cabinet, published as a parliamentary answer the same day, Goldsmith had apparently changed his mind, arguing that 'Authority to use force against Iraq exists from the combined effect of Resolutions 678, 687 and 1441.'[35] Under pressure from Downing Street, all the caveats and balanced discussion that had been present in the earlier advice had been removed, giving the cabinet and parliament the false impression that the legal basis for war was clear. Many others, including Wilmshurst, were not so certain.

Much later it came to light that Goldsmith had written a letter to Blair on 29 July 2002 – eight months before the invasion – explaining that he did not believe that military action to depose Saddam Hussein could in any way be justified under international law (although, admittedly, this was written before the Security Council passed resolution 1441 in November 2002, which Goldsmith later relied on in his 17 March 2003 advice to the cabinet).[36] It has also since come to light that the Foreign Secretary, Jack Straw, had serious reservations as well. As Foreign Secretary, Straw's support for Blair was crucial in winning the parliamentary vote that took Britain to war. But a year earlier he had written a private letter to the Prime Minister arguing that 'the weight of legal advice here is that a fresh mandate may well be required' and that 'regime change per se is no justification for military action'.[37]

In August 2004, a cross-party group of MPs began a campaign to impeach Blair for high crimes and misdemeanours, including misleading parliament and making a secret agreement with President Bush to overthrow Saddam Hussein. An impeachment motion was tabled a few months later but the three main parties barred their MPs from signing it and it was never debated by the House. Calls for Blair to be impeached or charged with war crimes continued throughout the rest of his premiership. Cook, though, distanced himself from attacks against the Prime Minister from the very beginning, saying in his resignation speech, 'I have no sympathy with, and I will give no comfort to, those who want to use this crisis to displace him.'

While Cook and others who opposed the Iraq War failed to stop the invasion, they did succeed in creating an environment where the government dared not rush Britain to war again against all good sense. This became apparent during 2006, when there were serious concerns that Bush and the neoconservatives were preparing the ground for US or Israeli air strikes against Iran's nuclear programme. The approach taken by the

Prime Minister and Foreign Secretary on that occasion was diplomacy and engagement with Iran, while publicly distancing the British government from possible military action. The political fallout and public outcry had the government supported the United States and adopted the same strategy as they had against Iraq would have been too great.

On 6 August 2005, Cook collapsed and died while hiking in the Scottish Highlands with his second wife, Gaynor. It cut short a political career that had lasted over thirty years and might well have seen him return to the cabinet when Gordon Brown became Prime Minister. Despite such a long and respected career, it is for his principled resignation over Iraq that he will be best remembered. Tellingly, Cook's gravestone in Grange Cemetery in Edinburgh bears the epitaph: 'I may not have succeeded in halting the war, but I did secure the right of parliament to decide on war.' These words, taken from Cook's memoirs, neatly sum up both his greatest failure and, more importantly, his greatest success.[38]

House of Commons, London, England

17 MARCH 2003

This is the first time for twenty years that I have addressed the House from the back benches. I must confess that I had forgotten how much better the view is from here. None of those twenty years were more enjoyable or more rewarding than the past two, in which I have had the immense privilege of serving this House as Leader of the House, which were made all the more enjoyable, Mr Speaker, by the opportunity of working closely with you.

It was frequently the necessity for me as Leader of the House to talk my way out of accusations that a statement had been preceded by a press interview. On this occasion I can say with complete confidence that no press interview has been given before this statement. I have chosen to address the House first on why I cannot support a war without international agreement or domestic support.

The present Prime Minister is the most successful leader of the Labour Party in my lifetime. I hope that he will continue to be the leader of our party, and I hope that he will continue to be successful. I have no sympathy with, and I will give no comfort to, those who want to use this crisis to displace him.

I applaud the heroic efforts that the Prime Minister has made in trying to secure a second resolution. I do not think that anybody could have done better than the Foreign Secretary in working to get support for a second resolution within the Security Council. But the very intensity of those attempts underlines how important it was to succeed. Now that those attempts have failed, we cannot pretend that getting a second resolution was of no importance.

France has been at the receiving end of bucketloads of commentary in recent days. It is not France alone that wants more time for inspections. Germany wants more time for inspections; Russia wants more time for inspections; indeed, at no time have we signed up even the minimum necessary to carry a second resolution. We delude ourselves if we think that the degree of international hostility is all the result of President Chirac. The reality is that Britain is being asked to embark on a war without agreement in any of the international bodies of which we are a leading partner – not NATO, not the European Union and, now, not the Security Council.

To end up in such diplomatic weakness is a serious reverse. Only a year ago, we and the United States were part of a coalition against terrorism that was wider and more diverse than I would ever have imagined possible. History will be astonished at the diplomatic miscalculations that led so quickly to the disintegration of that powerful coalition. The US can afford to go it alone, but Britain is not a superpower. Our interests are best protected not by unilateral action but by multilateral agreement and a world order governed by rules. Yet tonight the international partnerships most important to us are weakened: the European Union is divided; the Security Council is in stalemate. Those are heavy casualties of a war in which a shot has yet to be fired.

I have heard some parallels between military action in these circumstances and the military action that we took in Kosovo. There was no doubt about the multilateral support that we had for the action that we took in Kosovo. It was supported by NATO; it was supported by the European Union; it was supported by every single one of the seven neighbours in the region. France and Germany were our active allies. It is precisely because we have none of that support in this case that it was all the more important to get agreement in the Security Council as the last hope of demonstrating international agreement.

The legal basis for our action in Kosovo was the need to respond to an urgent and compelling humanitarian crisis. Our difficulty in getting support this time is that neither the international community nor the British public is persuaded that there is an urgent and compelling reason for this military action in Iraq.

The threshold for war should always be high. None of us can predict the death toll of civilians from the forthcoming bombardment of Iraq, but the US warning of a bombing campaign that will 'shock and awe' makes it likely that casualties will be numbered at least in the thousands. I am confident that British servicemen and women will acquit themselves with professionalism and with courage. I hope that they all come back. I hope that Saddam, even now, will quit Baghdad and avert war, but it is false to argue that only those who support war support our troops. It is entirely legitimate to support our troops while seeking an alternative to the conflict that will put those troops at risk.

Nor is it fair to accuse those of us who want longer for inspections of not having an alternative strategy. For four years as Foreign Secretary I was partly responsible for the Western strategy of containment. Over the past decade that strategy destroyed more weapons than in the Gulf War, dismantled Iraq's nuclear-weapons programme and halted Saddam's medium- and long-range missile programmes. Iraq's military strength is now less than half its size than at the time of the last Gulf War.

Ironically, it is only because Iraq's military forces are so weak that we can even contemplate its invasion. Some advocates of conflict claim that Saddam's forces are so weak, so demoralised and so badly equipped that the war will be over in a few days. We cannot base our military strategy on the assumption that Saddam is weak and at the same time justify preemptive action on the claim that he is a threat.

Iraq probably has no weapons of mass destruction in the commonly understood sense of the term – namely a credible device capable of being delivered against a strategic city target. It probably still has biological toxins and battlefield chemical munitions, but it has had them since the 1980s when US companies sold Saddam anthrax agents and the then British government approved chemical and munitions factories. Why is it now so urgent that we should take military action to disarm a military capacity that has been there for twenty years, and which we helped to create? Why is it necessary to resort to war this week, while Saddam's ambition to complete his weapons programme is blocked by the presence of UN inspectors?

Only a couple of weeks ago, Hans Blix told the Security Council that the key remaining disarmament tasks could be completed within months.* I have heard it said that Iraq has had not months but twelve years in which to complete disarmament, and that our patience is exhausted. Yet it is more than thirty years since resolution 242 called on Israel to withdraw from the occupied territories. We do not express the same impatience with the persistent refusal of Israel to comply. I welcome the strong personal commitment that the Prime Minister has given to Middle East peace, but Britain's positive role in the Middle East does not redress the strong sense of injustice throughout the Muslim world at what it sees as one rule for the allies of the US and another rule for the rest.

Nor is our credibility helped by the appearance that our partners in Washington are less interested in disarmament than they are in regime change in Iraq. That explains why any evidence that inspections may be showing progress is greeted in Washington not with satisfaction but with consternation: it reduces the case for war.

What has come to trouble me most over past weeks is the suspicion that if the hanging chads in Florida had gone the other way and Al Gore had been elected, we would not now be about to commit British troops.

The longer that I have served in this place, the greater the respect I have for the good sense and collective wisdom of the British people. On Iraq, I believe that the prevailing mood of the British people is sound. They do not doubt that Saddam is a brutal dictator, but they are not persuaded that he is a clear and present danger to Britain. They want inspections to be given a chance, and they suspect that they are being pushed too quickly into conflict by a US administration with an agenda of its own. Above all, they are uneasy at Britain going out on a limb on a military adventure without a broader international coalition and against the hostility of many of our traditional allies.

From the start of the present crisis, I have insisted, as Leader of the House, on the right of this place to vote on whether Britain should go to war. It has been a favourite theme of commentators that this House no longer

---

* Hans Blix is a Swedish diplomat and politician who was head of the UN Monitoring, Verification and Inspection Commission (UNMOVIC) from March 2000 until June 2003.

occupies a central role in British politics. Nothing could better demonstrate that they are wrong than for this House to stop the commitment of troops in a war that has neither international agreement nor domestic support. I intend to join those tomorrow night who will vote against military action now. It is for that reason, and for that reason alone, and with a heavy heart, that I resign from the government.

❝ We cannot base our military strategy on the assumption that Saddam is weak and at the same time justify pre-emptive action on the claim that he is a threat. ❞

This is Anthony

— MARIE FATAYI-WILLIAMS —

The war in Iraq provoked angry reactions from Britain's diverse Muslim community. The British government chose to confront this backlash as part of the war on terror and gave the Home Secretary the power to detain suspects under house arrest – without trial or public evidence. Writing in a national newspaper in February 2005, Robin Cook warned that 'it will be British Muslims who will be the victims of the new powers of house arrest, giving fresh reason for the alienation among the many young Muslims who already believe that the security services regard them as suspects rather than allies in the war on terrorism'.[39] While the overwhelming majority of British Muslims are allies in the struggle against terrorism, a small handful have sought violent outlets for their anger and alienation.[40]

At 9.47 a.m. on 7 July 2005 an explosion tore through the top deck of a London bus. One of the dead was a young man called Anthony Fatayi-Williams: twenty-six years old and killed on his way to work. The explosion was part of a coordinated series of suicide-bomb attacks on the London public-transport system that killed fifty-two people and injured over seven hundred others (in what would become known as the 7/7 attacks). The attacks were carried out by four young Muslim men from the north of England and it was the youngest of them, eighteen-year-old Hasib Hussain, who detonated the bomb that killed Anthony and twelve others on the Number 30 bus. As with the other bombers, Hussain had been planning to target a tube train but for some reason, like Anthony, he chose a bus instead.[41] These two men had never met, yet one of them used a home-made bomb to murder the other in order to make a violent political statement. Such is the horror of terrorism.

Five days later, Anthony's mother, Marie Fatayi-Williams, made a passionate and deeply moving public plea for information on what had happened to her son, who was still listed as missing at that time. Anthony's friends had spent days searching local hospitals for him and Fatayi-Williams had flown to London from her home in Lagos, Nigeria, desperately seeking information on her son's whereabouts. Surrounded by friends and family, she was fighting back tears and holding a photo of Anthony as she addressed a group of journalists at an outdoor news conference near the scene of the bomb blast in Tavistock Square: 'This is Anthony, Anthony Fatayi-Williams, twenty-six years old, he's missing and we fear that he was in the bus explosion . . . on Thursday. We don't know.'

It was impossible not to be moved by Fatayi-Williams' words. They revealed the pain of a mother grieving the loss of her son even before she was certain he was dead: 'I am proud of him, I am still very proud of him but I need to know where he is, I need to know what happened to him. I grieve, I am sad, I am distraught, I am destroyed.' Although she condemned those who had carried out the attacks, she did not seek revenge – but she did have questions: 'How much blood must be spilled? How many tears shall we cry? How many mothers' hearts must be maimed?' And: 'What did he then do to deserve this? Where is he, someone tell me, where is he?' She linked the innocent victims of terrorist attacks in New York, Madrid and London, where she said, 'There have been streams of tears, innocent tears. There have been rivers of blood, innocent blood.'

Anthony was born in London in 1979 but he was a 'world citizen' according to his mother, with his childhood split between London, Lagos and Paris. His mother Marie is a devout Catholic and at the time worked as a marketing director for Elf. His father Alan is a Muslim and one of Nigeria's leading doctors. Anthony attended school in Sevenoaks, Kent, and went on to study for a degree in politics and economics at the University of Bradford (not far from Leeds, the city where three of the bombers grew up). He moved to London and joined Amec Offshore Services in 2002, and in 2005 became a regional executive developing new oil and gas opportunities in Africa. At the time of his death, Anthony was also studying through a distance-learning course for an MBA with Durham University. He was killed because the terrorists made no distinction between innocent British citizens and their government.

Three of the bombers had Pakistani parents and two of the bombers – Shehzad Tanweer and Mohammad Sidique Khan – spent some time in Pakistan in late 2004 and early 2005, and they no doubt received support and training for the attack from jihadi elements, possibly linked to al-Qaida, in Pakistan. However, it does not seem right to blame Pakistan rather than Britain for the bombers' radicalisation, given that three of the bombers were British (Jermaine Lindsay was Jamaican) and all were raised and educated in the UK – they were, in short, the products of a British upbringing. Instead of pointing the finger at Pakistan, answers to the bombers' motivations lay closer to home. We know from the video messages left by two of the bombers, Khan and Tanweer, that they considered themselves, however erroneously, to be soldiers of Islam – fighting against the perceived oppression of Muslims and hoping to force the British government to withdraw troops from Afghanistan and Iraq.

Two weeks after the 7/7 attacks, four men originally from East Africa attempted a repeat attack on London's public-transport system, again targeting three underground trains and a bus (a fifth bomber dumped his device without attempting to detonate it). However, only the detonators fired and the would-be bombers fled after their bombs failed to explode, sparking a massive manhunt and numerous security alerts. The next day, while the search for the failed bombers continued, armed police shot and killed an innocent man at Stockwell tube station. The man was twenty-seven-year-old Jean Charles de Menezes: a Brazilian living in London, who surveillance officers had mistakenly identified as Hussain Osman, one of the suspects from the failed attacks the previous day (Osman was finally caught in Rome a week later). Specialist firearms officers confronted de Menezes after he boarded a train on the Northern Line and, wrongly believing he was about to detonate a bomb, two of them shot him seven times in the head at close range without warning.

It is clear that around this time the police and security services were on the brink of losing control of the terrorist threat. They were operating under intense pressure and lacking the necessary resources to untangle and track the various elements of the growing web of international jihadi networks and al-Qaida-inspired groups that threatened the United Kingdom (by September 2007 it was even worse, with MI5 reportedly tracking at least two thousand individuals, two hundred terrorist networks and thirty active plots).[42] It also seemed to many that the British government was more interested in protecting its own political reputation and special relationship with the United States than understanding the role its foreign policies were playing in this dynamic, denying any link between its support for the war on terror and the occupations of Afghanistan and Iraq and the growing terrorist threat to the UK. Yet at their trial in 2007, the failed 21/7 bombers clearly explained that their actions were in protest against the invasion and occupation of Iraq (as was one of the likely motivations of the 7/7 bombers).[43] Similar motivations were also claimed by Bilal Abdulla, one of the men behind the 2007 attack on Glasgow airport and the failed car-bomb attacks in London, who was in part inspired by insurgents in Iraq.[44]

Although the actions of people such as this may be cloaked in and justified by a dangerous perversion of Islam, their motivations are primarily socio-political grievances, not religious fundamentalism. However, they do see Islam to be a religion under attack – in Afghanistan and Iraq, as well as in Palestine, the Balkans, Chechnya, Kashmir, Lebanon and elsewhere – and are motivated by injustices against Muslims around the world: from the refugee camps of Gaza and the West Bank to torture, abuse and civilian deaths in Iraq. They feel called to defend their cultural heritage in the face of perceived Western social, political, economic and military dominance. Extremist groups offer radical philosophies that provide these people with an explanation of what is happening around them and suggest violent actions that may make sense from within an environment of humiliation, despair or anger. This is not to excuse violence – to attempt to understand is not to condone – but it is only through understanding what motivates such people that we can work to undermine the causes of terrorism.

It should be noted that while perhaps the greatest threat still comes from Islamist terrorism – because of the risk of al-Qaida-inspired mass-casualty attacks on civilians – during the period from 2006 to 2008 (for which there is Europol data) of the over fifteen hundred failed, foiled or successful terrorist attacks in Europe only five, or 0.3 per cent, were attributed to Islamist terrorism. Europol distinguishes between various different types of terrorist organisation based on their primary motivation:

Islamist, ethno-nationalist and separatist, anarchist and left wing (predominantly Marxist–Leninist), right wing (predominantly National Socialist) and single issue (predominantly animal rights or environmentalist). The vast majority of attacks during the period in question were carried out by Basque and Corsican separatist movements in Spain and France.[45] However, Europol report that 'A number of member states judge that they continue to face a high-level threat from Islamist terrorism for reasons that include military presence in Iraq or Afghanistan or accusations of anti-Muslim attitudes.'[46]

There is clearly a very real jihadist threat to countries in Europe and elsewhere (the Europol data does not, for example, include the successful March 2004 Madrid train bombings or the failed Christmas Day 2009 attempt to blow up an airliner en route to Detroit). However, attempts to sway such people away from violence must move beyond the failed policies of the war on terror. An effective strategy should be based on engagement: bringing those attracted to radical ideologies into dialogue wherever possible by attempting to draw them into a political process where their voice may be heard and legitimate grievances addressed. Community dialogue can encourage cohesion across diverse societies and moderate mosques and clerics can help the younger generation understand and integrate their Muslim and Western identities and show them peaceful interpretations of Islam. Efforts must also be made to counter the spread of jihadi propaganda on the Internet, through monitoring extremist websites and chat rooms and supporting more moderate online voices. At the same time, police and intelligence agencies can critically disrupt the recruitment, training and financing of terrorist groups. This would be a far more sustainable and effective approach – addressing some of the underlying causes of terrorism, intervening before individuals are persuaded by radical arguments and restricting the ability of terrorist groups to operate.

By reaching out to people at a very human level Fatayi-Williams had her own way of addressing the terrorist threat and coping with the pain of her loss. At Anthony's funeral mass in Westminster Cathedral on 23 July 2005, her husband announced that they were establishing the Anthony Fatayi-Williams Foundation for Peace and Conflict Resolution in order to seek alternatives to war, terror and violence. A year later she published a book recounting her experiences over the days and weeks that followed 7/7 and donated the proceeds to supporting the work of the foundation.[47] The day before her book was published, Fatayi-Williams urged Hussain's mother to stand side by side with her to condemn suicide attacks and has since worked hard to promote a message of peace and forgiveness.

The last word should go to Fatayi-Williams, who despite her intense personal grief showed more understanding than most: 'It's time to stop and think. We cannot live in fear because we are surrounded by hatred. . . . Hatred begets only hatred. It is time to stop this vicious cycle of killing. We must all stand together, for our common humanity.' It is in this way – not through division and war – that together we must face those who would seek to use violence for political gain, whether terrorist organisations or our elected politicians.

Bloomsbury, London, England

11 JULY 2005

This is Anthony, Anthony Fatayi-Williams, twenty-six years old, he's missing and we fear that he was in the bus explosion . . . on Thursday. We don't know. We do know from the witnesses that he left the Northern Line in Euston. We know he made a call to his office at Amec at 9.41 from the NW1 area to say he could not make it by the tube but he would find alternative means to work.

Since then he has not made any contact with any single person. Now New York, now Madrid, now London. There has been widespread slaughter of innocent people. There have been streams of tears, innocent tears. There have been rivers of blood, innocent blood. Death in the morning, people going to find their livelihood, death in the noontime on the highways and streets.

They are not warriors. Which cause has been served? Certainly not the cause of God, not the cause of Allah because God Almighty only gives life and is full of mercy. Anyone who has been misled, or is being misled to believe that by killing innocent people he or she is serving God should think again because it's not true. Terrorism is not the way, terrorism is not the way. It doesn't beget peace. We can't deliver peace by terrorism, never can we deliver peace by killing people. Throughout history, those people who have changed the world have done so without violence, they have won people to their cause through peaceful protest. Nelson Mandela, Martin Luther King, Mahatma Gandhi, their discipline, their self-sacrifice, their conviction made people turn towards them, to follow them. What inspiration can senseless slaughter provide? Death and destruction of young people in their prime as well as old and helpless can never be the foundations for building society.

My son Anthony is my first son, my only son, the head of my family. In African society, we hold on to sons. He has dreams and hopes and I, his mother, must fight to protect them. This is now the fifth day, five days on, and we are waiting to know what happened to him and I, his mother, I need to know what happened to Anthony. His young sisters need to know what happened, his uncles and aunties need to know what happened to Anthony, his father needs to know what happened to Anthony. Millions of my friends back home in Nigeria need to know what happened to Anthony. His friends surrounding me here, who have put this together, need to know what has happened to Anthony. I need to know, I want to protect him. I'm his mother, I will fight till I die to protect him. To protect his values and to protect his memory.

Innocent blood will always cry to God Almighty for reparation. How much blood must be spilled? How many tears shall we cry? How many mothers' hearts must be maimed? My heart is maimed. I pray I will see my son, Anthony. Why? I need to know, Anthony needs to know, Anthony needs to know, so do many others unaccounted for innocent victims, they need to know.

It's time to stop and think. We cannot live in fear because we are surrounded by hatred. Look around us today. Anthony is a Nigerian, born in London, worked in London, he is a world citizen. Here today we have Christians, Muslims, Jews, Sikhs, Hindus, all of us united in love for Anthony. Hatred begets only hatred. It is time to stop this vicious cycle of killing. We must all stand together, for our common humanity. I need to know what happened to my Anthony. He's the love of my life. My first son, my first son, twenty-six. He tells me one day: 'Mummy, I don't want to die, I don't want to die. I want to live, I want to take care of you, I will do great things for you, I will look after you, you will see what I will achieve for you. I will make you happy.' And he was making me happy. I am proud of him, I am still very proud of him but I need to now where he is, I need to know what happened to him. I grieve, I am sad, I am distraught, I am destroyed.

He didn't do anything to anybody, he loved everybody so much. If what I hear is true, even when he came out of the underground he was directing people to take buses, to be sure that they were OK. Then he called his office at the same time to tell them he was running late. He was a multi-purpose person, trying to save people, trying to call his office, trying to meet his appointments. What did he then do to deserve this? Where is he, someone tell me, where is he?

❝ Throughout history, those people who have changed the world have done so without violence, they have won people to their cause through peaceful protest. ❞

A New Beginning

— BARACK OBAMA —

Relations between the West and the Muslim world were severely strained by the time Barack Obama became the 44th President of the United States in 2009. The Middle East had suffered through colonialism, the Cold War, globalisation and the war on terror and Muslims around the world were railing against perceived and actual oppression and undue Western influence. During his election campaign Obama had promised to repair the damage that his predecessor George Bush had caused to these relations and attempt to bridge the widening gulf by giving a major address to Muslims from a Muslim capital during his first few months in office. On the afternoon of 4 June 2009 in the Great Hall at Cairo University he fulfilled that promise, explaining that he had 'come here to seek a new beginning between the United States and Muslims around the world; one based upon mutual interest and mutual respect'.

It was an incredible speech, but in many ways Obama is an incredible person. He entered the White House in January 2009 on the back of a hugely successful grassroots campaign that saw him come to office with genuine popular support. His optimism, intelligence, charm and skill as a powerful public speaker stood him in stark contrast to his predecessor and left his electoral opponent John McCain struggling to compete. As America's first black President, Obama offered not just a break with the recent past of Bush and the neoconservatives but something approaching a brief moment of closure on America's dark history of slavery and segregation. The sight of veteran civil-rights campaigner Jesse Jackson reduced to tears on the night of Obama's election victory said it all. Jackson was with Martin Luther King when he was assassinated in 1968 and could probably never have imagined then that forty years later he would witness the election of an African American to the US presidency.

Obama's electoral victory was greeted by supporters with cries of 'Yes we can'. He told those gathered in Grant Park in Chicago to hear his election night speech, 'It's been a long time coming, but tonight, because of what we did on this day, in this election, at this defining moment, change has come to America.'[48] However, within a year of his taking office, a feeling was growing within liberal circles that his promises of transformative change were not being borne out in policy. The start of 2010 saw Obama heavily criticised for compromising on healthcare reform, delaying the closure of the Guantánamo Bay detention camp, sending more troops to Afghanistan and failing to make significant progress on climate-change legislation, gay rights, immigration reform or labour-union rights. By then, Obama's approval rating was only 50 per cent – down eighteen points from the beginning of his presidency. He was also proving to be a politically divisive figure: opinion polls showed that while an overwhelming majority of Democrats still approved of his job performance, less than half of independents and only a small minority of Republicans felt the same way.[49] But as he said on election night: 'The road ahead will be long. Our climb will be steep. We may not get there in one year or even in one term. . . . There will be setbacks and false starts. There are many who won't agree with every decision or policy I make as President'. 'But I will always be honest with you about the challenges we face', he said, 'I will listen to you, especially when we disagree.'[50]

Obama was born in Hawaii on 4 August 1961 to a black Kenyan father and white American mother and spent four years of his childhood in Indonesia before moving back to Hawaii to live with his maternal grandparents. Just as Obama was well placed to bridge the gap between white and black America he was perhaps uniquely placed to bridge the gap between the Muslim world and the West: his paternal grandfather, father and stepfather were Muslims; he was raised for several years in a Muslim country; and even his name – Barack Hussein – is a Muslim name. This is what helped make his Cairo speech so powerful. It is also what worried conservative commentators so much during the 2008 presidential election campaign: not only was he an African American and a Democrat but, they feared, erroneously, he might be a Muslim as well – the worst possible combination in their eyes. Unable to publicly attack him for the colour of his skin, they often used his alleged Muslim background as a simple proxy for race (some went further and claimed that he was not an American citizen at all).[51] For such commentators, Obama's Cairo speech was the height of his appeasement of Islam. Fortunately, post-Bush, their views are now largely confined to right-wing media such as Fox News and the stranger corners of the Internet and blogosphere, where they can appeal to the right-wing grassroots without causing more widespread damage.

What really mattered was the generally positive reaction to Obama's speech from the Muslim world. He received a standing ovation and cheers from the three-thousand-strong crowd when he finished speaking and his words were broadly welcomed across the region – although many rightly argued that they would need to be backed up with true policy changes if they were to have any real meaning.[52] This is something Obama himself recognised when he said that 'change cannot happen overnight. No single speech can eradicate years of mistrust, nor can I answer in the time that I have all the complex questions that brought us to this point.' His speech covered many of these complex questions, including violent extremism, nuclear weapons, religious freedom, democracy, women's rights and economic development (the last three were particularly interesting for a speech given in Egypt). For many Muslims, however, the key issues he touched upon were Israel–Palestine and the wider Arab–Israeli conflict.[53]

The shadow of the Israeli–Palestinian conflict hangs over the Muslim world. It is so deep-seated that it blocks progress on many other important issues. It is a scar on the Arab and Muslim psyche that is personally felt by many ordinary people across the Middle East and further afield. The continued presence of Israeli settlements on Palestinian land and the appalling human-rights situation for most Palestinians increases support for Hamas and other Islamist movements and maintains Israel's status as a regional, if not global, pariah state. Israelis demand security, while Palestinians demand a viable state of their own – the two are mutually dependent on each other. However, Israel's reliance on the military elements of security above all other mechanisms leads to disproportionate levels of civilian deaths and injuries amongst the Palestinian population, together with the destruction of property and infrastructure. Furthermore, international attempts to isolate Hamas are ignoring the legitimate political aspirations of those who handed the movement a clear mandate in the January 2006 elections. For its part, the continued refusal by Hamas to officially recognise the State of Israel and its rocket attacks on the civilian population of Israel are deeply counter-productive and only provoke further military responses. The cycle needs to be broken.[54]

The Israeli-Palestinian conflict is characterised by deep division, with people usually falling into one camp or the other: either pro-Israeli or pro-Palestinian – as if the two are mutually exclusive, which they are not. According to Obama, 'if we see this conflict only from one side or the other, then we will be blind to the truth'. People's attitudes are all too often informed by their political outlook, rather than an understanding of the region's history, national identities or security needs. Many of those who lean to the left tend towards supporting the Palestinians and many of those who lean to the right tend towards supporting the Israelis. The debate is also characterised by astonishing levels of ignorance, historical revisionism and intolerance – with anti-Semitism and Islamophobia appearing in equal measures.

The Palestine question is only one issue in the wider Arab–Israeli conflict, which is one of the principal drivers of insecurity in the Middle East. From the struggle for Jewish statehood in the 1940s to the wars of 1967 and 1973, Israel's existence has at times been perilous and consequently security dominates the domestic political agenda above all other issues. Today, though, Israel is seen by many of its neighbours as the most militarily aggressive country in the region. Its occupation of Palestinian territory and its attacks on Lebanon in 2006 and Gaza in 2008 did little or nothing to improve Israeli security but led to high numbers of civilian casualties (the United Nations has raised concerns that war crimes and crimes against humanity may have been committed by both sides during the three-week Gaza offensive).[55]

Israel sees itself as isolated, surrounded by potential enemies, both state and non-state, which it believes pose an existential threat. At the same time, the Muslim world sees that Israel benefits from the political and financial support of the US government and has the best equipped and trained military forces in the region, backed up by the ultimate weapon of last resort in its controversial nuclear arsenal. While at times it does display a willingness to use diplomacy and negotiation (such as with Egypt, Jordan and, most recently, Syria), the history of the conflict and the level of mistrust in the region mean diplomacy is viewed by many Israelis as a tool of the naive. Instead, Israel's approach to security is built on the principle of deterrence and all too often it allows relations with other countries to become militarised.[56]

Several developments have potentially isolated Israel even further, including the change from the Bush to the Obama administration in the United States, a political move to the right in Israel and disagreements between the two governments over new settlements in East Jerusalem and the Israeli blockade of Gaza. This may, however, eventually have the positive effect of encouraging Israel to take seriously the offer set out in the Arab Peace Initiative first proposed by Saudi Arabia in 2002 and endorsed by both the Arab League and the Organisation of the Islamic Conference. In short, this initiative offers Israel comprehensive peace agreements and the normalisation of relations with Arab countries in exchange for a withdrawal from all occupied Arab territories, recognition of an independent Palestinian state (with East Jerusalem as its capital) and a just solution for Palestinian refugees. However, as Obama argued, 'Arab states must recognise that the Arab Peace Initiative was an important beginning, but not the end of their responsibilities. The Arab–Israeli conflict should no longer be used to distract the people of Arab nations from other problems. Instead, it must be a cause for action to help the Palestinian people'. Just as the Israeli government must change tack, so too must the Arab governments who encourage anti-Semitic sentiment in order to divert attention from the serious social, economic and political problems in their own countries.

Obama ended his Cairo speech by saying, 'We have the power to make the world we seek, but only if we have the courage to make a new beginning, keeping in mind what has been written.' He then quoted from the holy books of Islam, Judaism and Christianity, before saying, 'The people of the world can live together in peace. We know that is God's vision. Now, that must be our work here on Earth.' In recognition of his efforts in this area, Obama was awarded the Nobel Peace Prize at the end of 2009. The Nobel Committee wanted to support his approach to strengthening international diplomacy and cooperation between peoples. The award was greeted with widespread surprise – including from Obama himself – and many felt it was somewhat premature, coming less than a year into his presidency. However, it was no doubt designed to encourage Obama to follow a cooperative international approach.

Such encouragement was essential as he pursued his early foreign-policy priorities, including nuclear disarmament, international action on climate change, an end to combat operations in Iraq, better relations with Russia, engagement with Iran, progress on Arab–Israeli peace and a way forward in Afghanistan. Such huge international issues severely tested Obama's commitment to diplomacy and cooperation, and the world was watching carefully for any sign of a return to the aggressive policies of the Bush era. Worryingly, less than two weeks before he accepted his peace prize Obama announced that he would be sending thirty thousand more US troops to Afghanistan, in an echo of Bush's Iraq 'surge'. He then used his Nobel lecture in Oslo to defend US actions in Afghanistan and to argue that non-violence had its limits and that war was sometimes justified.[57] Then a week after accepting his prize he attended the Copenhagen climate-change summit and gave a lacklustre speech that provoked China and left world leaders deeply disappointed.[58] It seems that the aspirations of Obama the global peacemaker will at times be overshadowed by the actions of Obama the US President.

But as I argued in the introduction to this book, words do matter. Obama's friend and fellow US politician Deval Patrick said, 'the right words, spoken from the heart with conviction, with a vision of a better place and a faith in the unseen, are a call to action'.[59] This was reflected by Obama in the closing section of his Cairo speech: 'All of us share this world for but a brief moment in time. The question is whether we spend that time focused on what pushes us apart, or whether we commit ourselves to an effort – a sustained effort – to find common ground, to focus on the future we seek for our children, and to respect the dignity of all human beings.' In other words, together we can and must work for a peaceful future.

Cairo University, Giza, Egypt

4 JUNE 2009

I am honoured to be in the timeless city of Cairo, and to be hosted by two remarkable institutions. For over a thousand years, al-Azhar has stood as a beacon of Islamic learning, and for over a century, Cairo University has been a source of Egypt's advancement. Together, you represent the harmony between tradition and progress. I am grateful for your hospitality, and the hospitality of the people of Egypt. I am also proud to carry with me the goodwill of the American people, and a greeting of peace from Muslim communities in my country: *assalamu alaikum*.*

We meet at a time of tension between the United States and Muslims around the world – tension rooted in historical forces that go beyond any current policy debate. The relationship between Islam and the West includes centuries of co-existence and cooperation, but also conflict and religious wars. More recently, tension has been fed by colonialism that denied rights and opportunities to many Muslims, and a Cold War in which Muslim-majority countries were too often treated as proxies without regard to their own aspirations. Moreover, the sweeping change brought by modernity and globalisation led many Muslims to view the West as hostile to the traditions of Islam.

Violent extremists have exploited these tensions in a small but potent minority of Muslims. The attacks of 11 September 2001 and the continued efforts of these extremists to engage in violence against civilians has led some in my country to view Islam as inevitably hostile not only to America and Western countries, but also to human rights. This has bred more fear and mistrust.

So long as our relationship is defined by our differences, we will empower those who sow hatred rather than peace, and who promote conflict rather than the cooperation that can help all of our people achieve justice and prosperity. This cycle of suspicion and discord must end.

I have come here to seek a new beginning between the United States and Muslims around the world; one based upon mutual interest and mutual respect; and one based upon the truth that America and Islam are not exclusive, and need not be in competition. Instead, they overlap, and share

* *Assalamu alaikum* is an Arabic greeting meaning 'peace be upon you'.

66 We meet at a time of tension between the United States and Muslims around the world 99

common principles – principles of justice and progress; tolerance and the dignity of all human beings.

I do so recognising that change cannot happen overnight. No single speech can eradicate years of mistrust, nor can I answer in the time that I have all the complex questions that brought us to this point. But I am convinced that in order to move forward, we must say openly the things we hold in our hearts, and that too often are said only behind closed doors. There must be a sustained effort to listen to each other; to learn from each other; to respect one another; and to seek common ground. As the Holy Koran tells us: 'Be conscious of God and speak always the truth.' That is what I will try to do – to speak the truth as best I can, humbled by the task before us, and firm in my belief that the interests we share as human beings are far more powerful than the forces that drive us apart.

Part of this conviction is rooted in my own experience. I am a Christian, but my father came from a Kenyan family that includes generations of Muslims. As a boy, I spent several years in Indonesia and heard the call of the *azaan* at the break of dawn and the fall of dusk.* As a young man, I worked in Chicago communities where many found dignity and peace in their Muslim faith.

As a student of history, I also know civilisation's debt to Islam. It was Islam – at places like al-Azhar University – that carried the light of learning through so many centuries, paving the way for Europe's Renaissance and Enlightenment. It was innovation in Muslim communities that developed the order of algebra; our magnetic compass and tools of navigation; our mastery of pens and printing; our understanding of how disease spreads and how it can be healed. Islamic culture has given us majestic arches and soaring spires; timeless poetry and cherished music; elegant calligraphy and places of peaceful contemplation. And throughout history, Islam has demonstrated through words and deeds the possibilities of religious tolerance and racial equality.

* *Azaan* is the Islamic call to prayer.

I know, too, that Islam has always been a part of America's story. The first nation to recognise my country was Morocco. In signing the Treaty of Tripoli in 1796, our second President, John Adams, wrote: 'The United States has in itself no character of enmity against the laws, religion or tranquillity of Muslims.' And since our founding, American Muslims have enriched the United States. They have fought in our wars, served in government, stood for civil rights, started businesses, taught at our universities, excelled in our sports arenas, won Nobel Prizes, built our tallest building, and lit the Olympic torch. And when the first Muslim American was recently elected to Congress, he took the oath to defend our constitution using the same Holy Koran that one of our founding fathers – Thomas Jefferson – kept in his personal library.

So I have known Islam on three continents before coming to the region where it was first revealed. That experience guides my conviction that partnership between America and Islam must be based on what Islam is, not what it isn't. And I consider it part of my responsibility as President of the United States to fight against negative stereotypes of Islam wherever they appear.

But that same principle must apply to Muslim perceptions of America. Just as Muslims do not fit a crude stereotype, America is not the crude stereotype of a self-interested empire. The United States has been one of the greatest sources of progress that the world has ever known. We were born out of revolution against an empire. We were founded upon the ideal that all are created equal, and we have shed blood and struggled for centuries to give meaning to those words – within our borders, and around the world. We are shaped by every culture, drawn from every end of the Earth, and dedicated to a simple concept: *E pluribus unum* – Out of many, one.

Much has been made of the fact that an African American with the name Barack Hussein Obama could be elected President. But my personal story is not so unique. The dream of opportunity for all people has not come true for everyone in America, but its promise exists for all who come to our shores – that includes nearly seven million American Muslims in our country today who enjoy incomes and education that are higher than average.

Moreover, freedom in America is indivisible from the freedom to practise one's religion. That is why there is a mosque in every state of our union, and over one thousand two hundred mosques within our borders. That is why the US government has gone to court to protect the right of women and girls to wear the hijab, and to punish those who would deny it.

So let there be no doubt: Islam is a part of America. And I believe that America holds within her the truth that regardless of race, religion, or station in life, all of us share common aspirations – to live in peace and security; to get an education and to work with dignity; to love our families, our communities, and our God. These things we share. This is the hope of all humanity.

Of course, recognising our common humanity is only the beginning of our task. Words alone cannot meet the needs of our people. These needs will be met only if we act boldly in the years ahead; and if we understand that the challenges we face are shared, and our failure to meet them will hurt us all.

For we have learned from recent experience that when a financial system weakens in one country, prosperity is hurt everywhere. When a new flu infects one human being, all are at risk. When one nation pursues a nuclear weapon, the risk of nuclear attack rises for all nations. When violent extremists operate in one stretch of mountains, people are endangered across an ocean. And when innocents in Bosnia and Darfur are slaughtered, that is a stain on our collective conscience. That is what it means to share this world in the twenty-first century. That is the responsibility we have to one another as human beings.

This is a difficult responsibility to embrace. For human history has often been a record of nations and tribes subjugating one another to serve their own interests. Yet in this new age, such attitudes are self-defeating. Given our interdependence, any world order that elevates one nation or group of people over another will inevitably fail. So whatever we think of the past, we must not be prisoners of it. Our problems must be dealt with through partnership; progress must be shared.

That does not mean we should ignore sources of tension. Indeed, it suggests the opposite: we must face these tensions squarely. And so in that spirit, let me speak as clearly and plainly as I can about some specific issues that I believe we must finally confront together.

“ the challenges we face are shared, and our failure to meet them will hurt us all ”

Violent Extremism

The first issue that we have to confront is violent extremism in all of its forms.

In Ankara, I made clear that America is not – and never will be – at war with Islam. We will, however, relentlessly confront violent extremists who pose a grave threat to our security. Because we reject the same thing that people of all faiths reject: the killing of innocent men, women, and children. And it is my first duty as President to protect the American people.

The situation in Afghanistan demonstrates America's goals, and our need to work together. Over seven years ago, the United States pursued al-Qaida and the Taliban with broad international support. We did not go by choice, we went because of necessity. I am aware that some question or justify the events of 9/11. But let us be clear: al-Qaida killed nearly three thousand people on that day. The victims were innocent men, women, and children from America and many other nations who had done nothing to harm anybody. And yet al-Qaida chose to ruthlessly murder these people, claimed credit for the attack, and even now states their determination to kill on a massive scale. They have affiliates in many countries and are trying to expand their reach. These are not opinions to be debated; these are facts to be dealt with.

Make no mistake: we do not want to keep our troops in Afghanistan. We seek no military bases there. It is agonising for America to lose our young men and women. It is costly and politically difficult to continue this conflict. We would gladly bring every single one of our troops home if we could be confident that there were not violent extremists in Afghanistan and Pakistan determined to kill as many Americans as they possibly can. But that is not yet the case.

That's why we're partnering with a coalition of forty-six countries. And despite the costs involved, America's commitment will not weaken. Indeed, none of us should tolerate these extremists. They have killed in many countries. They have killed people of different faiths – more than any other, they have killed Muslims. Their actions are irreconcilable with the rights of human beings, the progress of nations, and with Islam. The Holy Koran teaches that whoever kills an innocent, it is as if he has killed all mankind; and whoever saves a person, it is as if he has saved all mankind. The enduring faith of over a billion people is so much bigger than the narrow hatred of a few. Islam is not part of the problem in combating violent extremism – it is an important part of promoting peace.

We also know that military power alone is not going to solve the problems in Afghanistan and Pakistan. That is why we plan to invest $1.5 billion each year over the next five years to partner with Pakistanis to build schools and hospitals, roads and businesses, and hundreds of millions to help those who have been displaced. And that is why we are providing more than $2.8 billion to help Afghans develop their economy and deliver services that people depend upon.

Let me also address the issue of Iraq. Unlike Afghanistan, Iraq was a war of choice that provoked strong differences in my country and around the world. Although I believe that the Iraqi people are ultimately better off without the tyranny of Saddam Hussein, I also believe that events in Iraq have reminded America of the need to use diplomacy and build international consensus to resolve our problems whenever possible. Indeed, we can recall the words of Thomas Jefferson, who said: 'I hope that our wisdom will grow with our power, and teach us that the less we use our power the greater it will be.'

Today, America has a dual responsibility: to help Iraq forge a better future – and to leave Iraq to Iraqis. I have made it clear to the Iraqi people that we pursue no bases, and no claim on their territory or resources. Iraq's sovereignty is its own. That is why I ordered the removal of our combat brigades by next August. That is why we will honour our agreement with Iraq's democratically elected government to remove combat troops from Iraqi cities by July, and to remove all our troops from Iraq by 2012. We will help Iraq train its security forces and develop its economy. But we will support a secure and united Iraq as a partner, and never as a patron.

And finally, just as America can never tolerate violence by extremists, we must never alter our principles. 9/11 was an enormous trauma to our country. The fear and anger that it provoked was understandable, but in some cases, it led us to act contrary to our ideals. We are taking concrete actions to change course. I have unequivocally prohibited the use of torture by the United States, and I have ordered the prison at Guantánamo Bay closed by early next year.

So America will defend itself, respectful of the sovereignty of nations and the rule of law. And we will do so in partnership with Muslim communities which are also threatened. The sooner the extremists are isolated and unwelcome in Muslim communities, the sooner we will all be safer.

Israel, Palestine, and the Arab World

The second major source of tension that we need to discuss is the situation between Israelis, Palestinians, and the Arab world.

America's strong bonds with Israel are well known. This bond is unbreakable. It is based upon cultural and historical ties, and the recognition that the aspiration for a Jewish homeland is rooted in a tragic history that cannot be denied.

Around the world, the Jewish people were persecuted for centuries, and anti-Semitism in Europe culminated in an unprecedented Holocaust. Tomorrow, I will visit Buchenwald, which was part of a network of camps where Jews were enslaved, tortured, shot, and gassed to death by the Third Reich. Six million Jews were killed – more than the entire Jewish population of Israel today. Denying that fact is baseless, ignorant, and hateful. Threatening Israel with destruction – or repeating vile stereotypes about Jews – is deeply wrong, and only serves to evoke in the minds of Israelis this most painful of memories while preventing the peace that the people of this region deserve.

On the other hand, it is also undeniable that the Palestinian people – Muslims and Christians – have suffered in pursuit of a homeland. For more than sixty years they have endured the pain of dislocation. Many wait in refugee camps in the West Bank, Gaza, and neighbouring lands for a life of peace and security that they have never been able to lead. They endure the daily humiliations – large and small – that come with occupation. So let there be no doubt: the situation for the Palestinian people is intolerable. America will not turn our backs on the legitimate Palestinian aspiration for dignity, opportunity, and a state of their own.

For decades, there has been a stalemate: two peoples with legitimate aspirations, each with a painful history that makes compromise elusive. It is easy to point fingers – for Palestinians to point to the displacement brought by Israel's founding and for Israelis to point to the constant hostility and attacks throughout its history from within its borders as well as beyond. But if we see this conflict only from one side or the other, then we will be blind to the truth: the only resolution is for the aspirations of both sides to be met through two states, where Israelis and Palestinians each live in peace and security.

That is in Israel's interest, Palestine's interest, America's interest, and the world's interest. That is why I intend to personally pursue this outcome with all the patience that the task requires. The obligations that the parties have agreed to under the road map are clear. For peace to come, it is time for them – and all of us – to live up to our responsibilities.

Palestinians must abandon violence. Resistance through violence and killing is wrong and does not succeed. For centuries, black people in America suffered the lash of the whip as slaves and the humiliation of segregation. But it was not violence that won full and equal rights. It was a peaceful and determined insistence upon the ideals at the centre of America's founding. This same story can be told by people from South Africa to South Asia; from Eastern Europe to Indonesia. It's a story with a simple truth: that violence is a dead end. It is a sign of neither courage nor power to shoot rockets at sleeping children, or to blow up old women on a bus. That is not how moral authority is claimed; that is how it is surrendered.

Now is the time for Palestinians to focus on what they can build. The Palestinian Authority must develop its capacity to govern, with institutions that serve the needs of its people. Hamas does have support among some Palestinians, but they also have responsibilities. To play a role in fulfilling Palestinian aspirations, and to unify the Palestinian people, Hamas must put an end to violence, recognise past agreements, and recognise Israel's right to exist.

At the same time, Israelis must acknowledge that just as Israel's right to exist cannot be denied, neither can Palestine's. The United States does not accept the legitimacy of continued Israeli settlements. This construction violates previous agreements and undermines efforts to achieve peace. It is time for these settlements to stop.

Israel must also live up to its obligations to ensure that Palestinians can live and work and develop their society. And just as it devastates Palestinian families, the continuing humanitarian crisis in Gaza does not serve Israel's security; neither does the continuing lack of opportunity in the West Bank. Progress in the daily lives of the Palestinian people must be part of a road to peace, and Israel must take concrete steps to enable such progress.

Finally, the Arab states must recognise that the Arab Peace Initiative was an important beginning, but not the end of their responsibilities. The Arab–Israeli conflict should no longer be used to distract the people of Arab nations from other problems. Instead, it must be a cause for action to help the Palestinian people develop the institutions that will sustain their state; to recognise Israel's legitimacy; and to choose progress over a self-defeating focus on the past.

America will align our policies with those who pursue peace, and say in public what we say in private to Israelis and Palestinians and Arabs. We cannot impose peace. But privately, many Muslims recognise that Israel will not go away. Likewise, many Israelis recognise the need for a Palestinian state. It is time for us to act on what everyone knows to be true.

Too many tears have flowed. Too much blood has been shed. All of us have a responsibility to work for the day when the mothers of Israelis and Palestinians can see their children grow up without fear; when the Holy Land of three great faiths is the place of peace that God intended it to be; when Jerusalem is a secure and lasting home for Jews and Christians and Muslims, and a place for all of the children of Abraham to mingle peacefully together as in the story of Isra, when Moses, Jesus, and Mohammed (peace be upon them) joined in prayer.

Nuclear Weapons

The third source of tension is our shared interest in the rights and responsibilities of nations on nuclear weapons.

This issue has been a source of tension between the United States and the Islamic Republic of Iran. For many years, Iran has defined itself in part by its opposition to my country, and there is indeed a tumultuous history between us. In the middle of the Cold War, the United States played a role in the overthrow of a democratically elected Iranian government. Since the Islamic revolution, Iran has played a role in acts of hostage-taking and violence against US troops and civilians. This history is well known. Rather than remain trapped in the past, I have made it clear to Iran's leaders and people that my country is prepared to move forward. The question, now, is not what Iran is against, but rather what future it wants to build.

It will be hard to overcome decades of mistrust, but we will proceed with courage, rectitude, and resolve. There will be many issues to discuss between our two countries, and we are willing to move forward without preconditions on the basis of mutual respect. But it is clear to all concerned that when it comes to nuclear weapons, we have reached a decisive point. This is not simply about America's interests. It is about preventing a nuclear arms race in the Middle East that could lead this region and the world down a hugely dangerous path.

I understand those who protest that some countries have weapons that others do not. No single nation should pick and choose which nations hold nuclear weapons. That is why I strongly reaffirmed America's commitment to seek a world in which no nations hold nuclear weapons. And any nation – including

Iran – should have the right to access peaceful nuclear power if it complies with its responsibilities under the nuclear non-proliferation treaty. That commitment is at the core of the treaty, and it must be kept for all who fully abide by it. And I am hopeful that all countries in the region can share in this goal.

Democracy

The fourth issue that I will address is democracy.

I know there has been controversy about the promotion of democracy in recent years, and much of this controversy is connected to the war in Iraq. So let me be clear: no system of government can or should be imposed upon one nation by any other.

That does not lessen my commitment, however, to governments that reflect the will of the people. Each nation gives life to this principle in its own way, grounded in the traditions of its own people. America does not presume to know what is best for everyone, just as we would not presume to pick the outcome of a peaceful election. But I do have an unyielding belief that all people yearn for certain things: the ability to speak your mind and have a say in how you are governed; confidence in the rule of law and the equal administration of justice; government that is transparent and doesn't steal from the people; the freedom to live as you choose. Those are not just American ideas, they are human rights, and that is why we will support them everywhere.

There is no straight line to realise this promise. But this much is clear: governments that protect these rights are ultimately more stable, successful, and secure. Suppressing ideas never succeeds in making them go away. America respects the right of all peaceful and law-abiding voices to be heard around the world, even if we disagree with them. And we will welcome all elected, peaceful governments – provided they govern with respect for all their people.

This last point is important because there are some who advocate for democracy only when they are out of power; once in power, they are ruthless in suppressing the rights of others. No matter where it takes hold, government of the people and by the people sets a single standard for all who hold power: you must maintain your power through consent, not coercion; you must respect the rights of minorities, and participate with a spirit of tolerance and compromise; you must place the interests of your people and the legitimate workings of the political process above your party. Without these ingredients, elections alone do not make true democracy.

Religious Freedom

The fifth issue that we must address together is religious freedom.

Islam has a proud tradition of tolerance. We see it in the history of Andalusia and Cordoba during the Inquisition. I saw it first hand as a child in Indonesia, where devout Christians worshipped freely in an overwhelmingly Muslim country. That is the spirit we need today. People in every country should be free to choose and live their faith based upon the persuasion of the mind, heart, and soul. This tolerance is essential for religion to thrive, but it is being challenged in many different ways.

Among some Muslims, there is a disturbing tendency to measure one's own faith by the rejection of another's. The richness of religious diversity must be upheld – whether it is for Maronites in Lebanon or the Copts in Egypt. And fault lines must be closed among Muslims as well, as the divisions between Sunni and Shia have led to tragic violence, particularly in Iraq.

Freedom of religion is central to the ability of peoples to live together. We must always examine the ways in which we protect it. For instance, in the United States, rules on charitable giving have made it harder for Muslims to fulfil their religious obligation. That is why I am committed to working with American Muslims to ensure that they can fulfil *zakat*.*

Likewise, it is important for Western countries to avoid impeding Muslim citizens from practising religion as they see fit – for instance, by dictating what clothes a Muslim woman should wear. We cannot disguise hostility towards any religion behind the pretence of liberalism.

Indeed, faith should bring us together. That is why we are forging service projects in America that bring together Christians, Muslims, and Jews. That is why we welcome efforts like Saudi Arabian King Abdullah's Interfaith dialogue and Turkey's leadership in the Alliance of Civilisations. Around the world, we can turn dialogue into interfaith service, so bridges between peoples lead to action – whether it is combating malaria in Africa, or providing relief after a natural disaster.

Women's Rights

The sixth issue that I want to address is women's rights.

I know there is debate about this issue. I reject the view of some in the West that a woman who chooses to cover her hair is somehow less equal, but

---

* *Zakat* is the systematic giving of 2.5 per cent of one's wealth each year to help the poor and is the third pillar of Islam.

I do believe that a woman who is denied an education is denied equality. And it is no coincidence that countries where women are well educated are far more likely to be prosperous.

Now let me be clear: issues of women's equality are by no means simply an issue for Islam. In Turkey, Pakistan, Bangladesh, and Indonesia, we have seen Muslim-majority countries elect a woman to lead. Meanwhile, the struggle for women's equality continues in many aspects of American life, and in countries around the world.

Our daughters can contribute just as much to society as our sons, and our common prosperity will be advanced by allowing all humanity – men and women – to reach their full potential. I do not believe that women must make the same choices as men in order to be equal, and I respect those women who choose to live their lives in traditional roles. But it should be their choice. That is why the United States will partner with any Muslim-majority country to support expanded literacy for girls, and to help young women pursue employment through micro-financing that helps people live their dreams.

Economic Development

Finally, I want to discuss economic development and opportunity.

I know that for many, the face of globalisation is contradictory. The Internet and television can bring knowledge and information, but also offensive sexuality and mindless violence. Trade can bring new wealth and opportunities, but also huge disruptions and changing communities. In all nations – including my own – this change can bring fear. Fear that because of modernity we will lose control over our economic choices, our politics, and most importantly our identities – those things we most cherish about our communities, our families, our traditions, and our faith.

But I also know that human progress cannot be denied. There need not be contradiction between development and tradition. Countries like Japan and South Korea grew their economies while maintaining distinct cultures. The same is true for the astonishing progress within Muslim-majority countries from Kuala Lumpur to Dubai. In ancient times and in our times, Muslim communities have been at the forefront of innovation and education.

This is important because no development strategy can be based only upon what comes out of the ground, nor can it be sustained while young people are out of work. Many Gulf states have enjoyed great wealth as a consequence of oil, and some are beginning to focus it on broader development. But all of us must recognise that education and innovation will be the currency of the twenty-first century, and in too many Muslim communities there remains underinvestment in these areas. I am emphasising such investments within my country. And while America in the past has focused on oil and gas in this part of the world, we now seek a broader engagement.

On education, we will expand exchange programmes, and increase scholarships, like the one that brought my father to America, while encouraging more Americans to study in Muslim communities. And we will match promising Muslim students with internships in America; invest in online learning for teachers and children around the world; and create a new online network, so a teenager in Kansas can communicate instantly with a teenager in Cairo.

On economic development, we will create a new corps of business volunteers to partner with counterparts in Muslim-majority countries. And I will host a summit on entrepreneurship this year to identify how we can deepen ties between business leaders, foundations, and social entrepreneurs in the United States and Muslim communities around the world.

On science and technology, we will launch a new fund to support technological development in Muslim-majority countries, and to help transfer ideas to the marketplace so they can create jobs. We will open centres of scientific excellence in Africa, the Middle East, and Southeast Asia, and appoint new science envoys to collaborate on programmes that develop new sources of energy, create green jobs, digitise records, clean water, and grow new crops. And today I am announcing a new global effort with the Organisation of the Islamic Conference to eradicate polio. And we will also expand partnerships with Muslim communities to promote child and maternal health.

All these things must be done in partnership. Americans are ready to join with citizens and governments, community organisations, religious leaders,

" We have the power to make the world we seek, but only if we have the courage to make a new beginning "

and businesses in Muslim communities around the world to help our people pursue a better life.

Conclusion

The issues that I have described will not be easy to address. But we have a responsibility to join together on behalf of the world we seek – a world where extremists no longer threaten our people, and American troops have come home; a world where Israelis and Palestinians are each secure in a state of their own, and nuclear energy is used for peaceful purposes; a world where governments serve their citizens, and the rights of all God's children are respected. Those are mutual interests. That is the world we seek. But we can only achieve it together.

I know there are many – Muslim and non-Muslim – who question whether we can forge this new beginning. Some are eager to stoke the flames of division, and to stand in the way of progress. Some suggest that it isn't worth the effort – that we are fated to disagree, and civilisations are doomed to clash. Many more are simply sceptical that real change can occur. There is so much fear, so much mistrust. But if we choose to be bound by the past, we will never move forward. And I want to particularly say this to young people of every faith, in every country – you, more than anyone, have the ability to remake this world.

All of us share this world for but a brief moment in time. The question is whether we spend that time focused on what pushes us apart, or whether we commit ourselves to an effort – a sustained effort – to find common ground, to focus on the future we seek for our children, and to respect the dignity of all human beings.

It is easier to start wars than to end them. It is easier to blame others than to look inward; to see what is different about someone than to find the things we share. But we should choose the right path, not just the easy path. There is also one rule that lies at the heart of every religion – that we do unto others as we would have them do unto us. This truth transcends nations and peoples – a belief that isn't new; that isn't black or white or brown; that isn't Christian, or Muslim, or Jew. It's a belief that pulsed in the cradle of civilisation, and that still beats in the heart of billions. It's a faith in other people, and it's what brought me here today.

We have the power to make the world we seek, but only if we have the courage to make a new beginning, keeping in mind what has been written.

The Holy Koran tells us: 'O mankind! We have created you male and a female; and we have made you into nations and tribes so that you may know one another.'

The Talmud tells us: 'The whole of the Torah is for the purpose of promoting peace.'

The Holy Bible tells us: 'Blessed are the peacemakers, for they shall be called sons of God.'

The people of the world can live together in peace. We know that is God's vision. Now, that must be our work here on Earth. Thank you. And may God's peace be upon you.

Afterword

Looking to the Future

"Could a greater miracle take place
than for us to look through
each other's eyes for an instant?"

Henry David Thoreau,
Walden; or, Life in the Woods
(1854)

In the introduction to this book I briefly set out two differing views of the world. There are so-called idealists who believe that all people are created equal and that division and confrontation often only lead to violence. In contrast, there are those who might call themselves realists (although, in truth, they hold a great deal of idealism). They see the world as divided into good and evil and argue that the powerful have a responsibility to use force to make the world a safer place. I hope this book has led you to question who, in fact, can rightly be described as realists and who base their behaviour on dangerous ideals.

What else can we learn from this brief tour through the tides of events that have shaped the last one hundred years and brought us to where we are now in the twenty-first century? There are many lessons that history can teach us but there are four motifs that are worth high-lighting here.

First, despite the fact that no injustice can last forever, too many of those who benefit from an unjust status quo attempt to resist change and oppress those who would bring about that change. In response, citizens may employ the methods of non-violent resistance and civil disobedience to obtain and protect their rights. However, all too often frustration in the face of repression or a lack of real political progress can erupt in anger and violence. We need an alternative approach. We must critically examine the relationship between the state and the individual, the governors and the governed, and ensure that all people have their political voice.

Secondly, there appears to be a persistent human need to divide the world into 'them and us'. So much conflict results from this often artificial division. It is clear, though, that there can be no them and us in the face of the serious environmental and socio-economic problems that will shape the course of this century – they will affect us all. Governments may be tempted to increasingly use the police to suppress dissent at home and the military to secure resources overseas but such an approach will not succeed in creating a fortress state safe from others. There is only one planet Earth and we all share it.

Thirdly, while many of the speeches in this book are positive and inspiring, others point to mistakes and missed opportunities that were either obvious at the time or have become clear with the benefit of hindsight. Individuals or groups will continue to rise who will encourage us to great deeds or great harm. Let us learn from those who are a positive light in the world but tear down those who would have us do wrong. We must be alert to those silver-tongued persuaders who would seduce us into fatal inaction or unnecessary confrontation. Do not fall for their false charm.

Fourthly, we should understand that the perception of events changes over both time and place. We need to be able to view these events through others' eyes. This does not mean blindly accepting all points of view as true or embracing moral relativism at the expense of your own sense of justice; but we should at least be able to empathise. We should not simply seek out those who share our opinions and will confirm what we already think. We need to challenge our assumptions and engage with those individuals with whom we may disagree. To assume that one is entirely correct in one's views is arrogance and to not question those views is laziness. In the same vein, do not just accept what I have written; check the facts, test the analysis – it is all part of the debate.

In conclusion, we need to accept that our own world views – the ways we see the world – are exactly that: ways of seeing. By examining these frameworks of beliefs and ideas and exploring how they have developed, we can hopefully come at least a step closer to understanding others and avoiding the mistakes of the past. And that must surely be a good thing.

Acknowledgements

So many friends, family members and colleagues have supported me in writing this book. I would like to thank Thomas Phipps, James Kemp and John Groom for early discussions on the book concept; Paul Rogers, Dan MacLeod and, especially, Louise Broadbent for their valuable comments on the draft text; and my editor Sue Lascelles for her patience and guidance, which helped make this book possible. There are far too many others to list here but I hope you know who you are and my thanks go out to you all.

I would like to thank the following individuals and organisations for permission to reproduce the transcripts featured in this book.

Just words, Deval Patrick: Reproduced with the permission of the Deval Patrick Committee.

I have a dream, Martin Luther King: Copyright, Dr Martin Luther King, Jr. (1963); copyright renewed, Coretta Scott King (1991). Reproduced with the permission of The Heirs to the Estate of Martin Luther King, c/o Writers House as agent for the proprietor, New York. *Rivers of blood*, Enoch Powell: Reproduced with the permission of the J. Enoch Powell Literary Trust. *A second chance*, Napoleon Beazley: Reproduced with the permission of the Texas Department of Criminal Justice. *Apology to the stolen generations*, Kevin Rudd: Reproduced with the permission of the Attorney General's Office of the Australian Government.

Ash heap of history, Ronald Reagan: Reproduced with the permission of the Ronald Reagan Presidential Library Foundation. *Our war on terror*, George Bush: Reproduced with the permission of AmericanRhetoric.com. *Your security is in your own hands*, Osama bin Laden: Reproduced with the permission of Al-Jazeera. *The case for climate security*, Margaret Beckett: Reproduced with the permission of the British Foreign & Commonwealth Office.

We shall fight on the beaches, Winston Churchill: Parliamentary material is reproduced with the permission of the Controller of HMSO on behalf of parliament. Reproduced under Parliamentary Licence P2009000034. *The Falklands factor*, Margaret Thatcher: Reproduced with the permission of the Margaret Thatcher Foundation. *Doctrine of the international community*, Tony Blair: Crown copyright. Reproduced with the permission of the Office of Public Sector Information. *The mark of Cain*, Tim Collins. Reproduced with the permission of Colonel Tim Collins.

Let no one commit a wrong in anger, Mohandas Gandhi: Reproduced with the permission of Mani Bhavan Gandhi Sangrahalaya. *The military–industrial complex*, Dwight D. Eisenhower: Reproduced with the permission of AmericanRhetoric.com. *With a heavy heart*, Robin Cook: Parliamentary material is reproduced with the permission of the Controller of HMSO on behalf of parliament. Reproduced under Parliamentary Licence P2009000034. *A new beginning*, Barack Obama: Reproduced with the permission of the White House under a Creative Commons Attribution 3.0 License: http://creativecommons.org/licenses/by/3.0/us/.

Every effort has been made to identify and contact copyright holders. However, the publishers will be glad to rectify in future editions any errors or omissions brought to their attention.

This book would not have been realised without the support of three important women. My thanks go to my mother, Barbara, and my sister, Helen, whose love and encouragement has always given me the confidence to believe in my own abilities. Above all, though, I would like to thank my partner, Lou, who quite simply means the world to me. This book is dedicated to her.

References

PART I: ALL THE WORLD IS HUMAN

1   Hillary Clinton, Speech at the UN World Conference on Women (Beijing: 5 September 1995).

2   'Mrs Pankhurst: A Pioneer of Women Suffrage', *The Times* (15 June 1928).

3   Cathy Zimmerman et al., *Stolen Smiles: The Physical and Psychological Health Consequences of Women and Adolescents Trafficked in Europe* (London: The London School of Hygiene & Tropical Medicine, 2006).

4   Sandra Dickson, *Sex in the City: Mapping Commercial Sex Across London* (London: The POPPY Project, 2004).

5   Mimi Silbert and Ayala Pines, 'Victimization of Street Prostitutes', *Victimology*, Vol. 7, pp.122–133 and Kelly Weisberg, *Children of the Night: A Study of Adolescent Prostitution* (Lanham: Lexington Books, 1985), p.155.

6   *Perpetual Minors: Human Rights Abuses Stemming from Male Guardianship and Sex Segregation in Saudi Arabia* (New York: Human Rights Watch, 2008).

7   Inter-Parliamentary Union, *Women in National Parliaments* (31 December 2009), http://www.ipu.org/wmn-e/world.htm (accessed 4 February 2010).

8   Ruth Sealy et al., *The Female FTSE Board Report 2009* (Cranfield: Cranfield University, 2009).

9   *Greater Expectations: Final Report of the EOC's Investigation into Discrimination Against New and Expectant Mothers in the Workplace* (Manchester: Equal Opportunities Commission, 2005).

10 *Gender (In)equality in the Labour Market: An Overview of Global Trends and Developments* (Brussels: International Trade Union Confederation, 2009).

11 United Nations Development Programme, *Human Development Report 1995: Gender and Human Development* (New York: Oxford University Press, 1995), p.36.

12 Lisa Rein, 'Mystery of VA's First Slaves Is Unlocked 400 Years Later', *Washington Post* (3 September 2006).

13 Robin Kelley and Earl Lewis (eds.), *To Make Our World Anew, Volume I: A History of African Americans to 1880* (New York: Oxford University Press USA, 2005).

14 David Eltis, *Economic Growth and the Ending of the Transatlantic Slave Trade* (New York: Oxford University Press USA, 1987), p.47 and Anthony Tibbles, *Transatlantic Slavery: Against Human Dignity* (Liverpool: Liverpool University Press, 2005), p.13.

15 Nell Painter, *Creating Black Americans: African-American History and its Meanings, 1619 to the Present* (New York: Oxford University Press USA, 2006), pp.32–33.

16 Robin Kelley and Earl Lewis, op. cit., pp.71–74.

17 Craig Werner, *A Change is Gonna Come: Music, Race & the Soul of America* (Ann Arbor: University of Michigan Press, 2006), p.10 and Robin Doak, *The March on Washington: Uniting Against Racism* (Mankato: Compass Point Books, 2008), p.12.

18 Robin Doak, op. cit., p.15.

19 James Cone, *Martin & Malcolm & America: A Dream or a Nightmare* (New York: Orbis Books, 1991).

20 Malcolm X, Speech to the Northern Negro Grass Roots Leadership Conference (Detroit: 10 November 1963).

21 Malcolm X, *The Autobiography of Malcolm X: As Told to Alex Haley* (New York: Grove Press, 1965), p.229.

22 Malcolm X, Speech at the founding rally of the Organisation of Afro-American Unity (New York: 28 June 1964) and Malcolm X, 'The ballot or the bullet' speech (Cleveland: 3 April 1964).

23 'Man Of The Year: Martin Luther King Jr, Never Again Where He Was', *Time* (3 January 1964).

24 James Cone, op. cit.

25 Peter Kihss, 'Malcolm X Shot to Death at Rally Here', *New York Times* (22 February 1965).

26 Telegram from Martin Luther King to Betty al-Shabazz (26 February 1965), http://mlkkpp01.stanford.edu/index.php/encyclopedia/documentsentry/telegram_from_martin_luther_king_jr_to_betty_al_shabazz/ (accessed 22 February 2010).

27 Jack Nelson and Nicholas Chriss, 'Ray Pleads Guilty, Gets 99 Years in King Death', *Los Angeles Times* (11 March 1969).

28 Martin Luther King, Speech at the Mason Temple (Memphis: 3 April 1968).

29 Isidor Stone, 'The Fire Has Only Just Begun', *I.F. Stone's Weekly*, Vol. 16, No. 8 (15 April 1968), p.1.

30 Jeffrey Ogbar, *Black Power: Radical Politics and African American Identity* (Baltimore: John Hopkins University Press, 2005), pp.69–158.

31 Barack Obama, Election night victory speech (Chicago: 5 November 2008).

32 Scott Gold, 'Trapped in an Arena of Suffering', *Los Angeles Times* (1 September 2005) and David Gonzalez, 'From Margins of Society to Center of the Tragedy', *New York Times* (2 September 2005).

33 Julia Stapleton, *Political Intellectuals and Public Identities in Britain Since 1850* (Manchester: Manchester University Press, 2001), pp.182–83.

34 HC Deb 27 July 1959 cc 232–237, Hansard.

35 Simon Heffer, *Like the Roman: The Life of Enoch Powell* (London: Weidenfeld & Nicolson, 1998), p.361.

36 Enoch Powell, Speech on immigration (Wolverhampton: 25 March 1966), Enoch Powell, Speech on immigration (Walsall: 9 February 1968) and Enoch Powell, 'Facing Up to Britain's Race Problem', *Daily Telegraph* (16 February 1967).

37 Enoch Powell, Speech on immigration (Eastbourne: 16 November 1968).

38 Robert Shepherd, 'The real tributaries of Enoch's "rivers of blood" ', *Spectator* (11 March 2008).

39 Ludi Simpson, 'Ghettos of the mind: the empirical behaviour of indices of segregation and diversity', *Journal of the Royal Statistical Society*, Series A 170, Part 2 (2007), pp.405–424 and Ludi Simpson and Nissa Finney, 'Ethnic ghettos in Britain: a fact or a myth?', *Significance*, Vol. 6, No. 2 (June 2009), pp.72–75.

40 Office for National Statistics, *Focus on People and Migration: 2005* (London: Her Majesty's Stationery Office, 2005), p.13, 135, 117.

41 Bernard McGrane, *Beyond Anthropology: Society and the Other* (New York: Columbia University Press, 1989) and Tim Ingold, *The Perception of the Environment: Essays in Livelihood, Dwelling and Skill* (London: Routledge, 2000).

42 Department of Economic and Social Affairs, *Trends in Total Migrant Stock: The 2005 Revision* (New York: United Nations, 2006), p.1.

43 Amnesty International, *Figures on the Death Penalty*, http://www.amnesty.org/en/death-penalty/numbers (accessed 3 January 2010).

44 *Media Advisory: Napoleon Beazley Scheduled to be Executed* (Austin: Office of the Attorney General, 24 May 2002), http://www.oag.state.tx.us/newspubs/newsarchive/2002/20020524beazleyfacts.htm (accessed 10 January 2010).

45 William Sabol, *Bureau of Justice Statistic Bulletin: Prisoners in 2008* (Washington DC: US Department of Justice, 2009), p.5 and Michael Tonry, *Malign Neglect: Race, Crime, and Punishment in America* (New York: Oxford University Press USA, 1996), pp.49–79.

46 Texas Department of Criminal Justice, *Executed Offenders*, http://www.tdcj.state.tx.us/stat/executedoffenders.htm (accessed 10 January 2010).

47 Harvey Rice, 'Teenage murderer executed', *Houston Chronicle* (29 May 2002).

48 Letter from Desmond Tutu to the Chairman of the Texas Board of Pardons and Paroles (16 May 2002), http://www.abanet.org/crimjust/juvjus/beazleytutu102.html (accessed 3 January 2010).

49 National Inquiry into the Separation of Aboriginal and Torres Strait Islander Children from Their Families, *Bringing Them Home* (Sydney: Human Rights and Equal Opportunities Commission, 1997).

50 Colin Tatz, *Genocide in Australia* (Canberra: Aboriginal Studies Press, 1999).

51 Text of the Apology to the Stolen Generations (13 February 2008), http://www.dfat.gov.au/indigenous_background/national_apology.html (accessed 13 December 2009).

52 National Inquiry into the Separation of Aboriginal and Torres Strait Islander Children from Their Families, op. cit.

53 Commonwealth of Australia, House of Representatives, Parliamentary debates (Official Hansard): Thursday, 26 August 1999 (Canberra: Commonwealth Government Printer, 1999), p.9165.

54 Brendan Nelson, Address to parliament on the apology to the Stolen Generations (Canberra: 13 February 2008).

55 Andrew Gunstone, 'The Howard government's approach to the policy of indigenous self-determination', *MAI Review*, No. 1 (January 2006), pp.1–3.

56 Northern Territory Board of Inquiry into the Protection of Aboriginal Children from Sexual Abuse, *Ampe Akelyernemane Meke Mekarle: 'Little Children Are Sacred'* (Darwin: Northern Territory Government, 2007).

57 Ibid., p.13.

58 Allan Gyngell, *Australia and the World: Public Opinion and Foreign Policy* (Sydney: Lowy Institute for International Policy, 2007) and 'Australians Back Apology for Stolen Generations, *Angus Reid Global Monitor* (27 February 2008), http://www.angus-reid.com/polls/view/australians_back_apology_for_stolen_generations/ (accessed 14 December 2009).

59 Amnesty International, *The Human Rights of Indigenous Peoples*, http://www.amnesty.ca/themes/indigenous_overview.php (accessed 30 March 2010) and Survival International, *Tribes & Campaigns*, http://www.survivalinternational.org/tribes (accessed 30 March 2010).

60 Centre for Indigenous Australian Education and Research, http://www.healthinfonet.ecu.edu.au (accessed 15 December 2009).

61 *A Statistical Overview of Aboriginal and Torres Strait Islander Peoples in Australia* (Sydney: Australian Human Rights Commission, 2008), http://www.hreoc.gov.au/Social_Justice/statistics/index.html (accessed 15 December 2009).

Part II: You're Either With Us or Against Us

1 'Obituary: Alexander Solzhenitsyn', *Sunday Telegraph* (3 August 2008).

2 Tore Frängsmyr and Sture Allén (eds.), *Nobel Lectures in Literature, 1968–1980* (Singapore: World Scientific Publishing Co., 1993), pp.31–33.

3 Aleksandr Solzhenitsyn, *One Day in the Life of Ivan Denisovich* (New York: Signet Classics, 1963), Aleksandr Solzhenitsyn, *The First Circle* (Evanston: Northwestern University Press, 1968) and Aleksandr Solzhenitsyn, *The Gulag Archipelago* (London: Harper & Row, 1973).

4 Michael Kaufman, 'Solzhenitsyn, Literary Giant Who Defied Soviets, Dies at 89', *New York Times* (4 August 2008).

5 W. Seth Carus, *Bioterrorism and Biocrimes: The Illicit use of Biological Agents Since 1900* (Amsterdam: Fredonia Books, 2002), p.84.

6 Jared Diamond, 'What's your consumption factor?', *New York Times* (2 January 2008).

7 Francis Fukuyama, *The End of History and the Last Man* (New York: Free Press, 1992).

8 Christopher Andrew and Vasili Mitrokhin, *The Mitrokhin Archive: The KGB in Europe and the West* (New York: Basic Books, 2005), pp.416–419.

9 Aleksandr Solzhenitsyn, 'Two hundred Years Together, 1795–1995', in Edward Ericson (ed.), *The Solzhenitsyn Reader: New and Essential Writings, 1947–2005* (Intercollegiate Studies Institute, 2006).

10 Helen Womack, 'Russians pay tribute to Solzhenitsyn', *Guardian* (5 August 2008).

11 Winston Churchill, 'Sinews of peace' speech at Westminster College (Fulton: 5 March 1946).

12 Paul Rogers, *Global Security and the War on Terror: Elite Power and the Illusion of Control* (Abingdon: Routledge, 2008), p.9.

13 Ibid., p.23.

14 Ibid., p.9–13.

15 US Department of State, *Reagan Doctrine, 1985*, http://www.state.gov/r/pa/ho/time/rd/17741.htm (accessed 16 February 2010).

16 Leon Trotsky, Speech to the Soviet Congress (Petrograd: 25 October 1917).

17 Richard Pipes, Remarks at a panel discussion on 'President Reagan's Westminster Address 20 Years Later' (Washington DC: 3 June 2002).

18 Ronald Reagan, Speech to the annual convention of the National Association of Evangelicals (Orlando: 8 March 1983).

19   Friedrich Frischknecht, 'The history of biological warfare', *EMBO Report*, Vol. 4 (June 2003), pp.47–52, Robert Wannemacher and Stanley Wiener, 'Trichothecene Mycotoxins', in Russ Zajtchuk (ed.), *Medical Aspects of Chemical and Biological Warfare: Textbook of Military Medicine* (Washington DC: Office of the Surgeon- General, US Army, 1997), pp.657–658 and *Report of the Group of Experts to Investigate Reports on the Alleged Use of Chemical Weapons* (New York: United Nations, 1982).

20   April Oliver and Peter Arnett, 'Did the US Drop Nerve Gas?', *Time* (15 June 1998) and William Blum, *Rogue State: A Guide to the World's Only Superpower* (London: Zed Books, 2006), pp.139–141.

21   Stephen Endicott and Edward Hagerman, *The United States and Biological Warfare: Secrets from the Early Cold War and Korea* (Bloomington, Indiana University Press, 1998) and William Blum, op. cit., pp.136–146.

22   Peter Duignan and Lewis Gann, *The Cold War: End and Aftermath* (Stanford: Hoover Press, 1996), pp.5–23.

23   Paul Rogers, op. cit., p.9.

24   Samuel Huntington, *The Clash of Civilizations and the Remaking of World Order* (New York: Simon & Schuster, 1996).

25   Douglas Garthoff, *Directors of Central Intelligence as Leaders of the US Intelligence Community, 1946–2005* (Washington DC: Central Intelligence Agency, 2007), p.221.

26   George Bush (Bentonville: 6 November 2000).

27   Presidential Daily Brief (6 August 2001; declassified 10 April 2004), http://www.gwu.edu/~nsarchiv/NSAEBB/NSAEBB116/pdb8-6-2001.pdf (accessed 21 October 2009).

28   9/11 Commission, *The 9/11 Commission Report: The Final Report of the National Commission on Terrorist Attacks Upon the United States* (Washington DC: US Government Printing Office, 2004).

29   Department of Defense, *Report of the Defense Science Board Task Force on Strategic Communication* (Washington DC: Department of Defense, September 2004), p.48.

30   Federal Bureau of Investigation, *Photos of Anthrax Letters to NBC, Senator Daschle, and NY Post* (23 October 2001), http://www.fbi.gov/pressrel/pressrel01/102301.htm (accessed 27 October 2009).

31 Sam Perlo-Freeman et al., 'Military Expenditure', in Stockholm International Peace Research Institute, *SIPRI Yearbook 2009: Armaments, Disarmament and International Security* (Oxford: Oxford University Press, 2009), pp.185–189.

32 George Bush, Address before a joint session of congress on the State of the Union (Washington DC: 29 January 2002).

33 Daniel Kimmage, *The Al-Qaeda Media Nexus: The Virtual Network Behind the Global Message* (Washington DC: Radio Free Europe/Radio Liberty, 2008) and Evan Kohlmann, *Al-Qaida's Online Couriers: The Al-Fajr Media Center and the Global Islamic Media Front* (Charleston: NEFA Foundation, 2009), http://nefafoundation.org/fajrchart.html (accessed 6 November 2009).

34 'Tale of the Tapes: Bin Laden's Messages', *CBS News*, http://www.cbsnews.com/htdocs/america_under_attack/bin_laden/framesource_tapes.html (accessed 1 November 2009).

35 'Bin Laden deplores climate change', Al-Jazeera (29 January 2010), http://english.aljazeera.net/news/middleeast/2010/01/20101277383676587.html (accessed 9 January 2010).

36 George Orwell, *Nineteen Eighty-Four* (London: Secker and Warburg, 1949).

37 9/11 Commission, op. cit., p.170.

38 Jason Burke, *Al-Qaeda: The True Story of Radical Islam* (London: Penguin Books, 2004), p. 79.

39 Ibid., pp.1–2.

40 Ibid., pp.1–14.

41 Alastair Crooke, *Resistance: The Essence of the Islamist Revolution* (London: Pluto Press, 2009), pp.80–81.

42 Paul Rogers, 'Al-Qaida: A question of leadership', *openDemocracy* (17 November 2005).

43 *FBI Ten Most Wanted Fugitive* [sic]: *Usama bin Laden* (June 1999, revised November 2001), http://www.fbi.gov/wanted/topten/fugitives/laden.htm (accessed 2 November 2009).

44 US Senate Committee on Foreign Relations, *Tora Bora Revisited: How We Failed to Get Bin Laden and Why it Matters Today* (Washington DC: US Government Printing Office, 2009).

45 Michael Smith, *Killer Elite: America's Most Secret Special Operations Team* (London: Weidenfeld & Nicolson, 2006).

[46] The Pew Global Attitudes Project, *Most Muslim Publics Not so Easily Moved: Confidence in Obama Lifts U.S. Image Around the World* (Washington DC: Pew Research Center, 2009), pp.83–86 and WorldPublicOpinion.org, *Public Opinion in the Islamic World on Terrorism, al Qaeda, and US Policies* (Maryland: University of Maryland, 2009), pp. 5–6.

[47] Jason Burke, op. cit., p.39.

[48] Eric Holder, Testimony before the House Appropriations Commerce, Justice and Science Subcommittee, US House of Representatives (Washington DC: 16 March 2010).

[49] Chris Abbott, Paul Rogers and John Sloboda, *Beyond Terror: The Truth About the Real Threats to Our World* (London: Rider, 2007).

[50] *National Security and the Threat of Climate Change* (Alexandria: The CNA Corporation, 2007).

[51] Thomas Fingar, *National Security Assessment on the National Security Implications of Climate Change to 2030: Statement for the Record* (Washington DC: Office of the Director of National Intelligence, 25 June 2008).

[52] Security Council 5663rd meeting, *Security Council holds first-ever debate on impact of climate change on peace, security, hearing over 50 speakers* (17 April 2007), http://www.un.org/News/Press/docs/2007/sc9000.doc.htm (accessed 9 December 2009).

[53] Chris Abbott, *An Uncertain Future: Law Enforcement, National Security and Climate Change* (London: Oxford Research Group, 2008).

[54] Royal United Services Institute, http://www.rusi.org/climate/research/ and Institute for Environmental Security, http://www.envirosecurity.org/programmes/.

[55] Chris Abbott, op. cit.

[56] Rajendra Pachauri and Andy Reisinger (eds.), *Climate Change 2007: Synthesis Report* (Geneva: Intergovernmental Panel on Climate Change, 2007).

[57] Ibid.

[58] Met Office, *The impact of a global temperature rise of 4°C*, http://www.actoncopenhagen.decc.gov.uk/content/en/embeds/flash/4-degrees-large-map-final (accessed 9 December 2009).

[59] Committee on Abrupt Climate Change, National Research Council, *Abrupt Climate Change: Inevitable Surprises* (Washington DC: National Academies Press, 2002).

60 Norman Myers, 'Environmental Refugees: A Growing Phenomenon of the 21st Century', *Philosophical Transactions: Biological Sciences*, Vol. 357, No. 1420 (April 2002).

61 *Human Tide: The Real Migration Crisis* (London: Christian Aid, May 2007).

62 Cleo Paskal, *How Climate Change is Pushing the Boundaries of Security and Foreign Policy* (London: Chatham House, June 2007).

63 Chris Abbott, op. cit.

PART III: MIGHT IS RIGHT

1 Neville Chamberlain, Statement outside 10 Downing Street (London: 30 September 1938).

2 Winston Churchill, First speech as Prime Minister to the House of Commons (London: 13 May 1940).

3 Winston Churchill, *The Second World War, Volume 1: The Gathering Storm* (Boston: Houghton Mifflin Company, 1948).

4 *The Westminster Hour*, 'Churchill "greatest PM of 20th Century" ', BBC Radio 4 (4 January 2000), http://news.bbc.co.uk/1/hi/uk_politics/575219.stm (accessed 19 February 2010) and *Newsnight*, 'Churchill tops PM choice', BBC Two (1 October 2008), http://news.bbc.co.uk/1/hi/programmes/newsnight/7647383.stm (accessed 21 February 2010).

5 Norman Moss, *Nineteen Weeks: America, Britain, and the Fateful Summer of 1940* (Boston: Houghton Mifflin Harcourt, 2003), p.130.

6 W. J. R. Gardner (ed.), *The Evacuation from Dunkirk: Operation Dynamo, 26 May–4 June 1940* (London: Taylor & Francis, 2000).

7 James Millar and Susan Linz, 'The Cost of World War II to the Soviet People: A Research Note', *The Journal of Economic History*, Vol. 38, No. 4 (December 1978), pp.959–962 and Twentieth Century Atlas, http://users.erols.com/mwhite28/warstat1.htm#Second (accessed 18 February 2010).

8 Malgorzata Kuzniar-Plota, *Press Release: Decision to commence investigation into Katyn Massacre* (Warsaw: Departmental Commission for the Prosecution of Crimes Against the Polish Nation, 1 December 2004) and Antony Beevor, *Berlin: The Downfall, 1945* (New York: Viking, 2002).

9   Richard Drayton, 'An ethical blank cheque', *Guardian* (10 May 2005).

10 A. C. Grayling, *Among the Dead Cities: The History and Moral Legacy of the WWII Bombing of Civilians in Germany and Japan* (New York: Walker & Co., 2006).

11 Walter Boyne (ed.), *Air Warfare: An International Encyclopaedia, Volume 1* (Santa Barbara: ABC-CLIO, 2002), p.290, *Erklärung der Dresdner Historikerkommission zur Ermittlung der Opferzahlen der Luftangriffe auf die Stadt Dresden am 13./14. Februar 1945* (Dresden: Landeshauptstadt Dresden, 2008), p.2 and Beau Grosscup, *Strategic Terror: The Politics and Ethics of Aerial Bombardment* (London: Zed Books, 2006), p.68.

12 Radiation Effects Research Foundation, http://www.rerf.or.jp/general/qa_e/qa1.html (accessed 16 February 2010).

13 William Blum, *Killing Hope: US Military and CIA Interventions since World War II* (London: Zed Books, 2003), p.209.

14 Select Committee to Study Governmental Operations with Respect to Intelligence Activities, *Covert Action in Chile, 1963–1973* (Washington DC: US Congress, 1975).

15 Christopher Andrew and Vasili Mitrokhin, *The World Was Going Our Way: The KGB and the Battle for the Third World* (London: Penguin Books, 2000), pp.69–85.

16 Select Committee to Study Governmental Operations with Respect to Intelligence Activities, op. cit.

17 Ibid. and Maurice Hinchey, *CIA Activities in Chile* (Washington DC: US Congress, 2000).

18 James Whelan, *Out of the Ashes: The Life, Death and Transfiguration of Democracy in Chile, 1833–1988* (Washington DC: Regnery Gateway, 1989), p.114.

19 Shirley Christian, 'Leftist Journal Concludes Allende Killed Himself', *New York Times* (17 September 1990).

20 Select Committee to Study Governmental Operations with Respect to Intelligence Activities, op. cit.

21 Maurice Hinchey, op. cit.

22 Select Committee to Study Governmental Operations with Respect to Intelligence Activities, op. cit.

23 *Informe de la Comisión Nacional de Verdad y Reconciliación* (Santiago de Chile: Ministerio del Interior, 1991) and *Informe de la Comisión Nacional sobre Prisión Política y Tortura* (Santiago de Chile: Ministerio del Interior, 2004).

24 Robin Harris, 'Thatcher always honoured Britain's debt to Pinochet', *Daily Telegraph* (13 December 2006).

25 'Las frases para el bronce de Pinochet', *La Nation* (11 December 2006).

26 Rex Hunt, 'My war story', *BBC News* (2002), http://news.bbc.co.uk/hi/english/static/in_depth/uk/2002/falklands / my_story/hunt.stm (accessed 22 January 2010).

27 Ibid.

28 *Falkland Islands: Census Statistics 2006* (Stanley: Falkland Islands Government, 2006).

29 *The World Factbook 2009* (Washington DC: Central Intelligence Agency, 2009).

30 HC Deb 3 April 1983 cc 21/633–38, Hansard.

31 Ministry of Defence, *Falklands 25: Background Briefing*, http://www.mod.uk/DefenceInternet/FactSheets/Falklands25Back groundBriefing.htm (accessed 26 January 2010).

32 Vincent Bramley, *Excursion to Hell: Mount Longdon – A Universal Story of Battle* (London: Bloomsbury, 1991).

33 Lawrence Freedman, *The Official History of the Falklands Campaign, Volume 1: The Origins of the Falklands War* (Abingdon: Routledge, 2005).

34 Oliver Franks et al., *Falkland Islands Review* (London: Her Majesty's Stationery Office, 1983).

35 Alastair Finlan, *The Royal Navy in the Falklands Conflict and the Gulf War: Culture and Strategy* (Abingdon: Routledge, 2004), pp.25, 59.

36 Eric Evans, *Thatcher and Thatcherism: Making of the Contemporary World* (Abingdon: Routledge, 1997), p.23.

37 Ibid., pp.23–25.

38 Argentine submission to the UN Commission on the Limits of the Continental Shelf (21 April 2009), http://www.un.org/Depts/los/clcs_new/submissions_files/ submission_arg_25_2009.htm (accessed 25 January 2010).

39 British submission to the UN Commission on the Limits of the Continental Shelf (11 May 2009), http://www.un.org/Depts/los/clcs_new/submissions_files/submission_gbr_45_2009.htm (accessed 25 January 2010).

40 Constitution of the Argentine Nation, http://www.argentina.gov.ar/argentina/portal/documentos/constitucion_ingles.pdf (accessed 26 January 2010).

41 Graeme Baker, 'Argentina's military threat raises fears over Falklands', *Daily Telegraph* (8 July 2008).

42 Robert Booth, 'Falkland islanders say Argentina is waging economic warfare', *Guardian* (14 June 2009).

43 Rory Carroll, 'Argentina appeals to UN over Falkland oil drilling', *Guardian* (25 February 2010).

44 John Kampfner, *Blair's Wars* (London: The Free Press, 2003).

45 International Commission on Intervention and State Sovereignty, *The Responsibility to Protect* (Ottawa: International Development Research Centre, 2001).

46 John Kampfner, op. cit., pp.51–52.

47 Chris Abbott, *Rights and Responsibilities: Resolving the Dilemma of Humanitarian Intervention* (Oxford: Oxford Research Group, 2005).

48 Iraq Body Count, www.iraqbodycount.org (accessed 15 October 2009).

49 Andrew Rawnsley, *The End of the Party: The Rise and Fall of New Labour* (New York: Viking, 2010).

50 Richard Norton-Taylor and Nicholas Watt, 'The Blair defence: September 11 changed the "calculus of risk" ', *Guardian* (29 January 2010).

51 Tony Blair, Speech to the Labour Party Conference (Brighton: 2 October 2001).

52 Iraq Inquiry, *Oral evidence by date*, http://www.iraqinquiry.org.uk/transcripts/oralevidence-bydate.aspx (accessed 2 February 2010).

53 Tony Blair, Evidence to the Iraq Inquiry (London: 29 January 2010).

54 Tim Collins, *Rules of Engagement* (London: Headline Review, 2006), p.159.

55 Sarah Oliver, 'The fires of Hell await Saddam', *Daily Mail* (20 March 2003).

56 Tim Collins, op. cit., pp.364–65.

57 'Colonel wins libel damages', *BBC News* (2 April 2004), http://news.bbc.co.uk/1/hi/northern_ireland/3593027.stm (accessed 2 March 2010).

58 Doug Beattie, *An Ordinary Soldier* (London: Simon & Schuster, 2008).

59 Tim Collins, 'We've failed in Iraq: Let's get it right in Afghanistan', *Daily Telegraph* (6 August 2006).

60 New Century Consulting, www.newcentcorp.com (accessed 1 November 2009).

61 Antonio Taguba, *AR15-6 Investigation of the 800th Military Police Brigade* (Washington DC: Department of Defense, 2004) and Seymour Hersh, 'The General's Report', *New Yorker* (25 June 2007).

62 United Nations High Commissioner for Refugees, *Country Operations Profile: Iraq* (UNHCR, 2009), http://www.unhcr.org/cgi-bin/texis/ vtx/page?page=49e486426 (accessed 4 November 2009).

PART IV: GIVE PEACE A CHANCE

1 Mohandas Gandhi, Statement at the Great Trial of 1922 (Ahmedabad: 18 March 1922).

2 Raghavan Iyer (ed.), *The Moral and Political Writings of Mahatma Gandhi, Volume III: Non-violent Resistance and Social Transformation* (New York: Oxford University Press, 1987), p.69.

3 Mohandas Gandhi, *The Story of My Experiments With the Truth* (Ahmedabad: Navajivan Trust, 1927) and Raj Kumar Gupta, *The Great Encounter: A Study of Indo-American Literature and Cultural Relations* (New Delhi: Abhinav Publications, 1986), pp.228–232.

4 Mohandas Gandhi, op. cit.

5 Kusoom Vadgama, *India in Britain: The Indian Contribution to the British Way of Life* (London: R. Royce, 1984).

6 William Hunter et al., *Report of the Committee appointed in the government of India to investigate the disturbances in the Punjab, etc* (London: His Majesty's Stationery Office, 1920).

7 K. Swaminathan et al. (eds.), *The Collected Works of Mahatma Gandhi, Volume 19: September 29, 1919 – March 24, 1920* (New Delhi: Government of India, 1984), p.350.

8   Frank Moraes, *Jawaharlal Nehru* (Mumbai: Jaico Publishing House, 2007), p.164.

9   George Orwell, 'Reflections on Gandhi', *Partisan Review* (January 1949).

10   Louis Fischer, *The Life of Mahatma Gandhi, Volume 2* (New Delhi: Bharatiya Vidya Bhavan, 1959), p.131.

11   'Pinch of Salt', *Time* (31 March 1930) and 'Man of the Year, 1930', *Time* (5 January 1931).

12   Scilla Elworthy, *Cutting the Costs of War: Non-military Prevention and Resolution of Conflict* (Oxford: Oxford Research Group and Peace Direct, 2004).

13   'Huge Crowd Honours Eisenhower; President to Leave India Today', *Associated Press* (14 December 1959) and 'Man of the Year, 1959: Dwight D. Eisenhower', *Time* (4 January 1960).

14   Dwight D. Eisenhower, Speech at the Canadian Club (Ottawa: 10 January 1946).

15   Stephen G. Rabe, *Eisenhower and Latin America: The Foreign Policy of Anticommunism* (Chapel Hill: University of North Carolina Press, 1988).

16   Charles Griffin, 'New Light on Eisenhower's Farewell Address', *Presidential Studies Quarterly*, No. 22 (Summer 1992), pp.469–479.

17   C. Wright Mills, *The Power Elite* (Oxford: Oxford University Press, 1956).

18   Andrew Mack (ed.), *Human Security Brief 2007* (Vancouver: Simon Fraser University, 2008), pp.37–40.

19   Martin J. Medhurst, 'Reconceptualizing Rhetorical History: Eisenhower's Farewell Address', *Quarterly Journal of Speech*, Vol. 80, No. 2 (May 1994), pp.195–218.

20   Daniel Michaels and Cassell Bryan-Low, 'BAE to settle bribery cases for more than $400 million', *Wall Street Journal* (6 February 2010).

21   Special Committee on Investigation of the Munitions Industry, *Report of the Special Committee on Investigation of the Munitions Industry* (Washington DC: US Senate, 1936).

22   Sam Perlo-Freeman et al., 'Military Expenditure', in Stockholm International Peace Research Institute, *SIPRI Yearbook 2009: Armaments, Disarmament and International Security* (Oxford: Oxford University Press, 2009), p.179–211.

23 Richard F. Grimmett, *Conventional Arms Transfers to Developing Nations, 2001–2008* (Washington DC: Congressional Research Service, 2009).

24 Organisation for Economic Cooperation and Development, *International Development Statistics (IDS) online databases*, http://www.oecd.org/dac/stats/idsonline (accessed 19 December 2009).

25 Dwight D. Eisenhower, *Chance for Peace: Speech to the American Society of Newspaper Editors* (Reston: 16 April 1953).

26 Gary Wills, *Bomb Power: The Modern Presidency and the National Security State* (New York: Penguin, 2010).

27 *US National Space Policy* (Washington DC: Office of Science and Technology Policy, 2006).

28 US Air Force, *The US Air Force Transformation Flight Plan, 2003* (Washington DC: HQ USAF/XPXC, 2003).

29 Chris Abbott, Paul Rogers and John Sloboda, *Beyond Terror: The Truth About the Real Threats to Our World* (London: Rider, 2007), p.70.

30 Robin Cook, *Point of Departure* (London: Simon & Schuster, 2003).

31 UN Security Council Resolution 1441 (8 November 2002), http://www.un.org/Docs/scres/2002/sc2002.htm (accessed 20 October 2009).

32 See http://www.un.org/News/Press/docs/2002/SC7564.doc.htm (accessed 16 October 2009), http://www.undemocracy.com/securitycouncil/meeting_4644#pg0 04-bk01 (accessed 16 October 2009) and http://www.un.int/france/documents_anglais/021108_cs_france_ir ak_2.htm (accessed 17 October 2009).

33 Memo from Frank Koza, Defence Chief of Staff (Regional Targets), National Security Agency (31 January 2003), http://image.guardian.co.uk/sys-files/Observer/documents/ 2004/02/07/memo.pdf (accessed 20 October 2009).

34 Attorney-General's secret advice to the Prime Minister (7 March 2003), http://web.archive.org/web/20050428194646/http://www.number -10.gov.uk/files/pdf/Iraq+Resolution+1441.pdf (accessed 17 October 2009).

35 HL Deb 17 March 2003 cc WA2-3, Hansard.

36 Simon Walters, 'Iraq Inquiry bombshell: Secret letter to reveal new Blair war lies', *Mail on Sunday* (29 November 2009).

37 Jack Straw's private letter to Tony Blair (25 March 2002), http://www.timesonline.co.uk/tol/news/politics/article6991102.ece (accessed 25 January 2010).

38 Robin Cook, op. cit.

39 Robin Cook, 'Pass laws have no place in Britain', *Guardian* (25 February 2005).

40 *Attitudes to Living in Britain – A Survey of Muslim Opinion* (London: GfK NOP, 2006).

41 *Report of the Official Account of the Bombings in London on 7th July 2005* (London: Her Majesty's Stationery Office, 2006).

42 MI5, *International Terrorism and the UK*, https://www.mi5.gov.uk/output/international-terrorism-and-the-uk.html (accessed 29 November 2009).

43 '21/7 plan "was Iraq war protest" ', *BBC News* (19 March 2007), http://news.bbc.co.uk/2/hi/6466581.stm (accessed 29 November 2009).

44 Dominic Casciani, 'Iraqi doctor's road to radicalism', *BBC News* (16 December 2008), http://news.bbc.co.uk/1/hi/uk/7784799.stm (accessed 4 January 2010).

45 *EU Terrorism Situation and Trend Report 2007* (The Hague: Europol, 2007), p.13, *EU Terrorism Situation and Trend Report 2008* (The Hague: Europol, 2008), p.10 and *EU Terrorism Situation and Trend Report 2009* (The Hague: Europol, 2009), p.12.

46 *EU Terrorism Situation and Trend Report 2009*, op. cit., p.17.

47 Marie Fatayi-Williams, *For the Love of Anthony: A Mother's Search for Peace After the London Bombings* (London: Hodder & Stoughton, 2006).

48 Barack Obama, Election night victory speech (Chicago: 5 November 2008).

49 Lydia Saad, 'Obama Starts 2010 with 50% Approval', *Gallup* (6 January 2010), http://www.gallup.com/poll/124949/Approval-Obama-Starts-2010-Shaky-Spot.aspx (accessed 13 January 2010).

50 Barack Obama, op. cit.

51 Gary Younge, 'Even Charles Manson could beat him now', *Guardian* (16 January 2010).

52 Ron Synovitz and Andy Heil, 'Mideast, Islamic World React To Obama's Cairo Speech', *Radio Free Europe* (4 June 2009), http://www.rferl.org/content/Islamic_World_Reacts_To_Obamas_Cairo_Speech/1747113.html (accessed 12 January 2010).

53 'Poll delves deep into Egyptians' opinion about US president visit to Egypt', *IDSC Monthly Newsletter*, Vol. 1, No. 6 (July 2009), pp.8–10.

54 Chris Abbott and Sophie Marsden, *From Within and Without: Sustainable Security in the Middle East and North Africa* (London/Alexandria: Oxford Research Group and Institute for Peace Studies, 2009).

55 Human Rights Council, *Human Rights in Palestine and Other Occupied Arab Territories: Report of the United Nations Fact Finding Mission on the Gaza Conflict* (New York: United Nations, 2009).

56 Chris Abbott and Sophie Marsden, op. cit.

57 Barack Obama, Nobel lecture (Oslo: 10 December 2009).

58 Barack Obama, Remarks at the morning plenary session of the United Nations climate change conference (Copenhagen, 18 December 2009).

59 Deval Patrick, Speech on Boston Common (Boston: 15 October 2006).

Index

RUPA
23.6.12